Black Men on the Blacktop

D1279305

Black Men
on the
Blacktop

Basketball and the
Politics of Race

A. Rafik Mohamed

LYNNE
RIENNER
PUBLISHERS

BOULDER
LONDON

Published in the United States of America in 2017 by
Lynne Rienner Publishers, Inc.
1800 30th Street, Boulder, Colorado 80301
www.rienner.com

and in the United Kingdom by
Lynne Rienner Publishers, Inc.
3 Henrietta Street, Covent Garden, London WC2E 8LU

Library of Congress Cataloging-in-Publication Data
Names: Mohamed, A. Rafik, author.
Title: Black Men on the blacktop : basketball and the politics of race / A.
   Rafik Mohamed.
Description: Boulder, Colorado : Lynne Rienner Publishers, Inc., 2017. |
   Includes bibliographical references and index.
Identifiers: LCCN 2017014172|
   ISBN 9781626376663 (hardcover : alk. paper) |
   ISBN 9781626376786 (pbk. : alk. paper)
Subjects: LCSH: Streetball—Social aspects—United States. |
   Basketball—Social aspects—United States. | African American young
   men—Social conditions. | African American young men—Economic conditions.
Classification: LCC GV887.3 .M65 2017 | DDC 796.3230973—dc23
LC record available at https://lccn.loc.gov/2017014172

British Cataloguing in Publication Data
A Cataloguing in Publication record for this book
is available from the British Library.

Printed and bound in the United States of America

 The paper used in this publication meets the requirements
of the American National Standard for Permanence of
Paper for Printed Library Materials Z39.48-1992.

5 4 3 2 1

If a city lurks beyond the borders of the park, it's no more real than the ball games they play.
—John Edgar Wideman, *Philadelphia Fire*, 43

We younger Negro artists who create now intend to express our individual dark-skinned selves without fear or shame. If white people are pleased we are glad. If they are not, it doesn't matter. We know we are beautiful. And ugly too.
—Langston Hughes,
"The Negro Artist and the Racial Mountain," *The Nation*

Contents

Acknowledgments

Thanks to my amazing parents for every opportunity they gave me, and to my grandmother for all of the times she'd sit with me and pass along her lived wisdom. Great appreciation goes to my sisters, Rena and Shalisa, who have always been critical to my grounding. Love to Beverly for putting up with my idiosyncrasies over all of these years, for carting me to the numerous knee surgeries that came in part as a by-product of researching this book, and for everything else.

This wouldn't have been at all possible without Kitty Calavita's mentorship and her backing of my less than conventional approach to the study of law and society. I'm also indebted to Paul Jesilow, John Dombrink, and Richard Perry for all of their guidance and support.

Andrew Berzanskis! Thanks for asking me over that beer at that hotel bar a few years back, "What else are you working on?" Even though you bailed on me in the final stretch, cheers to you for taking this project to Lynne Rienner, for getting this book off the ground, and for everything else you did to make my work better. Of course, my greatest gratitude is also owed to Lynne Rienner and her amazing team at LRP.

To my dear friend Tamar, if only there were more folks like you . . .

Finally, I'd be remiss if I didn't acknowledge all of the ballers—mentioned and unmentioned in these pages—who breathed life into the blacktop on a daily basis and brought meaning to this text. And, a special shout-out is owed to J. "Clark" for serving as my sounding board in the final years of writing and for his other contributions to this work.

1

The Black Man's Game

Basketball's all we got left.
—Clark*

It was about 5:30 on a summer Saturday afternoon at the park. The day's heat had just begun to ebb, and there were only a few other players out on the courts, certainly not enough for a real game to start-up. As far as outdoor venues go, these courts were in better shape than the courts at some of the city's more neglected parks and recreation centers. During his 2009 campaign, the mayor had promised to transform the city's twenty-six recreation facilities into "activity centers" that provide inner-city youth with meaningful alternatives to street life. Unlike other politicians who often seem to leave their promises on the stump, the mayor kept true to his word. The department of parks and recreation resurfaced the courts, replacing the traditional asphalt with a more professional feeling acrylic surface, and the courts had been out-fitted with new baskets, backboards, and paint. The old and damaged single basketball rims had also been replaced, but with double rims to prevent them from breaking or bending from overly enthusiastic dunks. Nobody prefers double rims, because the greater surface area creates more friction and bounce, and the rims require greater accuracy for a shot to go in. Basically, they can make average shooters look bad and bad shooters look worse.

While I waited for other players to show up, I began shooting around to warm up. After about twenty minutes a few others had arrived, but

---

*With the exception of academic sources, names used throughout this book have been changed to protect the privacy of individuals interviewed or observed.

none were among the regular ballers who frequented this court, at least not anyone that I knew. Since we still didn't have enough players to run a full-court game, those of us shooting on my end of the court decided to play twenty-one. While some of the rules for twenty-one vary depending on where you are in the country, in essence twenty-one is an every-man-for-himself game in which the objective is to score twenty-one points before your opponents.

Whenever games of full court are about to start, there is a sizing-up process where players casually try to estimate the skill level of others on the court. And the good thing about twenty-one is that this evaluation process can be accomplished fairly quickly. Usually, when sizing up another player, you pay attention to their height, general athleticism, jumping ability, and the overall style of game they play in a one-on-one setting. Basketball is a game of matchups, and this process can be critical to determining a team's success. You try to figure out who on the court might be a slasher, an individual who can drive the ball to the basket; who might be a shooter, someone who can score from mid- and long range consistently; who might be a balanced player capable of doing a little of everything; and who might be a scrub, someone whose skill-level commands little attention as either a teammate or opponent.

The other benefit of twenty-one is that it is a good way to find your shot. In basketball, shooting is largely mechanics, and even professional basketball players have a shoot-around to fine-tune their jumper and "find their stroke" before they begin an actual game. Over the course of our three games of twenty-one, eight additional players arrived, all black. Even though this court had one of the best runs around, rarely did white players venture out to play here. And when a white player did show up, you knew he brought "game." Many of the brothers assembled this afternoon were regular ballers who frequented this court, and it was obvious that the time had come to get the real action underway.

The protocol varies from place to place in determining who gets to play in the first full-court game and how particular teams are chosen. In some places the first ten guys to show up automatically get to play. On other courts, regardless of when players arrive, once it's determined that full-court will be played, players shoot for a spot on a team by making a free throw or three-pointer or are chosen by captains. The selection of captains offers another procedural layer, usually involving some form of shoot-out in which, for example, the first two players to make three-point baskets are chosen as team leaders and take turns selecting which players they want to man their squads.

In this day's contest, the winner of the final twenty-one game was designated as one team captain and the first of the remaining players to hit a three-point shot was designated the second captain. I was neither, but I was picked up fairly early. Teams were quickly chosen and the evening's games of pickup were nearly underway. By this time the temperature had cooled off enough to draw a small crowd of kids and young women, many of whom were there to cheer on a boyfriend or father. A couple of "old heads," whose basketball days were well in their rear view, took the sidelines and would soon begin their ritualistic public discourse, "Back in the day, when I played . . . " seemingly unwilling to move on from their prior status as a baller. Other passersby, drawn to the energy of the court, stood off in the shade to take in the scene.

Even though nothing of material value was typically at stake in pickup ball, I always get a bit anxious before the start of a competitive full-court game. Today was certainly no exception. I could feel my heart rate elevating and a little churning in my stomach as we determined our defensive assignments and more informally gauged what respective roles we would play on offense. On the offensive end, I've always been more of an assist and "garbage man," someone who cleans things up through rebounding and either kicking the ball back out to a teammate or putting the ball back up off the rebound for an easy score. In more recent years, as age has nibbled away at my athleticism, I have developed a decent mid-range game—but I still wouldn't consider myself a "shooter" and pose no consistent long-range threat. Therefore, depending on the size of the other team, on offense I'll either play down in "the block" closer to the basket or, because I've always had a fairly good sense of where a missed shot is going to come off the rim, I "crash" in from the perimeter for rebounds. On the defensive end, I like physical play and tend to guard bigger men who present a tougher defensive test for more wiry teammates. There were some fairly big guys on the court this afternoon, so I figured my offensive role in the first game to focus more on mid-range shooting and crashing in for offensive rebounds. Playing in the block with my back to the basket in an attempt to post-up the bigger defenders would be a challenge, and next to having an opposing player slam-dunk over you, there's nothing more embarrassing in basketball than having your shot thrown back at you by a defender.

One of the captains took a shot from the three-point line to determine which team would start on offense. His shot sailed through the rim and splashed through the fresh net, and my team started on defense. We went down early, five to three, but we rallied back and won the first game eleven to nine. The next game began in much the same way; we fell behind early. But the tenor of this game was different from the first. As they pulled ahead, our opponents began to trash-talk. Their point guard—the guy on their squad who was most trusted to bring the ball up-court because he had the best "handles"—was slowly dribbling the ball between his legs from right-to-left and left-to-right, staring down his defensive matchup and saying to no one and everyone at the same time, "This scrub can't guard me." I was playing defense down in the block, matched up against one of their team's bigger players, who had his back to the basket in a "post-up" position and called out to the point guard "ball, ball" as a public declaration that I wasn't capable of defending him. To communicate to my opponent that I didn't appreciate his disrespect, I hooked him with my elbow and "fronted" him, positioning myself between him and the point guard, daring the point guard to try to get the ball down low. Their jawing at us was clearly intended to demoralize our squad, but it instead proved to be a motivator for us; no one wants to lose to someone or some team that's been talking trash the entire game. Without speaking, we collectively tightened up our defense and began to play more physically and aggressively, and we ended up winning the second game eleven to ten. As a mark of ownership, none of us left the court to cool down, chat with friends, or get water from the nearby fountain until our opponents fully cleared the court.

The third game started differently from the two previous games. We jumped out to an early four-to-zero lead and began playing with a little too much swagger. Basketball is a game of rhythm and runs, and before we knew it, our opponents scored eight unanswered points. Aside from the bewilderment and dismay that comes from being on the receiving end of a run like that, I could tell that my teammates were becoming fatigued. We were giving up wide-open jump shots, had guys not getting back from the offensive end to play defense, and began openly bickering with each other. Instead of focusing on our opponents, we berated each other for poor shot selection—"Fool, pass the goddamned ball!" or lazy defensive play—"Get your ass back on D!" When you start yelling at teammates, it's lights out.

We ended up losing the game eleven to eight on an uncontested layup. By this time, about ten new players had arrived, meaning that we were effectively finished playing for the day as the next game for us wouldn't come for at least an hour. I decided to hang around, watch the next few games, and engage in some superficial chatter with some of the guys who were still waiting for their turn to play. Pickup games can be special because they represent basketball and basketball culture in their most pure forms. There are no scouts evaluating your skills for the next level. There are no referees interrupting the flow of the game. There are just ten guys competing to win and to be the best on that court and on that day. It's an often ludic escape, a rare space in which one can be temporarily freed from life's worries and life's stressors. I think that's why so many black boys and men play the game: pickup basketball offers them a transitory departure from society's ordinary hierarchy and a rare arena for them to earn a complete stranger's respect, something I suppose we all strive for in life.

Ballers

In ways that go well beyond a ubiquitous presence on city courts and symbolic domination of the sport, for decades the world of pickup basketball has belonged to black men. It is no understatement to say that black men have defined basketball as we know it today; as Rick Telander said aptly in the introduction to his classic street-ball tome, *Heaven Is a Playground*, "Basketball is *the* black man's game" (Telander 2009, 1). More casual observations might suggest that the game in its outdoor asphalt context is just recreation, shucking and jiving, trash talking, and showboating. Perhaps to many onlookers and passersby of the public parks in and around American urban centers, the dozen or so primarily black men that might be found assembled on the asphalt during any given afternoon game of pickup basketball are engaged in little more than frivolous recreation. Spectators who find the pickup culture unappealing, threatening, and "too street" may feel not unlike early-twentieth-century social critic Thorstein Veblen, who referred to the proliferation of recreational sports as a "transient reversion to the human nature that is normal to the early barbarian culture" and saw passionate involvement in sports as "manifestations of the predatory temperament" rooted in "an archaic spiritual constitution" and markers "of an arrested development of the man's moral nature" (Veblen 1899, 117).

However, and in direct contrast to these narrower understandings of recreational sports, to many of those brothers running up and down urban blacktops, the pickup arena is not just about playing basketball. Rather, it is through this medium of sport, pickup basketball in particular, that these principally young black men, consciously or otherwise, carve a collective identity out of the unforgiving physical and economic landscapes that have come to characterize post-industrial US cities. For a half-century, these landscapes have increasingly told a tale of limited opportunity and the unfulfilled promises and dying dreams of a stunted civil rights movement. In James Baldwin's words from his essay "Many Thousands Gone," "The story of the Negro in America is the story of America. It is not a very pretty story: the story of a people very rarely is" (Baldwin 1998, 19).

That's what this book is about—an often un-pretty look at black life, and therefore American life, told in part through the lens of basketball. But, this isn't simply a story about basketball any more than Carlin's *Invictus* was a story about rugby, Buford's *Among the Thugs* was a story about soccer, or the documentary film *Hoop Dreams* was a story about high school ball. What it amounts to is a story about race, particularly blackness and especially in the context of how race politics are mediated through sports. By using ethnographic accounts, history and policy, media, and other lenses, race is placed in its curiously US framework; and I also contextualize American anti-black racism as a stain that our country still has yet to fully come to terms with.

Throughout the book, I use *ballers* as shorthand to describe the core group of participants who serve as the central figures of the pickup basketball world at the urban courts I frequented. To many of these ballers, the blacktop functions as a semi-public platform for exhilarative expressions of cultural relevance, black masculinity, and ultimately personhood for people who, because of structural opposition to social and economic inclusion and a history of requisite deference to an unyielding dominant culture, frequently find it difficult to establish a satisfactory identity in other ways. What Evelyn Hu-DeHart wrote two decades ago continues to ring true: "Most American institutions . . . still remain largely impenetrable to the vast majority of those on the wrong side of the color line" (Hu-DeHart 1993, 6). And, perhaps filling some of that void created by disconnect, as Charles P. Pierce wrote of the black man's game, "Basketball's basic appeal is that it offers fellowship, a sense of belonging, a means of drawing strength from something larger than oneself" (Pierce 1996, 59).

Coast to Coast

For legitimate reasons, most considerations of street basketball have focused on the East Coast, specifically New York and Philadelphia, and to a lesser extent, Chicago.[1] Beginning in the waning years of the Great Depression and carrying well into the 1970s, America's iconic East Coast cities were physically, structurally, and demographically transformed through urban renewal initiatives that created massive "tower" housing projects placed on city "superblocks." Perhaps the most significant policy shaping this transformation was the American Housing Act of 1949, which established a national housing agenda pledging "a decent home for every American family." In carrying out this promise the Housing Act called for "well planned, integrated residential neighborhoods" and included a requirement that housing projects reflect the racial demographics of the areas in which they were constructed. In spite of these provisions, for at least the first twenty years after the Housing Act became law, this integrated neighborhoods requirement "carried no greater legislative momentum than moral intent" and ultimately resulted in "massive displacement of lower-income and minority families" (Martinez 2000, 468).[2]

What does national housing policy have to do with basketball? Well, even though the Housing Act deliberately reshaped the way Americans lived across the nation, its unintended impact on East Coast urban housing and the proliferation of the racialized vertical poverty that came to characterize housing projects in Eastern cities[3] is of particular significance to the evolution of basketball in the United States and the central role that African Americans have come to occupy in the game. As Darcy Frey wrote in his now classic look at basketball dreams in New York's Coney Island housing projects, "The experiment of public housing, which has worked throughout the country to isolate its impoverished and predominantly black tenants from the hearts of their cities, may have succeeded here with even greater efficiency because of Coney Island's utter remoteness" (Frey 2004, 3). The same type of densely packed projects that became hallmark characteristics of larger East Coast cities did not form in the more rural, less densely populated South, where football dominates the sporting landscape, or in the sprawling cities of the American West. Neither region formed the concentration of basketball talent produced from these gritty urban conditions and generated by youth who, as Frey noted, seek "the possibility of transcendence through basketball" (Frey 2004, 5).

None of this is to suggest that great pickup basketball cannot be found on the West Coast, or that prodigious basketball talents have not arisen from the low-profile less-densely populated sprawl that is Southern California, the largely rural South, and of course the Midwest. Indeed, California's famed Venice Beach has long been a showcase for emerging and established basketball talent, and arguably some of the best pickup games in the country could be found in UCLA's Student Activities Center, on Santa Monica's well-maintained public courts, and farther south on the oceanside half-courts of Laguna Beach. It is only to point out that much of the scholarly and journalistic attention paid to pickup basketball has focused on eastern cities and neighborhoods where basketball is truly "king" over all other sports.

Therefore, partially in an attempt to fill this scholarly void, it was largely on Southern California's Westside blacktops and a few gyms open to the public—in places like Culver City, Encino, Santa Monica, Westwood, Van Nuys, and West Los Angeles—where this reading's observations were initially and chiefly focused. From a comparative standpoint, I also spent some time exploring basketball subcultures in the urban South. But again, Southern California was the locus of most of this research, and more than others, the courts at Veterans Park in Culver City and Encino Park in the San Fernando Valley served as an ethnographic backdrop for this book. It was also largely Southern California basketball players—principally young black men—who gave life and substance to the observations of everyday existence I describe and discuss throughout these pages.

Based on the years I spent on these Westside courts and elsewhere, playing basketball, talking and hanging out with, interviewing, and visiting the homes of these Southern California ballers, it is my conclusion that much more is at stake for many of these young black men than just the *game*. To some meaningful extent, for these men, whose daily lives involve and are showcased by pickup basketball contests, more central to their everyday basketball court encounters are subtle statements of how they perceive and define themselves as members of a distinct group within a dominant and often nativist American culture that rhetorically suggests inclusiveness but, in practice, frowns upon much beyond symbolic diversity. Ultimately, this book proved not to be a study of basketball per se; it is a study of a particular racial and ethnic American subculture and of one of the methods this subculture's members employ in a long-standing tradition of resisting cultural hegemony.

Culver City

Of all of the places where I played, watched, and talked with and got to know ballers, Culver City best captured the social contradictions characteristic of America's urban centers and the ongoing negotiations of race and class in the United States. Culver City itself is a small incorporated area located about halfway between downtown Los Angeles and the beachside community of Venice. The plans for the economically "balanced city" were originally drawn up by Harry Culver in 1913, and four years later the area was incorporated as an independent 1.2-square-mile city. Shortly after its incorporation, Los Angeles–based film studios including the movie giant Metro-Goldwyn-Mayer moved to Culver City, forming its early economic base and establishing it as "the heart of screenland." The movie industry was so vital to Culver City's early economic viability that in 1937 the Chamber of Commerce adopted the slogan "Culver City, Where Hollywood Movies Are Made" and one of the board members publicly suggested officially changing the city's name to Hollywood. Ultimately, Los Angeles rejected the name change initiative and formally established legal boundaries for Hollywood.[4] Culver City and Hollywood had a "bury the hatchet" ceremony later that year, and Culver City continued on under its original name. Over the next several decades through a series of forty annexations, Culver City expanded to a 5-square-mile footprint and currently counts 40,000 people among its residents.

In contrast to the surrounding area as a whole, Culver City is significantly whiter and conspicuously less Latino than the city enveloping it. In 2000, for example, Culver City was nearly 60 percent white while the city of Los Angeles was only 47 percent white. During the same period, Culver City's Latino population was only 24 percent in a metropolitan area that boasted a 47 percent Latino population overall. By 2010 the percentage of white residents in Culver City slightly increased as the percentage of Latinos declined slightly, even though the overall representation of Latinos in Los Angeles increased over this ten-year-period. While the black population in Culver City in 2000 was roughly consistent with the city of Los Angeles (12 percent, compared to 11 percent, respectively), the black population in Culver City dropped to 9.5 percent by 2010, a proportional decline greater than that experienced by Los Angeles as a whole. This conspicuous population imbalance was the outcome of a decades-long gentrification trend in Culver City and other similar incorporated areas in greater Los Angeles. Actually, as I began writing this book, Culver City had recently launched the early phases of a "revitalization program" targeted at renovating its downtown area. This project was an apparent success with, by 2012, Roger Vincent of the *Los Angeles Times* reporting that the city had established a "reputation as a pedestrian-friendly destination with upscale restaurants, gastropubs and a thriving art scene" all less than a decade old.

Veterans Park—the location of the most active basketball courts and pickup games in Culver City—is a 1.5-acre park that is surrounded on three sides by middle-class, disproportionately nonminority neighborhoods. The park itself was originally named Exposition Park, when the land was first acquired by the city in 1938. However, due to the post–World War II housing boom fueled largely by programs established under the National Housing Act of 1934[5] and the 1944 Veterans Administration (VA) home loan program, construction began on smaller single-family homes in neighborhoods throughout Los Angeles. In particular, veterans returning from World War II benefited from these programs, especially the low-interest zero-down-payment home loans, and drove the era's housing explosion and the creation of new suburbs. For example, in 1945 VA mortgages accounted for only 7.5 percent of all sales for the 325,000 newly constructed homes built in that year. But these VA-backed mortgages accounted for a whopping 40.5 percent of the 1 million new builds sold the following year, and 42.8 percent of the more than 1.25 million new homes sold only two years later at the peak of the postwar housing boom.[6] As a likely homage to the US troops returning home and their noticeable presence among the area's new home owners, a veterans memorial building was devoted at the park's east end, and the park was renamed Veterans Park in 1949.

Located at the western end of the park on Coombs Avenue just south of Culver Boulevard are Veterans Park's two side-by-side asphalt basketball courts. Clockwise, from north to south, the courts are bordered by two tennis courts, a baseball diamond, and a softball diamond. Counterclockwise, to the west and to the south of Veterans Park is Culver City's Park West neighborhood, a "low-density single-family" zoned area featuring attractive, mostly two and three bedroom, post–World War II bungalows. These homes were constructed for modest-income working-class families and the aforementioned veterans. But that demographic changed in the latter decades of the twentieth century, and even at the height of the great recession triggered by the 2009 real estate lending crisis, homes for sale in the Park West neighborhood started in the mid-$500,000 range and soared to well over $1 million.

At most parks and recreational facilities where pickup basketball games may be found, if there is more than one basketball court there typically is a preferred court where the more competitive games with higher-skilled participants play. For example, at Los Angeles's famed Venice Beach basketball courts, three north-south courts radiate from the boardwalk toward the Pacific Ocean. In the many times I played at Venice or just stopped by to watch the games, the court nearest the boardwalk with the highest degree of visibility for the often showboating players always featured the highest level of play, and the skill level of players would generally decrease as the courts moved farther from the gaze of passersby. A newer "stadium-sized" court adjacent to the original courts was more recently added to Venice Beach's offerings to host tournament and league games.

Back in Culver City, at Veterans Park, the premier court is a regulation (94 feet in length) court situated nearest the tennis courts. The adjacent court is slightly shorter than regulation, but still long and wide enough to run four-on-four full-court games or to play half-court games of two-on-two or three-on-three. In spite of this second court's typical availability, regular players at Veterans would almost never play on this court. In fact, while waiting for their game to come up on the premier court, which could easily take an hour or more on crowded days, ballers would not even warm up or shoot around on the secondary court. Instead, they would practice their jump shots, layups, and dunks on the premier court as the action transitioned to the opposite end. Often times, this ritual would result in arguments as one of the players warming up or one of their balls would still be on the court when a stolen ball or fast break quickly brought the action back toward the court's other end.

Everyday Resistance

In direct response to the persistent structural inequalities experienced by underrepresented populations, African Americans have historically formed and continue to construct structures of opposition and resistance. Accordingly, in their capacity to push back against social and political oppression, I situate present-day black Americans in a place not entirely different from that of slave and peasant classes currently or in history. This isn't to suggest that the existing status of black Americans is literally akin to the condition of chattel that established the foundation for the African in the Americas. However, as I briefly outline in a moment, the measurable equality gap between black Americans and Americans of other racial and ethnic groups, particularly white Americans, speaks to pervasive inequalities undeniably rooted in the US "original sin" of slavery and carried forward through a full century of postemancipation formally racialized caste. As can be seen in numerous accounts of Maroon,[7] slave, and peasant resistance, members of oppositional subcultures routinely utilize some of the same instruments traditionally used in their repression (e.g. religion, music, language, and sport) as tools in their quest to carve out spaces of cultural identity.

In this book I explore one of these oppositional realities and examine historical ways in which sport has been manipulated by both participants and organizers as an accessible vehicle to challenge political and social institutions. By taking into account the intrinsic needs, aspirations, and intentions of localized resistant behavior, I seek to explore the potential of sport—using pickup basketball as a specific example—to produce and reproduce structures of resistance. In the specific case of black US athletes, I look at some of the ways sport has been used as a vehicle for black people—as *New York Sun* editor Charles Dana xenophobically cautioned his readers in 1895—to "rise against white supremacy" (Rhoden 2006, 1). I also bring in the socialization process of pickup basketball in the United States and the extent to which it too has become a medium of black national identity formation and resistance for principally African American male youth.

The emphasis on pickup basketball to the exclusion of the more formally organized forms of basketball that can be observed at the youth league, collegiate, and professional basketball levels is deliberate. In my experience, greater structure, organization, and supervision—markers of which include the presence of officials, coaches, league rules, and similar constraints on individualism—tend to inhibit the expressive aspects of the sport. Discussing this distinction in his book *Black Gods of the Asphalt*, former Yale University basketball standout Onaje Woodbine (2016, 5) wrote, "Yale basketball contrasted sharply with the expressive culture of Boston street basketball. Yale basketball felt more corporate."

Along these same lines, as she was contemplating not returning to her college basketball team for her junior year, Ice Lady—one of a handful of female ballers I had the fortune of getting to know while working on this book—captured this difference between recreational forms of basketball and the more competitive college game in the following way:

> I'm just honestly tired of it. I'm tired of the "be here, now, at this time."
> There's no freedom, there's no life to it. My passion isn't as into it. And
> it's kind of hard when you do something and you're not as passionate as
> you used to be. . . . It's just changed so much. Because it got so serious.
> Then you meet asshole coaches and you meet punk-ass teammates. It
> changed. . . . Basketball went from fun to business.

Certainly, more subdued and relatively mild expressionism does exist in these more formal arenas, but the freedom afforded by the pickup court has greater potential to serve as a theater where hyper-expressions of self and masculinity are accepted and often encouraged. Unlike on the refined hardwood, on the raw blacktop there exists a level of comfort and liberty from formal societal constraints that give African American youth the opportunity to express what James C. Scott (1992) called *the intermediate transcript*. This acted text exposes, in a way that is not entirely transparent but also not entirely hidden, ordinarily suppressed aspects of black male identity and sheds a sliver of light on what black male participants actually think about dominant social institutions and their status in American society. Touching upon this theme, Woodbine (2016, 4) shared, "On the blacktop, we also learned a street style, a way of moving our bodies, an attitude toward life that fostered resilience amid the hardships of the ghetto."

In this particular study of blacktop basketball and black life in America, I try not to delve too deeply into the social conditions that have led up to the present-day inequalities experienced by African Americans. Based on the brief sketch given in this chapter and in subsequent discussions, I consider the following four statements to be accepted: first, blacks in America have historically, and continue to have, less social, political, and economic power than most other members of society. Second, this inequality is directly linked to a history of overt and, more contemporarily, masked institutional racism and discrimination. Third, black Americans are largely aware of this unequal existence. And finally, as Campbell (1988, 10) wrote, "Under ordinary circumstances, human beings will not tolerate their own subordination, and given a chance, they will resist in one way or another."

Twenty-First-Century Black

Focusing on this first understanding for a moment, socially, economically, and politically, American society continues to operate in ways that are openly hostile toward black people. In contrast to the increasingly popular "postracial" and "level playing field" narratives, virtually all data indicate that race still plays an essential role in determining life outcomes and that the playing field remains anything but level. Certainly, there has been improvement since the days of Jim Crow. But study after study of actual and perceived racial inequality continues to uphold John Howard Griffin's conclusion from his impermanent pre–civil rights journey into blackness titled *Black Like Me*. Writing about the plight of African American men, Griffin (1961, 48) bluntly announced, "His day-to-day living is a reminder of his inferior status."

More recent examples of these perceptional disparities were evident through reactions to the acquittal of George Zimmerman in the death of unarmed teenager Trayvon Martin, and through responses to separate grand jury refusals to indict white police officers for the killings of unarmed black men Michael Brown and Eric Garner. In a July 2013 poll conducted by the Pew Research Center, 86 percent of black adults polled indicated dissatisfaction with the Zimmerman verdict while only 30 percent of whites expressed dissatisfaction.[8] Similarly, in a *Washington Post*–ABC News poll following the non-prosecution decisions in the Brown and Garner killings, a majority of white respondents indicated that blacks and other minorities receive equal treatment as whites in the criminal justice system, whereas nearly 90 percent of black respondents indicated the opposite. Similar disparities were found in questions asking whether officers have good relationships with the community, whether officers are adequately trained to avoid the use of excessive force, and whether officers are held accountable for misconduct.

At the turn of the century W. E. B. DuBois wrote that the black man in America was conscious of his impotence and skeptical of the desire of dominant social institutions to ensure true racial equality in America. Accordingly, "the Negro of today," DuBois wrote, "faces no enviable dilemma" (DuBois 1903, 123). Again, the status of black America is substantially and undeniably different today than it was during the time of DuBois's reflections. Nonetheless, it would be an insult to contemporary African Americans to assume they are not aware of ongoing and ubiquitous institutional and social inequalities that still befall them in contemporary society and the extent to which, across many key measures, conditions have not considerably changed for them since DuBois's time and, even more conspicuously, since the dawn of formal equality ushered in during the civil rights era (ca. 1954–1968).

The disparate criminal justice outcomes that have recently been thrust into our national conversation on race provide just one snapshot of continued inequalities. In certain categories of criminal law violation, for instance those linked to America's "war on drugs," the black arrest rate has tripled over the past thirty years and grown at a rate greater than that for any other racial group (Snyder, 2011). As my colleague Erik Fritsvold and I concluded in our book *Dorm Room Dealers: Drugs and the Privileges of Race and Class*:

> Perhaps the most widely commented upon and ethically problematic outcome of the war on drugs has been the disproportionate negative impact these policies have had on poor and minority communities, particularly African Americans. . . . This is despite the fact that drug-user data suggest that racial and ethnic groups in the United States tend to have

rates of drug use close to their representation in the US population. . . .
Clearly then, poor and minority populations along with the other "low
hanging fruit" upon whom the drug war primarily has been focused have
faced disproportionate consequences for their participation in illegal
drug activities. (Mohamed and Fritsvold 2009, 3–4)

In response to these enduring disparities, many of the recreational
pastimes taken up by black male youth—in the present case, pickup
basketball—serve to foster intensified intragroup solidarity and galva-
nize black consciousness, often at the expense of promoting intergroup
harmony. Put a bit more plainly, many of the leisure time and organized activities available to or embraced by young black men do a great
job of connecting them with other black folks, yet do little to address
the systemic problems of racial conflict in the United States or otherwise connect them to the rest of society.[9] Therefore, intergroup contact,
particularly more informal encounters where the threat of official sanc-
tions is lessened, provides an opportunity for black men to establish,
again in the words of Griffin, "proof of manhood for people who could
prove it no other way" (Griffin 1961, 23).

This phenomenon isn't unique to African Americans, of course. The
sport of capoeira in Brazil was historically used by members of subor-
dinated groups to articulate more significant sentiments of grievance
and frustration. Similarly, Latin American soccer has long underscored
the power of sport to articulate conflict, amplify contested social and
political spaces, and serve as a forum for resistance. As Joshua Nadel
summarized in his excellent analysis of soccer's prominence in Latin
America, "Soccer clubs and stadiums acted as spaces where Latin
American societies could grapple with the complexities of nationhood,
citizenship, politics, gender, and race. The sport eventually allowed
Latin American countries to show that, far from being inferior to
Europe, they could match their colonial and neocolonial masters
through sport" (Nadel 2014, 2).

In *Weapons of the Weak: Everyday Forms of Peasant Resistance*, a
definitive work on peasant resistance, James C. Scott (1985) contends
that traditional views of resistance[10] miss the continuous, informal,
undeclared, and disguised forms of autonomous struggle by the lower
classes—what he defines as *everyday resistance*. My ensuing description of the ritualistic and performative aspects surrounding pickup basketball is rooted in this perspective and places its emphasis on the
events and institutions that socialize principally young members of the
African American male community, creating for them alternative modes
of political expression and everyday resistance.

The argument put forth here is not that these movements are revolutionary in their intent or outcome. Rather, the position I take stresses a specific means by which black Americans in the United States defend themselves against the predations of ongoing prejudice, economic inequality, and formal political impotence. In the aggregate, to the extent that they succeed in altering the terms of social engagement, challenging the existing order, and otherwise reshaping American culture and society, these efforts can be viewed as successful and of historical significance.[11]

I suppose one might ask, do these sorts of statements really matter? Do these subtle and unorganized actions of everyday folks have any real impact? In short, the answer is yes. Ta-Nehisi Coates said of black resistance, "the struggle, in and of itself, has meaning" (Coates 2015, 69). And, as Campbell (1988, 10) more expansively reasoned regarding the plight of Maroon societies in the Caribbean:

> [The maroons'] fight for freedom, however prepolitical, represents another chapter in the history of the human struggle for the extension of freedom—with all the contradictions. And, in this respect, a study of this kind is not, in the words of Hobsbawm,[12] "merely curious, or interesting, or moving for anyone who cares about the fate of men, but also of practical importance."

Finally, as Forrest Colburn (1989, 2) noted in the introduction to his edited work on peasant insolence, in the course of their everyday resistance and defense of themselves, subordinate classes "also have an impact—unwitting, slow, and quiet as it may be—on elites and their endeavors. Peasants too are agents of historical change."

Contributions to Existing Literature

Having overt structural barriers to professional sport in large part torn down throughout the 1940s and 1950s, opportunity for and representation of blacks in sport have increased to the point where black males, and more recently black females, have been thrust to the forefront of various sports in the United States. This representation is most conspicuous in basketball, where more than three-quarters of National Basketball Association (NBA) players are African American. An effect of this genesis of the modern black athlete has been an increased interest in sociological studies related to race and ethnicity as they affect or are affected by sport. However, much of the scholarship concerning the African American male athlete (particularly nonprofessionals) has been and continues to be misdirected. The lingering foci on issues like sport as a vehicle for upward social mobility or as a means by which to produce intergroup harmony have overshadowed much of the critical theoretical evolution witnessed in other fields. As a result, many of the deeper race issues surrounding the black American athlete in the local community have been concealed.

The analytical focus has also been disproportionately trained on blacks in professional sports or highly organized amateur athletic settings, rather than on the everyday sports situations that more keenly capture the black experience in America. The outcome of this emphasis has been to draw attention away from the importance of using "diaspora," particularly the African diaspora, as a conceptual framework in problematizing widespread and lingering race-based inequalities in the United States. By recognizing the connected history of Africans in the Americas and "the ways in which collective memory and consciousness of displacement are produced and maintained across geography and through history," as sports sociologist Ben Carrington wrote, "Diaspora provides a framework to think about social movements, relations, and politics in a way that does not automatically defer to the nation state as either the primary or only unit of analysis" (Carrington 2015, 394).

In addition, studies on masculinity and sport have found that because of men's persistent presence in the foreground of organized sport, their experiences in sport *as men* have been obscured. This is to say that gender issues as they apply to men have been largely ignored due to the superordinate status of men in sport. A similar argument can be applied to race and sport scholarship centering on the plight of African American males. Due to their superordinate player status in premier American sports, many of the deeper intersecting race and gender issues revolving around young black men have been overlooked. It is worth noting, however, that several recent studies have shed some much-needed critical light on this deeper nexus among race, gender, sport, and class. In his excellent examination of high school basketball in inner-city Philadelphia, *Black Men Can't Shoot*, Scott Brooks (2009) provided a solid example of this emerging analytical style. Sociology professor Reuben May (2009) used a similar framework in his examination of a Northeast Georgia high school basketball team, *Living Through the Hoop*. Most recently, Woodbine's previously mentioned *Black Gods of the Asphalt* also makes important contributions to this literature.

With the notable exception of these books and a handful of other recent works like them, this study is different from past works in three primary ways. First, using the general framework of *everyday resistance*,

I identify sport as a vehicle for social and cultural resistance. I directly challenge the contact hypothesis, described in more detail later, which has tended to dominate the discourse revolving around minority participation in sport. Second, I draw attention to the social construction of identity formation in the black community. In this regard, I appeal to themes such as DuBois's *double life* or *double consciousness*, "this sense of always looking at one's self through the eyes of others, of measuring one's soul by the tape of a world that looks on in amused contempt and pity" (DuBois 1903, 2). This involves the idea that ethnically absolutist discourses arrange sociopolitical relationships so that black and white appear to be mutually exclusive social statuses, with the legitimate claim to "American" being "white." Dominant racial narratives in US society simultaneously claim to embrace diversity while frowning on public displays of cultural distinction—black culture in particular. And, as Paul Gilroy (1993, 1) wrote, "Occupying the space between [black and white] or trying to demonstrate their continuity has been viewed as a provocative and even oppositional act of political insubordination." This is the case because, in the words of Douglas Hartmann (2006, 322), "The very notion of a double (or split) consciousness almost invariably signals the problems and pathology of race in America" and debunks popular notions of inclusivity. Ultimately, through a legacy of imperialism, nationalism, and selective racial subservience, US society mandates that African Americans live a double life as black and as American. Again, as DuBois wrote in *The Souls of Black Folk* (1903, 122–123):

> Such a double life, with double thoughts, double duties, and double social classes, must give rise to double words and double ideals, and tempt the mind to pretence or to revolt, to hypocrisy or to radicalism. . . . Feeling that his rights and his dearest ideals are being trampled upon, that the public conscience is ever more deaf to his righteous appeal, and that all the reactionary forces of prejudice, greed, and revenge are daily gaining new strength and fresh allies, the Negro faces no enviable dilemma.

Third, I add to existing conversations about race by introducing and exploring several themes that were recurrent as I looked at the nexus between blackness and sports, basketball in particular. The first of these is what I identify as *reverse emulation*.[13] While it is not limited to black American culture, reverse emulation involves a process in which historically dominant groups appropriate the more superficial features of this reconstructed black male identity for seemingly cursory and cosmetic purposes, transforming them into fad and fashion. However, upon closer examination, this annexation of black urban culture by members of economically and politically dominant groups, while perhaps not as substantially definitional in the sense that it reconstructs the identity of the dominant class, or at least the public's perception thereof, may also serve as its own form of resistance for non-black participants. Essentially, walking and talking "black," listening to rap music, and adopting a hip-hop style of dress may all be ways in which non-black teens rebel against adult social institutions and their own voicelessness. However, they do so with the luxury of knowing that with a change of wardrobe and a different playlist on their iPod, they can easily slide back into their lives as accepted members of society.

The second thematic contribution to existing discourses on race, particularly those involving discussions of sports, is what I observed as the *black man's rules*. This concept characterizes the contextual status of black male supremacy in defining the rules of competition during interracial pickup basketball contests. It also captures the disproportionate power black men have in mediating contested foul calls and other disagreements that commonly occur on the pickup basketball court. Albeit very limited in scope, this position of black-over-white authority is qualitatively different from the regulatory and dispute resolution structures that black men experience in virtually every other aspect of their daily lives.

Finally, this book brought to bear what I have identified as the *Mandingo syndrome*, a term I use in reference to the conscious or unconscious formation of ideas that are rooted in and reinforce stereotypes of innate black male athleticism. I also explore how the biases incorporated into these stereotypes are often mobilized, internalized, and ultimately valued by black men themselves in ways that are counterproductive to debunking these myths and distract young black men from seeking success through avenues outside of sports.

Notes

1. There are several classic studies of street basketball or the intersection of street basketball set in major East Coast and Chicago basketball hubs. Examples include Pete Axthelm's *The City Game*, Scott Brooks's *Black Men Can't Shoot*, Darcy Frey's *The Last Shot*, and Rick Telander's *Heaven Is a Playground*. George Dohrman's *Play Their Hearts Out* focuses on youth basketball leagues in Southern California, not street basketball per se. However, his work offers strong insights into California basketball culture.

2. For more on the impact of the American Housing Act, see Martinez (2000).

3. The notable East Coast exception to this vertical poverty phenomenon is Washington, D.C. In 1899, as part of an effort to preserve D.C.'s "European feel" and in response to the 1894 construction of the fourteen-story Cairo Hotel in D.C.'s Dupont Circle neighborhood, Congress passed the Heights of Buildings Act (amended

in 1910), which effectively eliminated tall residential and commercial structures in the nation's capital.

4. See http://www.theatlanticcities.com/neighborhoods/2012/01/municipal-feud-made-hollywood/1007/# (last accessed January 20, 2013) for more information on the feud between Culver City and Hollywood.

5. The National Housing Act of 1934 significantly altered the availability and location of housing in the United States and was part of a major New Deal–era government effort to stimulate housing construction. Among other major developments, it authorized the newly created Federal Housing Administration (FHA) to create a national mortgage association to provide a secondary market where home mortgages could be sold, thereby allowing more money to be available for home loans.

6. These data were taken from Michael J. Bennett, *When Dreams Came True: The GI Bill and the Making of Modern America* (1999), as quoted in http://rortybomb.wordpress.com/2009/09/11/gi-bill-and-suburbanization/ (last accessed January 20, 2013).

7. Maroon societies were established by runaway slaves throughout the Caribbean and, to a lesser extent, North America. These establishments highlight the process through which the bands of runaways were able to alter their political condition at the height of colonization and the trans-Atlantic slave trade through both traditional and everyday resistive tactics.

8. See "Big Racial Divide over Zimmerman Verdict: Whites Say Too Much Focus on Race, Blacks Disagree," Pew Research Center for the People & the Press. Available at http://www.people-press.org/2013/07/22/big-racial-divide-over-zimmerman-verdict/ (last accessed September 6, 2013).

9. This claim contrasts with the social interactionist–oriented contact hypothesis, which suggests that prolonged exposure to members of different racial or ethnic groups, coupled with a common goal or theme, serves to mitigate racial hostility and promote the elimination of discrimination and prejudice (McPherson et al., 1989). It is argued that contact is most apt to be effective when the interaction occurs on an equal-status basis, is carried out in a noncompetitive and nonthreatening environment, and takes place on more than superficial levels. One of the more popular avenues through which contact theory has been translated into practice is in the promotion of intergroup involvement in sports. See "Basketball Teams for Peace," http://articles.cnn.com/2009-01-26/living/ypwr.evans_1_lapin-social-networking-northern-ireland?_s=PM:LIVING (last accessed October 30, 2011); and Cherner (2010). Specific to this study, the precarious history of the African in America, and the feeling among blacks of the ongoing pervasive nature of racial discrimination along with the simultaneous lack of recognition by whites of ongoing discrimination, the equal status essential for contact to be effective cannot or does not exist among certain significant groups of black Americans.

10. In its ordinary academic usage, the term *resistance* implies activity organized from above with the aim of enlightening, benefiting, and increasing levels of productivity among the citizens or subjects for whom it is intended.

11. In his wonderfully detailed analysis of Jamaican slave owner Thomas Thistlewood's diary, historian Trevor Burnard endorses the position that everyday attempts to disrupt systems of domination should not qualify as resistance. Citing Michel de Certeau's work, Burnard wrote that "resistance is only possible when the dominated group or dominated individuals act outside of the system of domination that encloses them" (Burnard 2004, 212). Rather, Burnard suggests that these everyday practices should be theorized as "opposition." While I certainly respect Burnard's position, I contend (supported by the work of James Scott and others) that it is nearly impossible for dominated groups to act fully outside of systems of

domination. Therefore, to accept Burnard's position is to accept the idea that true resistance is relatively rare and can only exist in a political vacuum in which power relations are suspended.

12. E. J. Hobsbawm, *Primitive Rebels: Studies in Archaic Forms of Social Movement in the 19th and 20th Centuries* (New York: W.W. Norton, 1965).

13. As far as I am aware, *reverse emulation* is an original term.

2

Sports and Basketball in Black American Culture

In basketball, you just embody that "cool." In black culture, there's not many other ways that you can judge your manhood.

—*Clark*

If for no other reasons than visibility, crossover appeal, and creative freedom, music and sport have proven to be the most prominent means by which public protestation has been possible for black Americans, especially young black men. And no sport is more linearly associated with black men in the United States or, for that matter, better captures the essence of male blackness in the United States than basketball. It is also reasonable to say that no specific racial or ethnic community in the United States has been more closely linked with a particular sport than black American men have with basketball,[1] and arguably no sport has offered a clearer reading of the state of US race relations than basketball.[2] As Hank— one of the ballers I came to know fairly well—summarized, "Basketball is a metaphor for race. All sports are racially coded, and basketball is black."

Toward the end of his ethnographic exploration of one Philadelphia basketball subculture and consistent with what I characterize as the Mandingo syndrome, Scott Brooks wrote, "Being a basketball player is undoubtedly attached to a black masculinity: a masculinity inherently defined in relation to and in contrast with ideas about white masculinity and black and white femininities" (Brooks 2009, 182). Even Barack Obama—the first black person to win the American presidency— proved to be a basketball player, prompting Scoop Jackson to write, "Twenty-one presidents and 117 years after Naismith invented the game, basketball has finally found a place inside the place that best symbolizes America" (Jackson 2010, 264). Further discussing the relationship between Obama's blackness and basketball, *Washington Post* journalist David Maraniss wrote, "With equally strong roots in the Kansas of his ancestors and the playgrounds of black America, basketball connected the disconnected parts of him" (Maraniss, 2012). Presidents before Obama have certainly been athletes and sportsmen, but, not at all ironically, it took a black man to bring basketball to 1600 Pennsylvania Avenue.

In exploring the significance of wrestling in Turkish society, Martin Stokes (1996, 22) characterized the ancient sport as "a repository of subversive knowledge," one that sheds light on other aspects of Turkish life and connects Turkish men to Muslim traditions. In an analogous way, basketball sheds similar light by defining moral, political, class, and gendered communities among significant segments of black American society. For at least a half century, the sport has represented "the kind of beauty torn from the pain and ecstasy of what it was to be a Negro in this country" (Mosley 2002, 17). And similar to Jeremy Mac-Clancy's (1996, 2) more general observations of sport and identity, for many late-twentieth-century and early twenty-first-century black Americans, basketball has provided "a sense of difference and a way of classifying themselves and others, whether latitudinally or hierarchically."

Making an assertion that can be cast toward virtually any place with throngs of black folks—and a point I similarly make later in a discussion of the "mobilization of bias"—Scott Brooks (2009, 15) argued, "Young black men learn early that their community values basketball, respects superior performance, and considers this integral to their masculinity." Linked to both the Mandingo image and the idea described earlier as reverse emulation, it is certainly also true that there exists a peculiar reciprocity of expectations in that much of mainstream white America values these same African American athletic attributes while often overlooking other traits that they value among themselves. Walter Mosley captures this exchange in the gaze of his fictive black detective Easy Rawlins: "Our potential was purely physical and necessarily short-lived. We could aspire to Joe Louis but never Henry Ford" (Mosley 2013, 173). But with that understood, and as Pete Axthelm wrote in his ground-breaking tome on 1970s street basketball, "Basketball is more than a sport or diversion in the cities. It is a part, often a major part, of the fabric of life. . . . Other young athletes may learn basketball, but city kids live it"[3] (Axthelm 1999, xvi).

During one of my many conversations with Clark, a black six-foot-five former youth league and high school basketball standout and

Division I college prospect, we discussed how he became a basketball player and the extent to which the sport became part of his overall identity. Clark explained that he was born and initially raised in a solidly middle class and largely white suburb of Dallas, Texas. His father was a former college basketball player, and an uncle with whom he had a close relationship was a former elite college player who transitioned into being a successful Amateur Athletic Union (AAU) coach in New England. The AAU claims that its primary mission is "to promote good sportsmanship and good citizenship" for "all people to have the physical, mental, and moral development of amateur athletes." While this may be in part true, since the early 1980s the AAU has been criticized for functioning as a de facto basketball farm system, allowing upper-echelon youth basketball players to showcase their talents as blue-chip collegiate and professional prospects. For example, current NBA stars LeBron James, Chris Paul, Dwayne Wade, Paul Pierce, Carmelo Anthony, and Blake Griffin were all groomed in the AAU and shopped for free to colleges and the NBA during their adolescence. A conversation with Hank, a baller from one of Atlanta's rougher neighborhoods, who played AAU summer league basketball from eighth grade until he graduated from high school with a basketball scholarship to a Division II university, exemplifies the AAU's precarious status:

> What are your thoughts about AAU?
>
> HANK: I think AAU is the best thing basketball brings to you. You know? AAU . . . like, those were my best days. You get all summer to hang with your teammates, would go on trips every weekend, to go play basketball. I think AAU is awesome. . . . But my uncle feels a certain way about it. What he feels AAU is, like, how you said they're looking for that player. You know what I'm saying? Like, teams aren't trying to develop players. They're trying to find that one player, throw a bunch of kids around him and just build him up.

Because of his family basketball legacy, Clark was involved in organized basketball from his early childhood and enjoyed his competitive playing days in the Dallas area. But, during his early teen years, his father lost his job and his family was forced to relocate to a working-class, all-black neighborhood in South Decatur (Atlanta), Georgia. Clark described his early basketball days, how he adapted to the change from Dallas to Decatur, and the role basketball played in this transition:

> ARM: Why did you start playing basketball?
>
> CLARK: I've been involved in playing basketball since I was five years old. . . . The main reason why I started playing basketball was because of my father and my godfather [the aforementioned uncle]. Because of how involved they were in the game. I don't think I really had an option. It was something that's just been ingrained in me since as long as I can remember. . . . My earliest memory is shooting with my father.
>
> ARM: Why did your father want to pass basketball on to you?
>
> CLARK: To keep that legacy going.
>
> ARM: I imagine life was a lot different for you moving from Dallas to Decatur. What did you do to adapt to life in Decatur?
>
> CLARK: Play basketball. . . . You break down the barriers with that. . . . The expectations were totally different in going from a white school [in Dallas] to a black school [in Decatur]. . . . You were expected to do well and go to your classes at the predominantly white school. But at the black school they were like, "eeeh" [suggesting that academics were secondary to athletic prowess].
>
> ARM: Why is it that we covet basketball the way that we do?
>
> CLARK: You can see the face . . . the whole personality . . . to be cool. . . . In basketball, you just embody that [cool]. . . . In black culture, there's not many other ways that you can judge your manhood.

This idea of being "cool" is explored more deeply in the next chapter, but to briefly quote Jeff Greenfield, "It is a question of style. For there is a clear difference between 'black' and 'white' styles of play. . . . 'Black' ball is the basketball of electric self-expression" (Greenfield 1999, 374–377). Hank—the earlier quoted Atlanta-area baller—said of this black-white distinction, "It's crazy, but I feel like with the blackness of basketball, it's like . . . it's more natural and it's a little bit more laid back." Indicative of "black man's rules" and the contextually limited black-over-white authority afforded by the court, and toward the point of the intersection between race, socioeconomic status, and masculinity, David Wolf contends that the pickup basketball court "is the only place [young black men] can feel true pride in what they do, where they can move free of inhibitions and where they can, by being spectacular, rise for the moment against the drabness and anonymity of their lives." For the young urban black male, echoing Clark's sentiments, Wolf reasons that basketball successes "become his measure as a man" (quoted in Greenfield 1999, 375).

I think it is also worth noting here that identity formation and fulfillment achieved by young black men through sports, basketball in particular, is learned behavior in much the same way that markers of other subcultures are. In his classic piece on becoming a marijuana user, sociological pioneer Howard Becker reached a similar conclusion about membership in marijuana-using subcultures. Becker wrote, "The presence of a given kind of behavior is the result of a sequence of social experiences during which the person acquires a conception of the meaning of the behavior, and perceptions and judgments of objects and situations, all of which make the activity possible and desirable" (Becker 1953, 235). Not at all associating black identity formation with social deviance, but connecting Becker's point to Clark's description of the role basketball played in defining his blackness and the broader conversation about black male self-awareness through sports, I suggest that becoming a basketball player involves an active process through which conceptions of self, behaviors, attitudes, and judgments are developed through the social experience of sport. And, this process is deeply rooted in American ideological structures, America's history of race and class relations, and widely held ideas of innate black male athleticism.

Where My Girls At?

While this book's focus intentionally centers on black masculinity, I think similar work exploring black femininity would have proven nearly impossible for the shear dearth of female participants. The world of pickup and recreation league basketball that I observed was desperately masculine. Only on the rarest of occasions did women venture onto the pickup courts. In those instances, as Clark describes later of white players in predominantly black pickup venues, those women could *really* play. They were typically former Division I basketball players and, on a few occasions, had made it to some level of professional play, either in the WNBA or in Europe. There were some women around the courts, particularly on the weekends and at the more public-friendly courts like Venice Beach. But, most of these women arrived as spectators—seeming to try to attract the attention of ballers—or were invited by men as atmosphere, to function as an accessory to be shown off by a baller, like "Hey, check out this cute chick I got with me." In total, over the entire time I spent working on this book, fewer than ten women played in any pickup or league games that I participated in or observed.

But that's not to say that the game didn't offer black women who played the same sense of escape, or pride, or identity formation that it did black men. The experiences of Peaches, one of the few women ballers I had the opportunity to interview, underscores this reality and sheds additional light on the link between "deep play" and black basketball discussed in the next chapter. At the time I interviewed her, Peaches was a twenty-three-year-old "she-baller"[4] who had been playing the game since she was a child.

> ARM: Give me a little bit about your background.
>
> PEACHES: Um, you could say I'm hood, ghetto, all that stuff. I was born and raised in the projects. . . . My parents were pretty much, like, big drug dealers and in the projects. That's pretty much where I started playing basketball. Kids my age were at the time selling drugs, and those are the kids that, like, pretty much put a ball in my hand. I was about five or six.
>
> ARM: So hold on. Before you get to basketball, let's go back to some of the other things that you just told me. You said both of your parents were involved in the game?
>
> PEACHES: Yeah, in the game.
>
> ARM: Alright, and what . . . how was that as a kid?
>
> PEACHES: I mean, I didn't know as a kid that that's what they were doing. But we lived in the projects and they pretty much ran, I wouldn't say they necessarily ran it out of the house but I wouldn't know any other place that they pretty much ran the business out of. . . . That's where my entire family was. That's where we were all born and raised. That's where my mom was raised. That's where my aunts and uncles were raised. So, I never understood why we didn't move. But, I mean, eventually we bought, bought

our own house. And my dad ended up being incarcerated for years and years.

ARM: Did your mother continue selling drugs after that?

PEACHES: Uh huh. Yeah. Actually, I think she stopped and then she got a new boyfriend who was also in the drug business, and she continued on with him. And so then they started working together. Umm, but I think by that time she stopped and, but he was doing it alone and I think . . . down the road we moved in the house together with him and I think the turning point was, somebody kicked in our door, robbed us, pistol whipped my mom. We watched; me and my sister watched the whole thing. And they threatened to kill her and rape her and this is all happening in front of me. And I think that was the turning point. After that she completely left it alone, including him.

ARM: And how old were you when that happened?

PEACHES: I was about ten or eleven.

ARM: How did you end up playing basketball?

PEACHES: Like I said, there were, there were, uh . . . I think I was like maybe five or six, so these kids had to be around eleven or twelve. But, like I said, they were all in the drug game. . . . I mean, they didn't have a choice.. . . They didn't have parents that led them down the right road. They didn't have anyone to look up to. I mean, they were all from the projects. But what happened inside the projects is, every projects you have a basketball court, and the basketball court was kind of in the center of the projects and that's where everybody would be from sun up to sun down, literally. They would still be playing ball at night with no street lights.

ARM: OK, so you started playing ball, and it began. Did you play rec ball?

PEACHES: Yeah, I played rec ball.

ARM: And so, did your parents put you in rec?

PEACHES: My mom, yeah. When the whole robbery thing happened . . . once that happened, she pretty much moved us away to [another] county that was majority white . . . and so it was a kind of a way to take us down another path than what we would have probably ended up, uh, growing up as everybody else in the neighborhood. I think that was just a way to allow me to focus on something else, other than project basketball.

ARM: OK, so you get into the rec league. What was the level of competition in the rec league? Was it a good rec league, or was it just a "kids off the street" rec league?

PEACHES: The first one was "keep kids off the street," definitely, because that was still in one of the rough parts of the city. And now that I think about it, all of the parents were like my mom and had gold teeth. So to me if you have gold teeth, you're hood, ghetto, whatever you wanna call it [chuckles]. Umm, they all used like really, really bad profanity. They were all, like, really loud. The common factor with the players and myself, I found that we all had the same background as far as where we came from and how our parents pretty much lived. I mean, if it wasn't the moms in the drug game, it was the dad, and if it was, or both! So . . .

ARM: And so how'd that make you feel? Did it create some solidarity, a kinship with your teammates?

PEACHES: Yeah. Yeah. Because when I went to my second team, these were the parents that had nice homes. Their parents were married. They went to really nice schools. They had nice homes; their parents drove nice cars and had . . . I mean, from the outside looking in, they had money. They all had sleepovers. Like, I didn't . . . I never had a sleepover. And so that made me feel like my parents weren't good enough, like they weren't doing something right. Like, I wanted my parents to be married, and I wanted us, I mean we had nice cars, but, I, at the time, I pretty much had an idea where it came from; drug money. And they had, like, two and three cars in the yard, the grass was cut. They had pets. . . . These are things that I didn't have growing up. Only thing I knew was guys with dreds, sagging pants, dirty shoes, nice chains, dads separated. This is the only thing that I knew. And I mean even at school, these are still the only things that I knew because obviously everybody that goes to [my elementary school] are really project kids because nine times out of ten the surrounding apartments are projects. So we all pretty much have the same thing.

ARM: And did you enjoy playing basketball?

PEACHES: I did.

ARM: What about basketball did you enjoy?

PEACHES: Everything about it. That was just something I was passionate about. As long as I did good in school and I never had behavioral problems, my mom would let me play. Emotionally, psychologically, it gave me confidence, especially when I got on the traveling team, 'cause I got all this gear, all this new stuff, and I started standing out more than others. I became real passionate about it, like that's all I wanted to do. Forget school. . . forget my parents, forget my siblings . . . as long as I could get that basketball in my hands. I was free; to me, that was my freedom.

ARM: Freedom from what?

PEACHES: My background, because, eventually, that started messing with me emotionally. Because once the drug money was gone, that was a long struggle. There was no more nice clothes, nice shoes. Mom actually had to get a job; and being in a single-parent home that whole time, all the way up until now, um, there was a long struggle.

ARM: So basketball became an escape of sorts?

PEACHES: Yep.

Learning to Walk

In Silver Spring, Maryland, just outside of Washington, D.C., proper, seemingly every young boy regardless of race or ethnicity or athletic ability played sports, and we all seemed to begin with soccer. At that age, soccer mostly involved the organized chaos that comes from a bunch of little kids running around without any real display of skill or risk of significant injury. Sure, there were ankle sprains, bruised shins, and scraped knees. But, a six year old didn't have to worry about the broken or mangled limbs, concussions, dislodged teeth, and other more serious injuries that accompany the contact sports many of us would ultimately move on to. At that age, soccer also didn't succumb as greatly to the stratification process that became glaringly apparent as kids got older and moved on to sports whose basic skills required greater coordination, like baseball, football, and basketball.

In the 1970s and 1980s, at least in the mid-Atlantic where I was raised, soccer was not thought of as a "country club sport"[5] that only relatively privileged kids played. When I relocated to Southern California in the 1990s, the dichotomous existence of recreational soccer was obvious. In public spaces, soccer appeared almost exclusively Latino. In stark contrast, however, soccer at the intercollegiate level seemed to be disproportionately populated by white men and women from Southern California's tonier zip codes.

In my youth, unlike today, recreational soccer was not pushed to the fringes because of nativistic and vitriolic prejudices marginalizing the world's most popular sport as the preferred pastime of "undesirable" Latin American and African foreigners. Soccer was just a hallmark of suburban life; a relatively inexpensive youth sport that kids from all different socioeconomic backgrounds could play in the ample green spaces that increasingly popped up around city centers as a result of post–World War II federal government programs[6] and, later, the changes in residential segregation that contributed to urban decentralization by permitting minorities to move out of city centers. But, as we got older, our soccer utopia would come to an end as talent became more important, the soccer teams became more selective, and the leagues became more competitive. Kids like me, who were not skilled enough to make the "select" teams but whose parents were willing to commit the time to continue with sports, were then generally steered into the entry-level ranks of Little League baseball and Pop Warner football. This migration also made practical sense as these sports, in ways that soccer couldn't, would play a key role in subcultural identity and defining status as we moved closer to high school. Conspicuously absent in organized youth league play at that time was basketball; outside of formal school-based programs, basketball was still "the city game."

To be sure, throughout my childhood and early teens, like most kids where I grew up, I played pickup basketball games with friends. We would congregate at one of the several houses in my neighborhood with the iconically suburban basketball goal in the driveway and get up games of one-on-one, two-on-two, twenty-one, and horse. Probably at my request but perhaps because he quietly wanted a son who was an athlete, somewhere in my "tweens" my father hired a carpenter to affix a basketball goal to the roof over our garage. Because of the height of our garage, the rim was easily a foot lower than the ten-foot regulation height. But that did not dissuade us, and, in our own unstructured fashion, we still "balled." The rim's relatively low height also attracted older kids from the neighborhood who wanted to experience the catharsis that comes from dunking a basketball, something I wouldn't understand for another decade. These were the days before the advent of breakaway rims that protect against rim damage; after a few years of teenagers dunking and hanging from the goal, the sagging rim became an eyesore and my father had it removed. From that point until I moved to California at the age of twenty-two, I probably only touched a basketball a dozen times.

Growing up in the metropolitan area of what was then one of America's iconic "chocolate cities," I never had to bother with being conspicuously black. As a late teen and early adult, I certainly had my bouts with racial profiling and prejudice. In years leading up to my relocation to California, America's drug war was in full swing and D.C. had earned the dubious distinction as the murder capital of the nation. Therefore, pretextual stops were common; my friends and I routinely found ourselves pulled over and detained by D.C. and Maryland police for questioning and searches for "driving while black." With that said, because I am racially "mixed"—my mother is a black American and my father was Guyanese, an ethnic Indian whose grandparents ended up in South America as a by-product of indentured servitude caused by Britain's empire building—and was surrounded by an abundance of black people in the D.C. area, many of whom were visually much "blacker" than I, the full brunt of the "black man's burden" was only rarely thrust upon me.

At my primarily white downtown D.C. undergraduate institution (lampooned on the front page of the *Washington Post* during my freshman year for its lack of African American students), I routinely found myself the lone representative of a black perspective. But as soon as I walked out of my dormitory building or lecture hall on the urban campus, I was right back to being invisible, or at least an inconspicuous person of color in D.C. This conspicuous blackness I experienced in the halls of my college has been a fairly common experience throughout my life since, and one shared by many black Americans who find themselves in principally white educational and work environments. Like comedian Wyatt Cenac said during a 2015 interview reflecting upon his time as the only black writer on Jon Stewart's *The Daily Show*, "I think that's the burden a lot of people have to have when you are 'the one.' You represent something bigger than yourself whether you want to or not" (Demby 2015).

But something happened upon my arrival in Southern California. I moved west to attend graduate school and quickly realized that I was suddenly very conspicuously and visibly black. This was partly the result of my choice of graduate institutions; on my prospective students tour of the Orange County campus, I asked about diversity among the university's student population. I was given percentages for white, Asian, and Latino students, but the black student population was apparently so insignificant that it was presented as an actual three-digit number on a campus of roughly 20,000 students. My conspicuous blackness was also the result of the acute race consciousness that emerged following the 1992 Los Angeles riots, which had occurred only five months before I moved to California. Sparked by the acquittal of city police officers who were videotaped brutally beating motorist Rodney King, the six-day unrest ripped off the scab that had never healed after the 1965 Watts Riot, the last time L.A. "exploded in rage against police abuse and institutional racism" (Davis 1992, 67).

Very much like my sudden hyper-visibility after September 11 as a man named Mohamed, in 1990s Southern California white people seemed acutely aware of the black people around them, particularly those who were formally educated and could therefore help them understand black consciousness. For example, during my first summer as a graduate student I worked as a resident consultant for a public-policy-oriented research organization. Aside from the groundskeeping and maintenance staff, and one other black resident consultant, I was the only other black person that I recall of the hundreds of people who worked out of the organization's Southern California offices. One afternoon, the resident consultant coordinator, a white economist, summoned me to his office. I entered, and he asked me to close the door and take a seat. On his desk was a copy of Nathan McCall's autobiography, *Makes Me Wanna Holler*, a candid account of how race is lived by young black men in America. My supervisor held up the book and asked, "Have you read this?" My mother had recently sent me a copy of McCall's book, but I hadn't had time to read it and told him as much. He said, "Well, after you read it, can you come back and talk to me about it? I want to know if this is how black people really feel."

Repeated encounters like these, coupled with the dearth of blackness on my new university's campus and in its surrounding Orange County communities, affirmed and intensified the black identity that I already held. But, a conspicuous stereotypical hole could easily be exposed in my blackness. In addition to the somewhat absurd expectation that I could legitimately serve as a spokesperson for all black

Americans any more than my Mexican friend and cohort-mate Luis could speak on behalf of all Latinos, like it or not, I was expected to play basketball. As Scott Brooks put it in his book *Black Men Can't Shoot*, "being a basketball player is undoubtedly attached to a black masculinity" (Brooks 2009, 182). So, as irrational as it may seem, as a means to affirm my black racial identity in the eyes of my new West Coast community and reaffirm it to myself, I bought a basketball.

Of course, possessing a basketball does not a baller make. And there was no basketball counterpart to the "beginners' golf" class that I would later enroll in during my second year as a graduate student in an effort to connect with my father, a social golfer. Not that I would have faced the humiliation of taking that class, had it been offered. But, our university did have a great research library, which had a small section of old basketball fundamentals books. And so, like the well-trained graduate student I was expected to be, I would quietly creep into the stacks and pull a couple of books from the shelf—and for hours at a time over the next few months I studied the game.

I explored the game's history, "Naismith's Original 13 Rules," the various positions and the players' roles, and ultimately graduated to technique. After I thought I'd digested the basics of proper shooting, I drove around through nearby well-manicured Orange County neighbor-hoods in search of public basketball courts where I could attempt to put theory into practice. This from-the-library-to-the-court process became a ritual I would repeat at least a dozen times over the next several months as I discovered the depths of my untried game's mechanical flaws. Always, I would settle in at isolated hoops where I could try to develop a game that wouldn't embarrass me or make me feel like a racial impostor. The hoops I found most suitable were at public schools after hours. Unlike grittier Los Angeles, this relatively privileged sec-tion of Orange County didn't have a need to secure their grounds with chain-link fences. At these courts, I would work on developing a jump shot, timing rebounds, dribbling, footwork, and other fundamentals, the mechanics and techniques of which I learned from the old library books. My favorite practice spot was tucked away behind a middle school in Irvine directly across a wide street from a public park where far more refined basketball skills were routinely put on display, predom-inantly by Asian American and white players. As John Edgar Wideman said of his neophyte "hoop roots," when I would glance over at the pickup game across the way, I was nothing but intimidated by the unlikely prospect that I would ever become as good as those I watched from afar (Wideman 2001, 4).

But I was a black man in Southern California and I therefore *had to* play ball. So, week after week, I continued to work on my game. While still foreign in many ways, the court began to feel like home, or perhaps, as a friend once said of the former correctional institution where he spent eight years of his life after being convicted for burglary and drug violations, the court seemed like where I "should" be. I felt, I suppose, that being an academically accomplished black person was all well and good, but it did not amount to a hill of beans if I could not also excel in activities at which I was "supposed" to be good. I finally worked up the nerve to take my game to the real court across the street from my training site, and, to my surprise, I held my own. After a couple of months running in that game, I was even offered a roster spot with a "Hoop it Up" squad that was going to play in an upcoming Southern California regional 3-on-3 tournament. I declined.

First in solitude and then gradually working my way up the ranks of increasingly more competitive pickup games, by the end of my personal training camp I had spent many months and countless hours developing some constituent of a *game*. Ultimately, pickup became my obsession, and rarely a day went by that I did not spend at least a couple of hours running up and down Southern California blacktops, gladly embracing the region's notorious traffic if at the end of that road was a good game. I was by no means an all-star, but I had become a solid role player even when playing with college players and the occasional past-their-prime and generally unknown former pros. By this time, it was not so much the racialized role or personal challenge that drew me to the courts day after day. What kept me coming back was the social and sociological world that was revealed to me after I earned what I suppose could be considered membership status at the handful of courts that became my home away from home.

On the day my father died, shortly after we removed him from life support after his year-long struggle with ALS, my best friend and I left my family behind at the suburban Maryland hospital not far from my childhood home and headed for a nearby gym to play basketball. It was all that I could think to do to pull me away from my unhappiness and feel normal, if only for a couple of hours. I had never set foot in that particular gym; almost a decade earlier I had moved to California, 3,000 miles away. But entranced by the familiar chatter that can be found on courts everywhere, the rhythm of the ball bouncing on the floor, and the sounds of sneakers squeaking on the hard wood, I was at home. Again, if only for a couple of hours.

About a year or so ago, I officially "retired" from basketball (although a good friend joked that I had retired well before that). While my soul was still in the game, my body wasn't. Knees damaged and repaired, only to be redamaged and repaired a couple more times, made that decision for me. I officially became one of the "old heads" who occasionally takes to the court and shoots a couple of jumpers but for the most part stands on the sidelines viewing the game in retrospect. When I realized that I wouldn't be playing anymore, at least not with any consistency, a part of me died. Basketball hadn't been with me all of my life, but it certainly had become a focal point of my life and my identity for nearly two decades. Even though age had caused me to "lose a step" and the distance between me and the rim seemed to grow greater every day, I still played for the love of the game, for the way the game had filled in holes in my racial identity, and for those challenging times when I just needed to find a home.

Being Struck by Lightning

Beyond identity formation and being something that American black men are "supposed to do," basketball and also significantly football (particularly in the southern United States) have become aspirations unto themselves with black men—and vicariously, their families, friends, and community members—investing a disproportionate amount of individual capital into the very unlikely prospect of earning a living as an athlete. I focus on this in greater detail later in the context of the Mandingo syndrome and its accompanying "mobilization of bias," but prevailing popular images of black men typically consign black worth to the ghettoes of physical prowess and other brutish accomplishments. Bad enough on its own, ongoing reinforcement of the "black man as athlete" stereotype has also triggered recent generations of black male youths to aspire to athletic success at the expense of pursuits far more likely to garner economic and social stability. Seemingly few young black men with athletic upside arrive at the epiphany reached by Onaje Woodbine, who quit Yale University's basketball team before his junior year after leading the team in scoring and earning "top ten player" tributes in the Ivy League. Explaining his decision to forgo basketball and his lifelong dream of playing in the pros, Woodbine wrote:

> Sure, I might have been the captain of the Yale basketball team or played in the NBA, but to me those are merely external accolades which often lead people in the deceptive direction of money and fame, instead of the

higher aims of divine purpose and truth. . . . If my goals are to become the person I am meant to be and to be happy, then the decision not to play basketball is easy. (Woodbine 2016, 2–3).

In the earlier stages of working on this book, I got to know a player named Zulu fairly well. He was born and raised on the edge of one of New York's dodgiest neighborhoods—a place well known for drugs, crime, and basketball—and became one of the area's premier high school ballers. In Zulu's public-housing-dominated community of nearly 50,000, being on the local varsity basketball team has been described as "close to royalty as there is" (Tucker 2012). Because of his six-foot-eight, 200-plus-pounds frame, affable demeanor, and his exceptional basketball ability, Zulu was one of the most heavily recruited high school players in the country. He committed to a marquis Division I college program not far from his New York home but ultimately transferred to a university in Southern California because of personality conflicts with a coach he described as an "abusive asshole." Before ever taking the court in California, Zulu was in a major car accident that left him temporarily in a coma and with severe head and leg injuries. The crash effectively ended his Division I basketball career and dashed any realistic hopes of using his NBA fortunes to pull his mother and sister out of poverty.

One cool evening several months after the accident, as he was fighting to regain the strength and agility that were once his trademarks, Zulu and I were shooting around on a pristine outdoor court in one of Southern California's nicer communities. The fact that Zulu survived the accident was seen as a miracle by many, including the first responders and medical staff who treated him, and he and I began discussing what might happen if he never played high-level basketball again. Zulu somberly explained that, if it was just about him, it would not bother him too much if he never made it "to the league" or if he never again played competitive basketball. Zulu loved the game, no doubt. Basketball was certainly what had defined him for most of his life, and he was intent on rehabilitation and playing professionally after college. But of greater concern to him was that his immediate family—his mother and his sister—and a host of other people around whom he grew up were counting on him to "make it." He wanted to get them out of the ghetto, to give his hardworking mother a break, and to bring a sense of pride to his family.

Zulu's lifelong investment in basketball bankrupted him, and, no longer able to compete at the Division I level, he withdrew from the Southern California institution and returned home to New York. Over my years formally and informally around intercollegiate athletics, I have seen dozens of basketball and football players suffer serious injury, but I had never seen anyone work so hard to get back on the court as Zulu. Because of his determination and, to be sure, his past basketball prominence, Zulu was able to secure a roster spot on a less competitive Division II team at an institution that was also significantly less academically selective. But, because of ongoing health issues related to his accident, Zulu was unable to keep his spot in the starting lineup. He did ultimately earn a degree, which he attributes to the opportunity afforded him by basketball.

For the wealthiest nation in the world, US poverty statistics are nothing short of embarrassing—with the associated economic hardships having a disproportionate impact on children of color.[7] Like Zulu, for countless black children growing up in the United States, the dream of getting out of the ghetto and one of the few pathways they see toward material success has come in the form of entertainment in general, and athletics in particular. As illustrated by Clark, this view is not just held by the athlete and his immediate family and friendship network but is also internalized, promoted, and encouraged by the community at large.

> ARM: You were talking about old guys at the court. Tell me a little about the "old heads" who used to hang around the courts.
>
> Clark: Especially when I was in New Haven [where he would spend summers with his uncle, the AAU coach], they have a lot more outside courts, more so than here in Atlanta. I think the competition is a little bit more competitive. You know, up north, hanging out outside, I think, is a little different than what I have found hanging out in the south. People are always just on the stoop. . . . On the court, you'd always see old guys always spouting advice to you. I remember one guy. This is when I was young; I was about thirteen and after a game he pulled me to the side like 'man, if you keep working hard you can play somewhere. At least play overseas or something.' You know, I'm thirteen years old and I'm sucking all this up. . . . Everybody's looking for that new sixteen, seventeen-year-old coming up in the pipeline.

As the cultural attributes that have come to characterize underclass urban black society has seeped into the mainstream and become the public face of blackness in America, an increasingly and distressingly significant percentage of middle-class blacks have placed on the back burner traditional pathways to success in order to follow sporting pipe dreams. Unfortunately, this monolithic quest has proven to be an ill-fated fantasy for most; a black child has a greater chance of being struck by lightning than signing an NBA deal.[8] Writing about her simultaneous love and loathing of basketball, economist and author Julianne Malveaux encapsulated:

> The race person in me has mixed feelings about basketball. On one hand, I enjoy seeing black men out there making big bank. . . . On the other hand, I'm aware of the minuscule odds that any high school hoop-ster will become a Michael Jordan. If some young brothers spent less time on the hoops and more in the labs, perhaps the investment in chemistry would yield the same mega-millions that professional basketball does. (Malveaux 2007, 399)

And, as Harry Edwards, iconic sport sociologist and lead organizer of the Olympic Project for Human Rights (OPHR), which ultimately culminated in the medal stand protest by Tommy Smith and John Carlos in the 1968 Olympic games, once lamented about these hoop dreams, "The result is a single-minded pursuit of sports fame and fortune that has spawned an institutionalized triple tragedy in black society: the tragedy of thousands upon thousands of black youths in obsessive pursuit of sports goals that the overwhelming majority of them will never attain" (Edwards 1998, 19). NBA star LeBron James more recently reflected via Instagram on this phenomenon saying, "We don't need more Le'Bron's, we need more physical therapists, scientists, police officers, teachers, doctors, professors, physicists, computer engineers, etc!! I want every kid to know there is absolutely NO LIMIT to what you can be...Open your heart and mind to the world around you . . . #WeNeedMore"[9] (Muhammad 2017).

Just to Get a Rep

While these misdirected material ambitions have fallen well short of bringing the fortunes associated with sporting celebrity to the overwhelming majority of black Americans, exemplifying everyday resistance, sport has been and remains one of the few arenas in which black boys and men have consistently used their athletic ability to make a push for respect and recognition. In much the same way that enslaved black people used musical satire as a weapon of resistance against oppression,[10] blacktop expressionism (along with other cultural art forms) has become a form of capital unto itself, allowing relatively disenfranchised black men to release anger, vent frustrations, and gain perceived respect from their peers while redirecting white American behavior and attitudes toward blacks (Piersen 1999).

Describing one of the players he observed in his ethnography of youth league basketball in Philadelphia, Scott Brooks wrote, "Petey expressed the hope that he would get better because basketball was one of the few ways he had available to earn more respect from others" (Brooks 2009, 16). Or, as John Valenti wrote in *Swee' Pea*, his classic chronicle of basketball playground legends, known street-ball players represent "the idea that people are remembered, honored and talked about on the streets and the playgrounds the way kids once talked about Old West gunfighters like 'Billy the Kid' and Jesse James" (Valenti 1990, 11). In essence, for the countless Peteys and other aspiring playground legends residing in America's chocolate cities, the court itself becomes a "strategic site," "a scene where litigiousness is regularly engaged and embraced" (DeLand 2013, 658) and "a place where a basketball reputation can lift a man above the din" (Valenti 1990, 12). As Edwards's own OPHR organizing efforts signified, sport has historically proved to be a space where African Americans have been able to establish collective identity and one of the few avenues through which blacks in America can engage in a transcript of resistance by publicly asserting their blackness.

But the question remains, in the great American melting pot, why is asserting blackness so important? And, why are such assertions largely relegated to nontraditional spheres like sports? The short answer to these questions is, the tradition in the United States has been to suppress minority voices and cultural representations as part of a broader effort to promote a largely idealized (and fictionalized) version of a harmonious and homogenous American culture. For most racial, ethnic, religious, and economic minorities in America, the pathway to full citizenship and equality has been a bumpy one at best. Therefore, "identity politics" have become an essential precondition for any effective politics of opposition (Carrington 2007). Expressions of cultural identity and distinction have served to underscore this reality while publicly debunking the triumphalist myth of an American ascendance to greatness rooted in the recognition of fundamental human rights and equality. Put another way, as Paul Gilroy wrote in his book *The Black Atlantic*,

> There are other ways in which the non-linear, self-similar pattern of these
> political conflicts can be periodised. They are, for example, battles over
> the means of cultural representation available to racially subordinated
> people who are denied access to a particular cultural forms (like literacy)
> while others (like song) are developed both as a means of transcendence
> and as a type of compensation for very specific experiences of unfree-
> dom. (Gilroy 1993, 123)

In a nation like the United States, which fancies itself culturally
pluralistic, insisting that you be heard as a black man not only bucks
that illusion but also forces nonblacks to consider the bizarre, schizo-
phrenically rooted, and ultimately tragic history of blacks in America,
particularly as it pertains to their interactions with whites. Thomas Sowell offers what I hold as a poorly constructed argument that black slavery in America was not specifically racist and was effectively no different from the various forms of human bondage that predate the Middle
Ages. In concluding that casting American slavery in racial terms is a
provincial liberal ruse "to score ideological points against American
society or Western civilization, or to induce guilt and thereby extract
benefits from the white population today," Sowell (2005, 111, 113)
argues, "For most of its long history . . . slavery was largely not the
enslavement of racially different people. . . . People were enslaved
because they were vulnerable, not because of how they looked." Eric
Williams, a historian and former prime minister of Trinidad, made similar claims about the origins of New World slavery, contending, "Slavery in the Caribbean has been too narrowly identified with the Negro. A
racial twist has thereby been given to what is basically an economic
phenomenon" (Williams 2002, 2).

What Sowell, Williams, and other folks of like minds seem too willing to overlook is the fundamental difference between "Old World" and
"New World" slavery, and the rather distinct role that race and specifically preexisting and evolving presumptions of Negro inferiority cast in
the "science" of the day played in the economic decision to enslave
Africans in the Americas. It is indeed true, as David Brion Davis points
out in *Inhuman Bondage*, his Pulitzer Prize–winning exploration of
slavery in the New World, "Various historians have shown that from
antiquity onward, slaves have been subjected to certain common stereotypes regardless of race, ethnicity, or time period" (Davis 2006, 50). But
it was not until the start of the Imperial Age that Europeans came into
considerable contact with the sub-Saharan Africans whom they would
ultimately characterize as the "beastly savage people," a classification
converted easily to the racialized Sambo ideology[11] that justified the

lifelong and generationally unalterable debasement of black slaves. It was this notion that "Negroes were a distinct and irredeemably inferior species" (Davis 2006, 76)—which gained momentum during the Age of Enlightenment—and the corresponding racial taxonomy that declared white Christians above and black heathens below all others that served as the foundation for the invention of New World slavery. Further explained by Winthrop Jordan (2002, 9), "In England . . . the firmest fact about the Negro was that he was 'black.' . . . No other color except white conveyed so much emotional impact." And as Ronald Takaki (1993), a historian of multicultural America, wrote of the seventeenth-century wedge driven between servant-class blacks and whites in the American colonies:

> Negative images of blacks that had predated the institutionalization of slavery in English America dynamically interacted with economic and political developments. . . . Increasingly, black servants were separated from white servants and singled out for special treatment. . . . Africans, unlike whites, were being degraded into a condition of servitude for life and even the status of property. . . . This division based on race helped to delineate the border between savagery and civilization. . . . The planter class saw that black slaves could be more effectively controlled by state power than white servants, for they could be denied certain rights based on the color of their skin. . . . Black was made to signify slave. (Takaki 1993, 76, 56, 57, 59, 66, and 67)

Clearly, and as a significant departure from slaveries past, the transformation of black Africans to American chattel was substantially part of a deliberate choice to debase blacks specifically because they were black. Therefore, to recognize that *black American* is in some ways distinct from just *American* conjures up this past and requires us to consider the role that race played and continues to play in the making of American culture and politics. In her book *Black Looks*, bell hooks pointedly asks readers to "consider the possibility that to love blackness is dangerous in a white supremacist culture" (hooks 1992, 9). Her suggestion here is twofold. First, the United States is a nation that both openly and discretely places a premium on attitudes and behaviors that are typically characterized as white. The history of legally mandated racial prejudice in the United States makes this point clear, as does the work of contemporary critical race scholars. Jane Hill's (2008) linguistic anthropological dissection of "the everyday language of white racism," for example, explores how our racial status quo is shaped and strengthened through ordinary language, highlighting that our history of privileging whiteness did not end with the era of formal equality ushered in during the 1960s civil rights revolution. Second, hooks proposes that the public embrace of a cultural or ethnic identity that deviates from whiteness is perceived as a threat to dominant social, political, and cultural institutions. The failure to fully assimilate to "American" culture and values is interpreted as disrespect and, more important, a danger to the status quo and social stability. In effect, resisting cultural diffusion is an act of social dissonance and political resistance. hooks further suggests that, for the historical reasons mentioned above and the lingering legacy of black slavery, this threat becomes particularly acute when the nonwhite ethnicity that is embraced is blackness.

For hooks, the idea of loving blackness, in and of itself, can be an effective political and resistive stance as it threatens the existing power structure and social hierarchy, and it highlights the fact that while we might all be American, we most certainly are not one nation culturally. The Mexico City Olympic Games medal stand black power salute by Tommie Smith and John Carlos and their subsequent expulsion from the Olympic village by Avery Brundage and the United States Olympic Committee offers but one clear example of the consequences associated with publicly "loving blackness." In a similar gesture against increasingly public embraces of black culture, in 2005 the National Basketball Association imposed a dress code requiring all players to wear "business casual attire" before and after games and during any official league event.[12] Among the dress code's explicitly excluded items were "chains, pendants, or medallions worn over the player's clothes," restrictions that many players in the overwhelmingly black league interpreted as an attack against African American culture. As Allen Iverson, one of the league's more notably outspoken and intemperate stars, said in response to the dress code, "They're targeting my generation—the hip-hop generation" (Wise 2005). More recently, San Francisco 49ers quarterback Colin Kaepernick publicly embraced blackness by refusing to stand during the playing of the pregame national anthem in protest of "the mistreatment of people of color" and police brutality disproportionately directed toward members of minority communities. The most audible public response was not to rally in defense of his First Amendment rights to free speech, nor was it to engage in public dialogue about considerations like the reasonableness of maintaining a national anthem penned by a slaveholding lawyer from Maryland and vehement defender of black slavery in the United States.[13] Rather, much of the public conversation on Kaepernick's protest was dominated by cries that he was "anti-American," accompanied by calls for his ouster from the National Football League (NFL).[14]

America's prevailing political and economic institutions, which remain overwhelmingly male and white, continue to have a disproportionate coercive and ideological influence over acceptable behavior and fail to reward (and often punish) that which deviates from the prescribed norm—a status quo that over the course of centuries has been forged by ideas and practices that do not support cultural diversity. Consequently, blacks, Asians, Native Americans, Latinos, and other distinctively ethnic subcultures are taught to put (white) country before (minority) community and have generally been reluctant to discuss their ethnicity in other than white emulative terms. But, it is also specifically because nonwhite ethnic identities have been suppressed and racial integration was not a social or legal possibility until relatively recently that black American subcultures of opposition were able to develop and take root.

A Deep Volcanic Force

Returning to the question of why contemporary assertions of blackness seem largely relegated to nontraditional spheres like sports—rather than more conventional political, economic, or educational arenas—the answer seems to be related to access and opportunity. Through intricate webs of policy and practice that existed on either side of the Mason-Dixon Line, for the majority of American history black people were systematically shut out from the conventional channels members of other racial and ethnic groups successfully utilized to claim political and economic opportunity.

But, for a number of reasons, even access to sports was not an easy road for African Americans. For starters, black Americans were never intended to participate in many of the sports in which they now excel, including basketball. Actually, basketball was not even envisioned to be a sport for black men. Driven by Victorian era ideas of "Muscular Christianity," the genesis of many modern sports—particularly their construction into formally structured undertakings—was primarily to provide upper-class white males with leisure-time character-building activities that "wouldn't be coopted by feminist and Chartist activists"[15] (Anderson 1997, 191). In mid- to late-nineteenth-century Britain, the broadening of women's roles, coupled with rural laborers displaced into newly developing urban centers, began challenging long-held ideas of masculinity to the point that "the men of the gentry and lower aristocracy were feeling the encroachment of the middle classes" (Rosen 1994, 20).

In an attempt to "recoup some notion of masculinity" that had deteriorated as the aforementioned movements advanced an agenda of social change, as machines progressively distanced men from the earth, and as prestige was increasingly becoming associated with money[16] rather than "manly labor," vocal religious-political leaders of the era began promoting an agenda of "self-actualization" and salvation in which "the fulfilling of manly potential, becomes a moral imperative" (Rosen 1994, 35). This ethos of masculine salvation through physical activity swiftly became more egalitarian, although still racially and religiously stratified, and expanded beyond the purely upper classes. During this era, the body had become a "site for the contestation and resolution of socio-political conflicts" (Hall 1994, 4) and came "to stand for work, for the land, and for England itself" (Sussman 1996, 292). Accompanying the eruption of this "deep volcanic force" of masculinity was the belief that men naturally belong in groups, and the sports that emerged during this era became the proving grounds for this muscular Christian ethos and "an important instrument of sex role differentiation and male supremacy" (Kampf 1977, 836).

The Brits' idea of collectively working on mind, body, and soul resonated with late nineteenth- and early twentieth-century Progressives in the United States. Rejecting the ideas of Social Darwinism, the Progressives felt that public-sector resources could be marshaled as a tool for positive social change and to combat many of the problems associated with rapid industrialization and the quickly shifting ethnic landscape of the United States. In addition to the perceived degradation of gender roles and erosion of character, there were substantial concerns for the maintenance of public order that might be compromised by this newly "displaced mass of humanity" (Kampf 1977, 836). Sports, like other social institutions, became a vehicle by which to promote public order. Without specifically naming sports, but certainly in a sentiment inclusive of sports' power as an agent of socialization, legal historian Lawrence Friedman said this of the era's ethos, "The 19th century relied upon self-control, which it tried to support the legal institutions, as well as other social processes" (Friedman 1994, 133).

In an article exploring the downside of America's contemporary obsession with high school sports, Amanda Ripley (2013, 74) offered the following account of the early twentieth-century Americanized incarnation of this movement:

> The United States was starting to educate its children for more years than most other countries, even while admitting a surge of immigrants. The

ruling elite feared that all this schooling would make Anglo-Saxon boys soft and weak, in contrast to their brawny, newly immigrated peers. Oliver Wendell Holmes Sr. warned that cities were being overrun with "stiff-jointed, soft-muscled, paste-complexioned youth." Sports, the thinking went, would both protect boys' masculinity and distract them from vices like gambling and prostitution. "Muscular Christianity," fashionable during the Victorian era, prescribed sports as a sort of moral vaccine against the tumult of rapid economic growth. "In life, as in a football game," Theodore Roosevelt wrote in an essay on "The American Boy" in 1900, "the principle to follow is: Hit the line hard; don't foul and don't shirk, but hit the line hard!"

Encompassed in these social and political values of the era, the Progressive platform as it related to athletics held that "sporting contests enhanced the educational mission of postsecondary schools: they helped to mold a public-spirited and physically courageous male citizenry by rewarding fair play, assimilating ethnic and cultural difference, encouraging cooperative behavior, and toughening the moral fiber of American youth" (Horger 2005, 49).

In the mid- to late-nineteenth century, organizations like the Young Men's Christian Association (YMCA) began resolutely embracing and institutionalizing the tenets of Muscular Christianity as well as the idea that sports could be an effective tool to keep working people distracted from political and class concerns. As a critique of more casually religious organizations like the YMCA and their use of sports as a tool of religious indoctrination, Thorstein Veblen summarized:

These lay religious bodies commonly devote some appreciable portion of their energies to the furtherance of athletic contests and similar games of chance and skill. It might even be said that sports of this kind are apprehended to have some efficacy as a means of grace. They are apparently useful as a means of proselyting, and as a means of sustaining the devout attitude in converts once made. (Veblen 1899, 137–138)

Veblen's suspicions aside, organized athletics became viewed as a pathway to reconstruct the manliness thought to be ebbing as a consequence of industrialization and the blurring lines between "manly" men and "womanly" women, and they simultaneously functioned to invigorate bodies and instill Protestant values in young men. Existing participatory sports like baseball, soccer, rugby, and football worked well within this framework during warmer months. However, in places like New England, winter weather proved prohibitive for these activities to be carried out year-round. While serving as an instructor of physical education at the

YMCA in Springfield, Massachusetts, James Naismith—a native Canadian who studied to become a Presbyterian minister and graduated from McGill University with a degree in theology—contemplated this wintertime conundrum and invented basketball as a solution to this dilemma of an indoor team sport that could mold young men and be played during the Northeast's relentless winters (Horger 2005).

The Brain and the Body

Basketball's path to blackness is understood to have similar roots. In spite of the game's origins as a mechanism to keep young white Christian males out of trouble and "every imaginable form of racism and Jim Crow restrictions against bringing physical education and basketball to black youth," the ideal of Muscular Christianity was also influential to many early twentieth-century black leaders who "saw no contradiction between a sound mind and a sound body" (Spivey 2006, 98). Believing that sport could be a key vehicle to Negro education, leadership, esteem, and overall well-roundedness, a basketball movement was introduced into the black urban landscapes of Washington and New York. In 1910 the game ultimately took hold at D.C.'s 12th Street YMCA, the organization's first African American chapter. The leader of this movement was Edwin Bancroft Henderson, an African American from Falls Church, Virginia, and graduate of Howard University who picked up the game during a 1904 summer physical training class for gym teachers held at Harvard University. Known as "the black James Naismith" and "the father of black basketball," Henderson is credited with creating "an organized force that would have national implications" (Spivey 2006, 97).

Having the same practical importance in densely populated and working-class urban areas that lacked the space and resources to fully engage in other organized outdoor sports, basketball fit perfectly into the context of the city. It was cheap, accessible, a beacon of hope as a vehicle for admission to college and therefore a pathway toward acceptance into dominant society, a "crowd-pleasing spectacle," and a diversion from Jim Crow and economic inequality. While suburban and rural white basketball certainly marched on and became part of the foundation for big-time intercollegiate athletics and professional leagues, its urban cousin quickly transformed into "the city game"— and from that emerged a distinctly black style of play fostered and encouraged by segregation.

In the late nineteenth and very early twentieth centuries, it was not uncommon for black and white athletes to compete against each other (Walter 1996). But increasing African American success in sports coupled with intensified northern racism that developed in response to the Great Migration[17]—the mass movement of southern blacks to northern cities in the early to mid-twentieth century—created a shift in attitudes toward interracial competition. The huge increases in northern urban black populations that stemmed from African Americans breaking through the South's "Cotton Curtain" also coincided with the development of new "scientific" theories asserting innate black intellectual inferiority, criminal tendencies, and, ironically enough, physical inferiority (Walter 1996). Without question, similar aspersions were cast upon white immigrant groups in northern cities, particularly those from places like Ireland and Southern and Eastern Europe. But America's history of black subjugation justified by even older theories of black savagery and the irrevocable stain of race that created the impossibility of physical assimilation afforded added credence to these now acutely visible northern prejudices, and rather quickly brought an end to this brief era of integrated competition.

In *Soul on Ice*, Eldridge Cleaver's seethingly candid collection of essays promoting an ideology of black liberation penned while serving a sentence in Folsom Prison for assault with intent to murder, Cleaver spoke to the tenuousness created by black achievements in historically white sports:

> The white man wants to be the brain and he wants us to be the muscle, the body. . . . It reminds me of two sets of handcuffs that have all four of us tied up together, holding all black and white flesh in a certain mold. . . . The white man doesn't want the black man, the black woman, or the white woman to have a higher education. Their enlightenment would pose a threat to his omnipotence. Haven't you ever wondered why the white man genuinely applauds a black man who achieves excellence with his body in the field of sports. . . . The mechanics of the myth demand that the Brain and the Body, like east and west, must never meet—especially in competition on the same level. . . . There can be no true competition between superiors and inferiors. This is why it has been so hard historically for Negroes to break the color bar in sport after sport. (Cleaver 1968, 151–152)

It is worth stating that, similar to the earlier-mentioned negative images of black people that prevailed in England at the dawn of the transatlantic slave trade, racially coded assumptions of white brain versus black brawn (like those embodied in the Mandingo stereotype) are certainly not limited to the United States. As the chairman of a prominent

English football (i.e., soccer) club said in 1991 during a nationally televised match, "The black players at this club lend a lot of skill and flair, but you need white players in there to balance things up and give the team some brains and common sense" (Goldblatt 2014, 147). And while football (soccer) certainly proved to be "among the most successful acts of social mobility achieved" by black and Afro-Caribbean immigrants in England (Goldblatt 2014, 146), no arena provided a more vivid harbinger of contested racial spaces and the staying power of the racialized black "Body" than twentieth-century American sports.

As if to foreshadow the ascendance of Tiger Woods in golf, Cleaver continued:

> Once the color bar falls, the magic evaporates, and when the black man starts to excel in a particular sport the question starts floating around: "Is boxing dying?" "Is baseball through?" "What happened to football?" "What is basketball coming to?" In fact, the new symbol of white supremacy is golf, because there the Brain dominates the Body. But just as soon as the Body starts ripping off a few trophies, they will be asking the question, "What happened to golf?" (Cleaver 1968, 151–152)

A League of Their Own

The end result of this emergent black athletic success and the corresponding intensification of anti-black racism, particularly in northern states, was the formal blockage of African Americans from organized sports throughout much of the modern sporting era. Perhaps the most well-known and often cited example of institutional discrimination in sports was the sixty-year exclusion of blacks from major league baseball, or what Russell Wigginton (2006) refers to as "baseball's whites-only clause." Segregation in "America's pastime" ended in the spring of 1947 when Jackie Robinson took the field as first baseman for the storied Brooklyn Dodgers franchise, effectively breaking the color barrier in professional sports.[18]

But it is equally important to note that racial exclusion was not limited to baseball; rather, the practice extended across all professional sports. It is true that African Americans played professional and club sports prior to the integration of professional baseball. However, rules in most leagues prescribed racial segregation until the mid-twentieth century. For example, a limited number of African Americans played in the NFL during its early years (including standouts Paul Robeson and Fritz Pollard), but blacks were banned from the NFL, in an attempt to "make their game more respectable," from 1934 to 1946 (Lomax 1999). Only when they were challenged by an upstart rival league, the AAFC, did NFL executives reconsider the league's policy on enlisting black players. And even after taking into account the 1946 "banner year" for African Americans entering the NFL's labor force, only twenty-six blacks played for the league by the end of the 1940s. Professional basketball was not racially integrated until the late 1940s, when the new Basketball Association of America, in an attempt to compete with the wealthier and more established National Basketball Association, signed its first African Americans to player contracts (LeFeber 1999). Regarding this first reintegrated wave of black players, Michael Lomax noted, "Many of these players had only one year careers and served primarily as 'tokens' on their respective teams" (Lomax 1999, 165).

Institutionalized segregation in sports mirrored the race-based discrimination and segregationist practices that existed throughout most of American society—in both the North and South—until the civil rights movement of the 1950s and 1960s. The southern states that openly embraced Jim Crow restrictions most certainly deserve the scorn they continue to receive for espousing and encoding American apartheid, but segregation based on racial classifications was also well-ingrained in northern states. Through a network of formal and informal policies and practices, racial exclusion in the North spanned many of the same institutions seen in the South, covering everything from education and housing to sports and other public recreational activities. Jeff Wiltse's monograph examining the history of public swimming pools offers a rare historical glimpse into these less formalized isolationist practices:

> The social melting pot that municipal pools became during the 1920s and 1930s was accompanied by the exclusion and segregation of black Americans. . . . Large metropolises, which operated many pools, generally segregated black swimmers at Jim Crow pools. In cities with a southern heritage such as St. Louis and Washington, D.C., segregation was officially mandated. . . . Further north, in cities such as New York and Chicago, city officials encouraged de facto segregation by locating pools within racially homogenous neighborhoods. When blacks sought admission to pools earmarked for whites, attendants discouraged them from entering but . . . enforcement then fell to white swimmers who often harassed and assaulted black Americans who transgressed this new racial boundary. In this way, segregation was frequently achieved through violence. (Wiltse 2007, 123)

In response to these multiple exclusionary fronts, enterprising blacks responded by forming their own professional baseball and basketball leagues as early as 1909,[19] a trend that became even more substantial in the 1920s (LeFeber 1999; Peterson 1970). These leagues did not simply give Negro athletes a stage upon which to display their athletic prowess but also provided blacks with everyday opportunities to challenge the existing structure through reaffirming black identity, demonstrating equally separatist capabilities, and asserting a new form of political and, to a lesser extent, economic viability for African Americans.

Ultimately the bastions of segregated sporting life were destined to fall apart in the decades following World War II, and professional sports in America gradually began desegregating in the 1940s and 1950s, mirroring—if not foreshadowing—racial desegregation in other visible public spaces, such as housing and education. These moves toward racial integration in sports have often been and continue to be heralded as indicative of significant social changes in white American attitudes toward domestic race relations as well as the genesis of middle-class economic opportunity for black Americans. As Donald Calhoun (1987, 33) states, "Whereas other careers were barred to blacks, athletics became an area in which it was possible for blacks to get ahead in money and recognition." And it is certainly true that access to professional and collegiate athletics continues to serve as an economic springboard for black men and women with superior athletic ability. However, a larger pool of evidence suggests that integration in sports was not primarily driven by broader ideas of social justice. Rather, these changes were principally compelled by a national political agenda espousing democratic values abroad and, not dissimilar to acquisition of the American Basketball Association by the larger and more powerful NBA in the 1970s, the realization that black athletes could significantly contribute to the financial success of professional sports franchises. Fundamentally, struggles for racial equality in twentieth-century America clearly demonstrate that formal legal equality and the recognition of the athletic talents of specific African Americans has never equaled racial equality. Instead, as David Goldblatt noted of the integration of English football leagues, "the silencing of overt public racism has come at the price that other forms of stereotyping and discrimination can be overlooked" (Goldblatt 2014, 149).

By Any Means Available

As the traditional stance of athletes on the whole began to change significantly during the late 1960s and early 1970s (Calhoun 1987), the corresponding shift in the cultural discourse that was largely directed by black ingenuity, white economic interests, and emerging Cold War politics permitted sports to emerge as a forum for black American cultural and political expression. And, as blacks gained a foothold and ultimately recognition in American sports, a window of political voice and opportunity was simultaneously opened. Perhaps the clearest example of the emergent politicization of sport in America, particularly for black athletes, came in the events leading up to and culminating in the 1968 Olympic Games in Mexico City. A few months before the start of the Mexico City games, the chief architect of the Olympic Project for Human Rights, Harry Edwards, organized a successful boycott of a prestigious track meet at the storied New York Athletic Club (NYAC).[20] The protest was designed to draw attention to the NYAC's discriminatory membership practices, described in a February 1968 *Sports Illustrated* article as "the crusty old Irish-dominated club's refusal to admit Negroes and all but a few Jews into its hallowed dining rooms and steambaths." In defense of its membership, the NYAC leadership "dismissed the undeniably lily-white makeup of the club as a right it had earned by many contributions to Negro youths through various track organizations" (Axthelm 1968).

Edwards's ambition was to have the NYAC boycott carry over to a larger-scale political expression in Mexico City. But, given the grandness of the Olympic stage and athletes' years of training and sacrifice, most of the African American Olympic athletes opted to forgo a boycott and participate in the games. This is not to say that the games went on without black athletes literally taking a stand for civil rights. In protest of ongoing racial discrimination in the United States and the International Olympic Committee's secret-ballot vote to allow South Africa back into the Olympics in spite of continued apartheid in that country, African American gold and bronze track medalists Tommie Smith and John Carlos conspired in the era's iconic expression of everyday resistance, raising black-gloved fists during the medal ceremony for the 200-meter track event. This gesture vividly conveyed their discontent for what they perceived to be American political farce; like Cleaver's "the Body," blacks were equal to represent America on the global athletic stage but continued to be denied full and equal access to political rights and economic opportunity within the United States. Similarly, South Africa had agreed to integrate its formerly segregated teams in order to regain access to the Olympics, but black South Africans were still subjected to harsh racially discriminatory practices in their homeland. The essence of the era and sports' centrality to the politics of race were framed clearly by the architects of the Olympic Project for Human Rights political platform, who wrote in the organization's founding statement:

> We must no longer allow this country to use a few so called Negroes to point out to the world how much progress she has made in solving her racial problems when the oppression of Afro-Americans is greater than it ever was. We must no longer allow the sports world to pat itself on the back as a citadel of racial justice when the racial injustices of the sports world are infamously legendary. . . . Any black person who allows himself to be used in the above matter is a traitor because he allows racist whites the luxury of resting assured that those black people in the ghettos are there because that is where they want to be. So we ask why should we run in Mexico only to crawl home? (Zirin, 2008)

Noted previously, in response to their 1968 Mexico City protest, Smith and Carlos were stripped of their respective medals and the track-stars-turned-activists were ordered by International Olympic Committee president Avery Brundage to leave Mexico within twenty-four hours. Brundage later referred to their protest as "the nasty demonstration against the American flag by Negroes." Earlier that same year, the Philadelphia Phillies baseball organization threatened a forfeit in order to force cancellation of a baseball game that Major League Baseball and, ironically, the Los Angeles Dodgers, were determined to have played on the day of Martin Luther King Jr.'s funeral. Years earlier and in the revolutionary spirit of the decade, after being refused service at a restaurant in his hometown of Louisville, Kentucky, Olympic boxing champion Muhammad Ali (then Cassius Clay) reportedly threw the cherished medal he earned at the 1960 Rome Games into the Ohio River. And, around the same period, through his play and his words as both a player and a player-coach, Bill Russell further pushed beyond the molds of the necessarily more passive Jackie Robinson and Jesse Owens, openly questioning the nonviolent strategies advocated by Dr. King to challenge America's ongoing racial double-standards. Basketball had been desegregated more than a decade earlier, but by the time of his retirement in 1969 during what Aram Goudsouzian referred to as "the basketball revolution," Bill Russell "became a unique touchstone of African-American pride. He succeeded within a racially integrated framework, but he never sacrificed his principles for mass adoration. He maintained an unapologetic black identity, even as the NBA grew into a viable commercial endeavor" (Goudsouzian 2006, 62).

These examples represent a small subset of the myriad cultural and political expressions afforded by organized sport that firmly took hold by the late 1960s, and the ways in which black Americans have used sport as a vehicle of resistance to challenge existing social and political structures. With this as a backdrop, it seems entirely conceivable that the scope of sport's significance in protest may also extend to less formalized and less structured sporting contests and that activities viewed by many as simple recreation may perhaps more accurately be interpreted as a "direct doorway into the rich field of meanings at the heart of daily life" (Lewis 1992, 2). Sport, as it was in the past and as it exists today, allows for self-representation not generally seen in other contexts or social outlets. It also permits those with less access to formal legal and political structures to play "with and in the key of law [that] transforms the significance of the game . . . [and] constitute the game with meaning and potentiate its significance for the players" (DeLand 2013, 257). The expressive freedoms permitted black men on the basketball court in particular to distinguish this sport from other popular leisure practices and allow an even greater opportunity for resistive statements and, like Leroi Jones's assertion of the blues, an ideal opportunity for cultural scrutiny. As Michael Novak wrote in 1976, when basketball began to creep out from the shadows of popularity cast by baseball and football, "Basketball is Jazz: Improvisatory, free, individualistic, corporate, sweaty, exulting, screeching, torrid, explosive, exquisitely designed for letting first the trumpet, then the sax, then the drummer, then the trombone soar away in virtuoso excellence" (Novak 1976, 109).

It's a Black Thing

It is my contention that basketball expressionism, especially that which takes place on the blacktops outside the more formal constraints of organized sports, has become a vehicle for self-identity and a focal point of community strength, structure, and everyday resistance among black Americans. Commenting on these aspects of basketball, baller Clark reflected:

> In a lot of ways you just you see that your manhood is judged on your athletic ability. It's like you can be the greatest dude ever but if you get on the court and you just look soft and you can't play, people just . . . your respect level is gonna be gone just from that. So I think that's just one of the biggest things. You know, I see that to this day . . . even now as I'm getting older and stuff, I'm like wow, so what am I gonna be judged now on, because obviously you can't play basketball forever. You know you can't, you just can't. And so, like, how's my masculinity gonna

be judged now if not athletically? . . . If you can't compete anymore, like, what arenas can we compete in? . . . The basketball court is one of the few avenues where, as a black man, you can let your emotions out and it's not going to be on a negative basis. You know, you let it out on the street, man, you're going to go to jail.

This function of basketball in black society extends back to its earliest days where "it was in the black communities of Washington and New York that the game initially flourished as an organized force that would have national implications" (Spivey 2006, 97). Clearly, many of the more political platforms that came to define the "golden age" of black sports as it relates to the struggle for recognition have ebbed, been quieted or coopted by the self-interest that comes from celebrity and fortune, or disappeared entirely. But the nexus between black identity and basketball is still profoundly there. For some, in the words of baller Clark, "basketball's all we got left," and the game exists as one of the few forums through which many black men feel they can define themselves in the context of America.

At the heart of this race-based subcultural resistance in urban black America stand black Americans who defy hegemony by openly embracing their interpretation of black culture in public spaces. It is here that, in their defiance of the whiteness that pervades most other aspects of their public lives, black males have the unique opportunity to reject their domination—both perceived and measurable—simply through the style of basketball that they play and behaviors associated with this playground spectacle. What occurs during these episodes of African American expression is more than just sport; it is a subtle yet distinct statement of the falsity, or at least incompleteness, of the American integrationist ideology. Through the insistence upon "black man's rules" and taking over public spaces in which, in the broader social context, superordinate systems privileging white males remain intact, black ballers carve out spaces of resistance and reject the idea that equality on any front can be accomplished without significant changes in public attitudes about race in general and blackness in particular.

In addition to its function as a focal point for black resistance, the surging popularity of the demonstrative schoolyard style of basketball play seen on the pickup court and the various other cultural statements made in this forum have served to alter the terms of engagement through the redefinition of American emulative popular culture. In a *Sports Illustrated* article, cultural critic Stanley Crouch observed of Michael Jordan's fame, "In 1960, if white girls in the suburbs had had posters of a Negro that dark on the wall, there would have been hell to pay. That kind of racial paranoia is not true of the country now. Today you have girls who are Michael Jordan fanatics, and their parents don't care" (Price 1997). To be sure, the racial ambivalence observed by Crouch offers an overly optimistic assessment of sport's ability to transcend racial boundaries and induce intercultural tolerance. It also speaks to what I identified earlier as *reverse emulation*, that tendency of historically dominant groups to appropriate superficially "cool" features from the culture of "the other" and transform them into fashion and occasionally microresistive statements to suit their own interests. Nonetheless, the impact that sports in general, but basketball in particular, have demonstrated on American popular culture is unmistakable; this effect is validated by corporate America's increased willingness to use more expressive black basketball players as product pitchmen. For example, in 2012 alone, NBA stars LeBron James, Kobe Bryant, Dwyane Wade, Kevin Durant, Derrick Rose, and Dwight Howard hauled in over $100 million in combined endorsement earnings.[21] The only white American athlete to eclipse the NBA's top endorsement earners was golfer Phil Mickelson, whose $57 million in endorsement earnings just barely nudged out Tiger Woods's $54.5 million pitchman bounty.

Conclusion

In spite of the game's increasing universal popularity and the notable globalization of basketball through the infusion of international players into the sport's professional ranks, basketball remains the "black man's game" and persists as a focal point of social life in black communities throughout America. Contrary to Avery Brundage's insistence that "revolutionaries are not bred on the playing field" and other attempts to idealize "sports as the venue where race [and politics] was supposed to be minimized" race certainly "still matters in sport" (Wigginton, 2006, xi, xii). Perhaps nowhere is this significance more evident than in basketball and the role it continues to play in defining black masculinity in the United States.

This connection is among the more contemporary examples of the compelling relationship for African Americans that sit parked at the intersection of sport and politics. It is also a relationship that has transcended simple recreation and has far more significance than offering blacks mere opportunities to interact with whites on the playing field, make it to college, or earn a living. Instead, the relationship carved out of this sociopolitical space has been most significantly characterized by the manipulation of sports toward political ends through what could perhaps best be classified as *by any means available*. While its meaning and interpretative significance are as diverse as those who participate in these activities, for many black Americans, sports have carried and continue to hold political implications equal, if not greater, to that of other more conventionally accepted forms of political activity. This makes sense since the black American "Body" has become central to sports and because more Americans, irrespective of race or class, pay attention to sports than they do anything else going on in the world around them. As Bruce Feldman (2007) noted in his examination of big-time college football recruiting, on National Signing Day[22] in 2007, one of the two main websites dedicated to information on college football recruits—Rivals.com—received nearly 75 million page views, compared to MSNBC.com's yield of approximately 15 million page views on election night in 2006.

Certainly, sports can be politics, particularly for subordinate groups like African Americans who have historically and consistently been denied more conventional access to power. The iconic example of this phenomenon is, of course, Muhammad Ali, who used his status as a sporting icon to demand equality for black people in America and, in the spirit of Black Nationalism, to draw attention to the broader struggles of black people throughout the African diaspora. In more recent times, Michael Jordan, Bill Bradley, Steve Largent, Tom Osbourne, Lynn Swann, Kevin Johnson, and numerous other sports figures have used their successes on the field to catapult into corporate and political arenas.[23] Still, historically and today, the most politically significant of these experiences occur at much more subtle everyday levels, where the gains, on the surface, seem negligible. Despite this relative marginality, in the eyes of the individual actors these gains are often akin to emancipation, even if only momentary. The point here is that subordinate classes of people have historically used whatever tools available to them, sport included, in their struggle for recognition, and the black experience with basketball seems a clear manifestation of this point.

Notes

1. Certainly, this is not to be dismissive of lacrosse and its strong historical association with Eastern Woodland Native Americans. However, European colonists significantly co-opted and transformed the game, and it is now largely known as a "country club" sport played by relatively privileged white Americans.

2. David Goldblatt (2014, 147) makes a similar suggestion about the significance of football in understanding race relations in England.

3. Gentrification and urban renewal have altered the racial makeup of many iconic American urban centers, and even famous "chocolate cities" like Washington, D.C., have lost their black majorities in the new millennium. However, in the context used here by Axthelm, for at least the past fifty years, *city* has been synonymous with or been used as code-speak for *black*. For example, in his 2016 presidential campaign, Donald Trump routinely referred to "inner cities" when discussing the lives of African Americans.

4. I chose this label for hard-core women basketball players from a piece of clothing worn by another female devout basketball player. A regular at the gym in Van Nuys, this particular woman often wore a pair of knee-length basketball shorts with the phrase "She-Baller" printed on the backside.

5. While a graduate student at the University of California Irvine, for approximately four years I served as a graduate assistant in the Department of Athletics, where I worked primarily with "at-risk" student athletes in the "revenue" sports, specifically men's and women's basketball. These student-athletes were disproportionately black and from more urban environments. In our internal code-speak at Irvine, we distinguished between the "revenue" (disproportionately black and working-class) sports and the "country club" (disproportionately white and solidly middle-class) sports like soccer, golf, and tennis.

6. Examples of post–World War II federal government programs include home mortgage insurance and the development of the interstate highway system. Inner-city racial tensions and concerns about crime have also been cited as factors in urban decentralization and suburban expansion (Baum-Snow 2007; Mieszkowski and Mills 1993).

7. In 2013 the proportion of black Americans falling beneath the government's poverty threshold was an astounding 27 percent and the poverty rate for African American children was an even more staggering 37 percent.

8. According to *National Geographic*, "The odds of becoming a lightning victim in the US in any one year is 1 in 700,000" and the odds of being a lightning strike victim over a lifetime shrinks to about 1 in 3,000 (http://news.nationalgeographic.com/news/2004/06/0623_040623_lightningfacts.html). In contrast, the NBA drafts only forty-eight players each year, and only about 1 percent of the nation's 17,500 NCAA college basketball players ever make it on to an NBA roster.

9. #WeNeedMore is part of Verizon's Innovative Learning initiative seeking to elevate youth interest in STEM by "inspiring tomorrow's creators to use technology to build brighter futures for themselves." The initiative is specifically targeted toward underserved schools and communities, and influential athletes like LeBron James have been enlisted to encourage underrepresented youth to explore alternative career choices outside of playing sports.

10. For more on this discussion, see Piersen (1999).

11. Quoted in David Brion Davis's book *Inhuman Bondage* (2006, 51), Stanley Elkins summarizes: "Sambo, the typical plantation slave, was docile but irresponsible, loyal but lazy, humble but chronically given to lying and stealing; his behavior was full of infantile silliness and his talk inflated with childish exaggeration. His relation with his master was one of utter dependence and childlike attachment: it was indeed this childlike quality that was the very key to his being."

12. Ostensibly, the 2005 NBA dress code was adopted as part of a package of "public relations alterations" in response to a 2004 brawl that took place during a game between the Indiana Pacers and Detroit Pistons dubbed "the Malice at the

Palace." The fight originally began between opposing players but shortly thereafter exploded into a melee involving players and fans, and was widely regarded as a league embarrassment and one of the lowest points in NBA history. But many players and social critics felt that the league merely used the brawl as an apology for pursuing a preexisting agenda of toning-down the league's blackness. As then-player Jason Richardson said, "They want to sway away from the hip-hop generation. . . . One thing to me that was kind of racist was you can't wear chains outside your clothing. I don't understand what that has to do with being business approachable. . . . You wear a suit, you still could be a crook. You see all what happened with Enron and Martha Stewart. Just because you dress a certain way doesn't mean you're that way. Hey, a guy could come in with baggy jeans, a 'do rag and have a PhD and a person who comes in with a suit could be a three-time felon. . . . Some [chains] have religious meanings behind their chains, others have personal messages behind their chains. Some guys just like to wear them. I think that was . . .indirectly racial." http://sports.espn.go.com/nba/news/story?id=2198089.

13. Multiple historical sources note that Francis Scott Key grew powerful and wealthy in part because of his personal stake in a slaveholding plantation. Beyond that, Key "harbored racist conceptions of American citizenship," holding that blacks in America were "a distinct and inferior race of people, which all experience proves to be the greatest evil that afflicts a community." According to one of Key's biographers, Jefferson Morley, Key "prided himself as a humanitarian and as a young lawyer relished defending individual colored people in court," earning the title "the Blacks' lawyer." But, "At the same time, Key shared a general view of the free people of color as shiftless and untrustworthy: a nuisance, if not a menace, to white people," and sought to repatriate free blacks to Liberia. See Morley's *Snow-Storm in August* (2012), Anchor Books; Christopher Wilson's essay "Where's the Debate on Francis Scott Key's Slave-Holding Legacy?" (2016), *Smithsonian Magazine* (available at http://www.smithsonianmag.com/smithsonian-institution/wheres-debate-francis-scott-keys-slave-holding-legacy-180959550/?no-ist); and Kobie Brown's OpEd "Colin Kaepernick and the Racist History of Our National Anthem" (2016), NBC News, available at http://www.nbcnews.com/news/nbcblk/oped-colin-kaepernick-racist-history-our-national-anthem-n642636.

14. At the time I wrote this, neither the 49ers nor the NFL had taken any action against Kaepernick. However, both organizations issued statements distancing themselves from Kaepernick's protest while acknowledging his right to not stand during the anthem. In their release, the 49ers stated: "The national anthem is and always will be a special part of the pre-game ceremony. It is an opportunity to honor our country and reflect on the great liberties we are afforded as its citizens. In respecting such American principles as freedom of religion and freedom of expression, we recognize the right of an individual to choose and participate, or not, in our celebration of the national anthem." More vaguely, the NFL released a statement saying, "Players are encouraged but not required to stand during the playing of the national anthem."

15. The Chartist movement—a decade-long British working-class movement that began in the late 1830s—emerged in response to the failure of the 1832 Reform Act to extend suffrage to citizens who did not own property.

16. Among the key "founders" of the Muscular Christianity movement was Charles Kingsley, a member of England's Protestant elite who advocated activities that simultaneously promoted moral, spiritual, and physical development. In Kingsley's view, the need for this shift in consciousness was particularly acute in the Victorian period as emerging industrialization and the consequent shift away

from more "manly labors" had created more sedentary lifestyles. Furthermore, Kingsley quarreled with the emerging middle class "artificial equation of money and power," arguing, among other things, that "money-making is an effeminate pursuit" (Hall 1994, 33).

17. Massive labor shortages in northern industrial centers triggered by war industries and the effective cutoff of European immigration during World War I created a huge demand for black workers. At the time, 90 percent of the nation's black population still lived in the South. But, in a span of twenty years, an estimated 2 million African Americans from the South (25 percent) moved to northern industrial areas. The black outflow continued until the Great Depression, and the result of this mass exodus was the creation of the first large, urban black communities in the North—a region that saw its black population increase approximately 20 percent between 1910 and 1930. The response in the North was anything but congenial as racially restrictive housing covenants were adopted to keep neighborhoods all-white, significant "white flight" to emerging suburbs became commonplace, northern schools were segregated, and union politics became increasingly racialized.

18. A few blacks did play integrated major league baseball in the nineteenth century, but due to increasing discrimination, by 1898 the last black player was successfully purged from what are now known as the major leagues (Peterson 1970).

19. There are accounts of black sporting leagues that predate the twentieth century. For example, a Negro baseball league located in New York City held its first recorded game in 1859. However, these leagues seem to have been local in their scope and formed in response to more general patterns of discrimination and a desire to play sports rather than the more formalized exclusion of blacks from professional sporting leagues.

20. The New York Athletic Club was founded in 1868 as an organization devoted to the growth and development of amateur sport in the United States. As of 2014, NYAC members have won 119 Olympic gold medals, 53 silver medals, and 59 bronze medals.

21. According to *Sports Illustrated*'s "Fortunate 50" list, in 2012 endorsement earnings alone, LeBron James earned $33 million; Kobe Bryant earned $28 million; Derrick Rose earned $18 million; Kevin Durant earned $12.5 million; Dwayne Wade earned $12 million; and Dwight Howard earned $11 million. http://sportsillustrated .cnn.com/specials/fortunate50-2012/# (last accessed May 23, 2013).

22. National Signing Day, the first Wednesday in February, is the day top high school football players sign binding letters of intent, formally committing to play football for a particular university.

23. During the 2000 presidential primaries, Michael Jordan used his status as a basketball superstar to endorse Bill Bradley (another former professional basketball player and recently retired US senator) as a candidate for the Democratic Party presidential nomination.

3

Everyday Resistance
and Black Man's Rules

Forget school, forget my parents, forget my siblings . . . as long as I could get that basketball in my hands. I was free; to me, that was my freedom.

—Peaches

When I began looking more deeply at pickup basketball, I wasn't considering the hidden structures of resistance that have been forged into black American culture or otherwise dot the landscapes of black America. In fact, in all of my years of formal education, I had been exposed to shamefully little about the plight of black Americans and had never come across the idea of everyday resistance. But, as I came to find, numerous studies have demonstrated that such structures have continuously existed in North America from the moment the first twenty Africans were brought to the shores of Virginia as indentured servants in 1619,[1] and in the Caribbean for more than a century before that.[2] The resistive capacity of these bondsmen and bondswomen only intensified as the majority of blacks in the New World suffered as chattel for centuries afterward and, in the case of the United States, de jure second-class citizens from the time of emancipation until the end of Jim Crow.

Perhaps naively, I didn't stop to think that political statements of this sort would be found in a contemporary environment as seemingly casual and apolitical as the basketball court. Instead, the original purpose of my research on pickup basketball in the black community was more functional in its design, aimed at determining the potential of sport to mitigate racial hostility among diverse racial and ethnic groups. Toward that end and around the time I began the book, I had read several pieces celebrating sport's ability to bridge cultural divides, to heal centuries-old political wounds, and to even encourage rival university faculty to set aside their philosophical and pedagogical differences for the good of the game.

The underlying premise of my intended approach was rooted in the contact hypothesis—the idea that prolonged exposure to members of different racial or ethnic groups, coupled with a common goal or theme, could serve to reduce racial conflict and promote the elimination of discrimination and prejudice (McPherson et al. 1989). Introduced earlier, this contact approach asserts that racial hostility, as well as other perceived differences, can be mitigated by showing people that their prejudices and fears about "out-groups" are social constructs—the results of racial projects created to support a particular economic or ideological structure—rooted in incomplete or flawed information rather than empirical realities. Put another way, "Under appropriate conditions interpersonal contact is one of the most effective ways to reduce prejudice between majority and minority group members" (Schiappa et al., 2005, 92). Accordingly, as a pathway toward racial healing, advocates of the contact hypothesis promote increases in meaningful intergroup interaction among people who have historically been on opposite sides of socially constructed racial divides. As Schiappa et al. (2005, 94) explain, "Because avoidance of members of specific groups is a form of negative social behavior that is consistent with negative attitudes, positive contact can create a sense of dissonance that can lead to attitude change." And consistent with this assertion, several studies have demonstrated that under the appropriate conditions[3] intergroup contact has been shown to reduce prejudice toward certain minority groups.[4]

One of the environments rather often held to support the aforementioned conditions and facilitate positive intergroup racial and ethnic relations through contact is sports. Perhaps one of the more interesting contentions of this contact effect has been made in regard to Native Americans, remarkably diverse groups of people who have borne the collective burden of their own version of "Mandingo," one that collectively periodized them as savages, drunks, and undeserving gambling moguls. The application of the contact hypothesis here suggests that such interaction has the ability not only to advance multicultural understanding among members of Native American tribes and other members of society, but also to bandage long-standing wounds that exist between groups of Native Americans.

For example, according to Charles P. Pierce (1996), since the late nineteenth century the Arapaho and Shoshone Indians have shared a physical space on the Wind River Indian Reservation. At one time these two tribes were mortal enemies. And, in what seems to be a real-life manifestation of the parable of the signifying monkey[5] (with the US Calvary serving as the monkey in this case), toward the tail end of what Helen Hunt Jackson (2003) referred to as "a century of dishonor,"[6] the Shoshones were convinced by the US government to join forces with US servicemen against the Northern Arapaho in the Bates Battle of 1874.[7] During the aftermath of the battle, which left the US government as the only clear "winner," the two tribes begrudgingly agreed to co-reside at Wind River. Pierce argues, however, that while they physically shared the reservation, members of the two tribes never truly coexisted until over a hundred years later—when they began playing basketball together. "In basketball, it seems, they have found a place where the old traditions can survive despite what time and circumstance have done to them" (Pierce 1996, 62). Per Pierce's account, the two tribes have set aside their ancient antipathies for the sake of basketball, and he ultimately concludes that it is through basketball that both Native American traditions and those of the Episcopalian missionaries who built the mission that introduced basketball on the reservation "could converge and rise."

While this seems to be a compelling account of the near-mystical powers of sport in overcoming historical divides, closer scrutiny suggests that basketball is more than just a place where "old traditions can survive." Superficially, in a very limited and specific sense it seems the tribal unification Pierce describes was somewhat consistent with contact theory; on the surface and from a distance, it appears as if the two formally feuding tribes used sport to bridge a gap with deep cultural roots and one that stood for over a century. However, another conclusion could just as easily be reached, one that highlights that everyday resistance is more probably at play.

What Pierce overlooks is the fact that the newfound solidarity established between the two tribes probably did not come as the result of the introduction of basketball on "the rez." Rather, the introduction of basketball was more likely a backdrop that afforded the two groups the opportunity to realize through interaction their mutually oppressed status—an epiphany that arguably could have been reached regardless of the presence of tribally integrated sports. What the basketball experience more aptly provided the two tribes was an opportunity to carve out a new-but-old national identity of shared circumstance, ongoing marginalization, and mutual subjugation. It allowed them to see what reflecting upon the nineteenth century made abundantly clear; like generations before as well as today, to the extent that they are regarded by dominant American society at all, Native Americans have been collectively looked upon as little more than pawns in the game of colonial conquest and inconvenient remnants of a seemingly ancient American past. The introduction of the game of basketball simply afforded members of these two tribes an occasion to resist the dominant culture and, particularly for the Shoshone, choose a better suited ally in a resurrected and reconstructed Bates Battle.

Pierce's vision of this social dynamic, while perhaps Pollyannaish and utopian, seems to be clouded by a misguided understanding of the hidden transcript of this particular aspect of Native American culture. Indeed, six years after Pierce's article was published, a 2002 PBS documentary titled *Chiefs* chronicled Wyoming Indian High School's basketball players, all of whom resided on the very same Wind River Indian Reservation. And while the players most certainly coalesce as a team—their five state basketball championships over their relatively short eighteen-year existence serves as a testament to their teamwork—they seem to do so more as a means to fight back against the overt racism they experience when playing white teams from off the reservation and as a means to counterbalance the poverty, alcoholism, and suicide that plague their daily existence as natives in America.

If we put aside the Native American experience for a moment, in principle, contact theory still is plausible. Because, if the core causes of prejudice and discrimination are ignorance and lack of interaction with out-groups, then increased interaction with and among these groups should provide some degree of enlightenment on any side of the racial divide. And because of the tradition of white-black racial segregation in the United States, especially in areas like housing and education, the impact of contact should be particularly pronounced when seeking to foster improved relations between those historically defined as black and white. I draw attention to this specific dichotomy because, for a host of reasons too expansive to be addressed here, more Americans have been exposed to the overt and subtle atrocities committed against African Americans by dominant white social institutions than they have similar abominations by these institutions against members of other racial or ethnic groups.[8] This is particularly the case for black males, who have repeatedly borne the brunt of publicly acknowledged social injustices as well as public displays of political, economic, and physical abuse at the hands of the state.

In their book *Cool Pose*, Richard Majors and Janet Mancini Billson wrote:

Historically, racism and discrimination have inflicted a variety of harsh injustices on African-Americans in the United States, especially on males. Being male and black has meant being psychologically castrated—rendered impotent in the economic, political, and social arenas that whites have historically dominated. Black men learned long ago that the classic American virtues of thrift, perseverance, and hard work did not give them the same tangible rewards that accrued to whites. (Majors and Mancini Billson 1993, 1)

Making a similar statement in *American Paradox: Young Black Men*, Renford Reese asserts, "More than a half-century after Ralph Ellison wrote the classic book *Invisible Man*, black men in America are still trying to become visible" (Reese 2004, xi).

The past paints a clear picture of black subordination predicated on a socially constructed idea of race, and the legacy of this subordination resonates in contemporary society. Given the history of the African in America and the awareness among blacks of ongoing racial discrimination, the problem with contact theory, particularly as it applies to black men, is quite simply that the equal status that the theory's proponents argue is necessary for contact to be fully effective does not and cannot presently exist between the vast majority of black and white Americans.[9]

As Haywood Burns notes in his discussion of law and race in early America, "The Revolution of Jefferson, Washington, and Madison was never intended to embrace the ebony" and "For all our gains, America remains a country deeply infected by racism" (Burns 1998, 280, 284). Notions of black inferiority helped lay America's foundation and, despite movements toward equality under the law (with the most significant progress occurring as a result of the civil rights movement of the 1950s and 1960s), there has never been true social or structural equality in America. The Supreme Court has highlighted in numerous cases,[10] both upholding and tearing down walls of de jure inequality, that legislation and formal policy have never proven effective in eliminating social distinctions based on race. Accordingly, in dealing with black-and-white relations in the United States, with the exception of certain "highly monitored" environments (e.g., the military, interracial housing projects), contact theory fails before it begins because the substantive playing field in America is currently not, nor has it ever been, level. Thus, at least in the context of US race relations in most social spaces and even more specifically in the context of sport and race, contact theory is an insufficient model to depend upon in the promotion of racial harmony.

Black Man's Rules

Accepting this inadequacy of the contact hypothesis as it applies to the present-day status of black Americans in most everyday contexts, the question then becomes, if prolonged exposure to members of different racial or ethnic groups does not promote understanding, what is its effect? Specifically in the framework of sport, if encouraging people of diverse racial and ethnic backgrounds to play together does not meaningfully mitigate racial prejudice, what impact do these encounters have on racial relations? Consistent with the fundamental proposition of play, that being the idea that the ordinary rules of society are temporarily suspended and replaced with a new code of conduct, the world of pickup basketball that I observed was one in which the racial status quo of "white over black"[11] was often provisionally suspended and replaced by a new network of rules, statuses, and mechanisms of informal social control that privileged black over white, a point I will return to momentarily.

For added context, in his participatory analysis of the dispute resolution process in pickup basketball, also set in Southern California, sociologist Michael DeLand appropriately noted that "a game of basketball can mean a variety of things. . . . In each situation, the meaning is constituted as participants 'key' their behavior to sustain the game's particular meaning" (DeLand 2013, 656). However, DeLand's analysis momentarily breaks down when he asserts:

> At the pick-up basketball court, the decision-making authority is non-hierarchical. No player arrives at the court with more authority than others to organize the game or impose a vision of how things ought to go. . . . On the basketball court, meaning is created as participants make and contest bids for authority. (DeLand 2013, 658–659)

On the contrary, at every court I visited in Southern California over the course of this study, including the court that served as the basis for DeLand's analysis, known basketball ability, off-the-court status, and race were key factors in determining decision-making authority, the types of permissible foul calls, and otherwise establishing court hierarchy. Just as the lead referee officiating a professional football or basketball game dictates to his crew how "tightly" the game is to be called, from start to finish, pickup players with more standing have very clear influence on a game's organization, flow, and dispute resolution process. In my observations, ballers with more on-the-court status would routinely organize games as they saw fit and breach court protocol if doing so created an outcome they preferred. For example, teams for the first game of any day's pickup contests can be selected in a number of different ways (e.g., shooting for captains, shooting for teams, "first five," and others), and usually the method is prescribed by the norms or traditions of a particular court. At Encino Park, for instance, the preferred method was to shoot for captains; after ten players had assembled, players would line up to shoot free throws and the first two players to make baskets would serve as opposing captains, picking their teams accordingly. But, on a number of occasions, higher-status ballers would ignore a court's folkways and dictate who would play on what squad to get the afternoon's games started. Similarly, if a higher-value player's team lost the previous game, a baller with "next" would frequently dismiss a lesser player he had already signed to his squad for the preferred player. And, in these instances, the lesser player may gripe, but the only recourse he had was to call "next" or, if someone already had next, try to get a slot on that team.

An interesting example of this question of status in the court's decision-making hierarchy took place on a summer afternoon in Culver City and involved Dula, a low-status member of the local basketball community. Dula was a first-generation Ethiopian immigrant in his late teens and was largely regarded as "soft" by the other players. On more selective days, Dula would have a hard time getting picked up by any squad, and he therefore knew to be at the courts when the first game was assembling if he wanted a chance to play. Dula was among the first ten players at the court that afternoon, and so he gained a spot on a team when the first full-court game began. His team was victorious in the first contest and held court for a second run. But, three points into the second game, Dula was frustrated because his teammates wouldn't pass him the ball. Annoyed, he quit the game in progress, offered his spot to a waiting player, sat down on the bench at the court's west end, and called out "I got next." One of his teammates responded, "Man, that's bullshit. He always does this shit." When Dula's game came up, he walked on the court to secure his "next," but ballers with more court status denied his claim. Instead, they ostracized him for violating court etiquette and, in spite of his protests, refused to let him play for the remainder of the day.

Respect for foul calls offered another often seen example of a player's status affecting decision-making authority. Essentially, ballers with more prestige had the power to ignore fouls called by players with less status, or to call phantom fouls committed against them by another player. As just one example of this point, when he was not in and out of jail for gang-related and other criminal activity, Jacques was a regular at Veteran's Park in Culver City. An Afro-Cuban man in his mid-twenties with a chipped front tooth and facial scars from fighting, Jacques was only about five-foot-seven, with a squat and muscular bulldog-like build. He was relatively quick and had slightly better-than-average basketball skills, but he played with the grace his physique would suggest, roughly hacking others on defense and routinely charging over opposing players on his way to the basket. Even though he had committed an offensive foul in making contact with a stationary defensive player, Jacques would almost always call a "blocking" foul on the defender, particularly if his shot missed. But, because Jacques was an active member of a local set of the Crips street gang and had an off-the-court reputation for violence, very few players ever dared to challenge his calls. And for players without status equal to Jacques's, their infrequent protests to his calls occasionally ended poorly. Perhaps even more interesting was that Jacques's younger brother, Luke, benefited from a form of transitive authority, often getting away with unchallenged fouls and calls because of his older brother's status.

Back to the question of race and pickup hierarchy, while the formal conventions of basketball might be the same for all players regardless of framework or environment, the rules governing social interaction and style of play in these pickup contests are what could best be described as *black man's rules*. Discussed in greater detail later, the world of pickup basketball I observed very clearly belonged to black men and created a zone in which black masculinity and black cultural authority carried more weight than that of any other racial or ethnic group. The predominance of black man's rules was so acute that at each court I frequented, white players made uncomfortable by black men overtly challenging their day-to-day authority organized separate pickup games at times when they knew black ballers wouldn't be present. These games typically occurred during the early morning hours on the weekends. Some groups of white players would go a step further by paying to reserve gym time at local high schools so that they could control who gained access and avoid what was described to me on several occasions as the "street" element. On numerous occasions I observed white players quietly exiting public basketball courts as black players began to arrive in any significant numbers. Bob, one of the white players who occasionally participated in afternoon pickup games in Culver City, began showing up less frequently. When I asked about his absence, Bob informed me that he had begun playing with a "group of guys" in the mornings, saying "it's a good run in the morning." Several times I showed up for this morning run and was either the only black person present or one of just a few.

Albeit in a necessarily limited scope, this suspension of the racial status quo on the pickup court affords African American men a blend of momentary domination and liberation not permitted them in most spheres of American life; a temporary foray into a symbolic "bizarro"[12] universe characterized by black male supremacy. Through a distinctive fusion of public and hidden transcripts[13]—what is perhaps best categorized as an "intermediate transcript"—the court offers younger black men a chance to weave a unique text through which the frustrations derived from being black in America are articulated in a public forum without fear of formal social repercussions. An exchange with Clark captures this well:

> ARM: You said that the basketball court was one of the few places where, as a black man, you could let your emotions out without consequences that might come in other contexts. Do you think other people have those same constraints?

> CLARK: Not really . . . like females, they can act wild and not much is going to happen to them. White guys can act wild and you know nothing much . . . I mean, you can just look at prison statistics. You know? For brown and black, it's just a different. . . . I would think with Latinos it would be soccer, not basketball. But . . . it's just somewhere where you can just let yourself . . . you know . . . not worry about what the next person is saying. Just be you, let your emotions out, and just play. You know, and whatever happens, happens. It's not going to be looked on as negative.

Escaping the Ethnoracial Prison

Similar to all popular American sports in which black men appear to predominate, basketball—as I noted earlier—was not organically developed by the principally black participants with whom the sport is commonly associated. In fact, basketball's 1891 invention in Springfield, Massachusetts, was rather deliberate and was certainly never intended to attract the ebony. On the contrary, it was generally held to be a sport for young white Christian men as part of a formal "Muscular

Christianity" campaign intended to develop the "mind, and soul," as well as the body of male college students (LeFeber 1999). As legal scholar Lawrence Friedman wrote about the era's regulation of perceived immorality, "the nineteenth century . . . relied on self-control, which it tried to support through legal institutions, as well as other social processes" (Friedman 1994, 133). Accordingly, the social policies that emerged were rooted in the belief that sources of living morality such as the church, the family, and the school could act in concert with sources of official morality to maintain norms needed for discipline and order. As a result of these ideas, on both sides of the Atlantic and ultimately throughout the European and US colonies, sports emerged as one of the more unique social processes used to reinforce late Victorian notions of personal morality. In spite of its parochial beginnings, in part due to internal colonial influences and minority cooptation of the sport, in the decades following its invention, the game of basketball developed into "the city game." And, through its claiming by minority urban ambassadors, the sport evolved to suit economically and politically unequal conditions not dissimilar to those experienced by the Afro-Brazilian peasants to whom capoeira belongs—conditions in which a theater of power inequality is played out on a daily basis.

It is precisely this adaptive quality of sport coupled with its generally nonthreatening superficial and ludic veneer that makes it the ideal portal through which to view the intermediate transcript, highlighting the incongruity of suppressing one's public self and simultaneously exposing parts of the inner self ordinarily bridled in day-to-day interaction. Among the core group of pickup basketball participants—the ballers—the game assumes this greater symbolic meaning; a meaning of struggle, resistance, and temporary triumph. On the pickup court, the game is agonistic in the sense that contest is dominant. But the contest is only partially about winning the game at hand. At the same time that the physical competition is being carried out, a parallel contest based on competitive self-expression through physical display is equally prominent. In this closer analysis of the pickup culture, issues like respect, poise, and dignity often become more important than the final score or any other quantitative outcome.

As Clifford Geertz (1973) and J. Lowell Lewis (1992) noted in their respective interpretations of Balinese cockfighting and Brazilian capoeira, what is seen in the culture of pickup basketball is a kind of "deep play." Despite who may win or who may lose any individual contest, with the game as backdrop, the real contest is social struggle and the real end is akin to liberation. It is a temporary emancipation from what Loïc Wacquant described as the American ethnoracial prison that "encages a dishonoured category and severely curtails the life chances of its members in support of the 'monopolization of ideal and material goods or opportunities' by the dominant status group dwelling on its outskirts" (Wacquant 2002, 51).

Hank, an Atlanta-based baller in his early twenties, offered his thoughts on growing up black and male in one of these ethnoracial prisons, and the role basketball played in offering escape, a portal not available to most:

> Growing up in the inner city is not always a good thing, although people take a lot of pride in saying that they are from the city. Growing up in the city was tough for me because I've seen a lot of things young boys should not see at my age. I knew who the drug dealers were, and the drug dealers knew me. I knew I wanted different and I wanted to do more than what I had seen the people on the streets doing. Basketball was an activity that took me out of the streets and placed me in a different context and group of peers. That is why I believe basketball saved my life. I have cousins who are the same age as me, and we are on totally different paths right now.

Ultimately, for a good number of black folks living contested existences, basketball offers an opportunity for momentary freedom from an enduring race- and economically based caste system; from class domination, continued exclusion and social isolation, denial of recognition, and savagely disproportionate poverty; and from the literal and metaphorical shackles placed upon black people by a society whose proclamation that "all men are created equal" consistently falls abusively short of fulfilling this promise.

The significance of black pickup basketball's statement is not, as Lewis suggests, because play "comes from a loosening of social restraints, a suspension of the rules of normal behavior" (Lewis 1992, 4). Instead, what I found and what I contend to more often be the case is that pickup basketball may indeed loosen conventional social restraints, but in the context of the city game, it simultaneously replaces them with a new social order in which black males sit atop the social hierarchy, affording them a temporary transcendence of ordinary social boundaries that I call "black man's rules." It presents an anomalous form of status inconsistency in which black males, while collectively still lacking in material wealth and other conventional markers of higher social position, interstitially claim a disproportionate share of power and prestige.

Treating Basketball as Text

The traditional "play" position in sports sociology holds that the game serves this function of suspending the rules of normal behavior because it is one of the rare episodes in social life in which participation is completely voluntary. By definition, it is certainly true that one cannot be forced to play. However, willing participation does not entirely or even primarily remove the actor from social restraints. And to further complicate matters, it is difficult to say to what extent participation in particular sports by specific groups of people is "voluntary" and to what extent it is a subcultural expectation or mandate. For example, as also discussed in the previous chapter, Clark, a six-foot-five baller who came of age in inner-city Atlanta, reflected that he personally enjoyed playing basketball. But, in addition to his affinity for the sport, his family and friends made it clear to him that as a black youth growing up in the city, he was *supposed* to play basketball. During his teen years, as he eclipsed the six-foot mark and began to develop the "long" physique typical of a basketball player, these cultural expectations only intensified. Clark captured these collective anticipations of others:

> Your identity is so intertwined with basketball and it's hard to separate
> that. And, like I said, my family members were like, "OK, you graduated,
> congrats. So what, you graduated. So you didn't play ball. So it never
> worked out for you, Clark." You know what I'm saying? So they'll still
> hit you with jabs like that. "So what happened? You didn't make it." You
> know they'll still hit you with a jab or something.

The way in which the public, hidden, and intermediate transcripts are conveyed is not always verbal. In fact, they typically are unspoken but are most certainly discursive as the social action that takes place becomes a kind of text. The meaning and interpretation of nonverbal interaction becomes as central as spoken words in the understanding of this discourse of race. The basketball court becomes more than simply an arena for ludic expression—a place where ten guys get together in playful cooperation, competing against one another for the sake of the game— and a sphere in which aspects of external reality are excluded as irrelevant. The goings-on are more than a mere social gathering. For many, the court serves a metaphorical battleground on which some African American men attempt to carve out new spaces of recognition and resist the ascribed social identity of inferiority cast upon them by centuries of subordination and the corresponding legacy of American racism. For them, sport becomes a mode of resistance that, consciously or not, is related to what Joy DeGruy Leary refers to as "post traumatic slave syndrome"—the transgenerational adaptations associated with the past traumas of slavery and on-going oppression (Leary 2005, 13).

In this sense, pickup basketball transcends play, adding an agonistic dimension—a state of defensive social interaction in which the contest is dominant and winning is everything. However, winning on the black-top is not solely determined by who scores the most points on whom. Instead, the measurement of victory lies in direct contrast to measures of success on other, more restrictive courts—those located in private gymnasiums, those reserved by particular organizations for league play, and those located in more exclusive communities typically not accessible to the majority of black youth. On the public blacktops where a significant African American representation is present, a ceaseless parallel contest is taking place in which indicators of victory include the challenging of the existing social structure and altering the terms of social engagement. Underneath the many superficial aspects of these games, the pickup court often becomes a public space where black men feel free to be themselves. The games provide a place to reject assimilation in mainstream white culture, providing poor black men a place of privilege and attracting middle- and upper-class black men trying to maintain an authentic street identity.

The performance, behavior, and contest in these pickup basketball arenas highlight a shared sense of antipathy and acrimony among African American males toward the dominant social institutions that many of them perceive to serve as constant reminders of their inability to get ahead or merely become "visible." Beyond the court, to many black males, day-to-day public interaction with white people underscores the fact that they are still not of equal status in American society. Aside from formal and overt racist encounters, there exist countless examples of what Jerelyn Eddings calls "stealth racism," the more subtle daily encounters blacks and other minorities have with prejudice and discrimination. These episodes, Eddings remarks, "remind blacks that they are often dismissed as less intelligent, less industrious, less honest, and less likely to succeed" (Eddings 2000, 198). Because of this, certain spaces become theaters for everyday resistance in which a formulaic public script of deference is cast aside and replaced by an often veiled, yet distinct, text of protest. UCLA history professor Robin Kelley brilliantly captures how some of these spaces exist on the "margins of struggle" and allow working-class black people to survive "without direct links to the kinds of organizations that dominate historical accounts of African American or US working-class resistance" (Kelley

1996, 4). Due to its physical construction, the level of necessary inter-action among willing participants, and the opportunity for subtle public expression afforded by the peculiar social dynamics displayed, the pickup basketball court has become an ideal stage for a performance of this sort. The following chapter explores and describes instances of how these statements of resistance are made.

Notes

1. In his book *A Different Mirror*, Ronald Takaki (1993) notes that the first twenty Africans arrived in the New World at the Jamestown settlement in 1619 and were, like most laborers to populate the early colonies in America, indentured ser-vants rather than slaves. However, over the course of that century, the white plan-tocracy found it politically and economically advantageous to discontinue white indentured servitude and institute a system of black bonded labor.

2. Records of African slavery in the New World date back at least to 1502, and the transatlantic slave trade, as an official enterprise, began in approximately 1526 with ships carrying cargoes of Africans to permanent enslavement in Portuguese and Spanish colonies in the New World.

3. According to most proponents of the contact hypothesis, these requisite conditions for the groups in contact are: (a) they must possess equal status, (b) they must share common goals, (c) they must interact cooperatively, and (d) they must have environmental support (Braddock 1980).

4. Schiappa et al. (2005) point to successes in reducing prejudice toward mem-bers of the LGBTQ community and Arabs. Other studies have shown support for the prejudice-reduction function of interracial contact in arenas like education, housing projects, and the military (Powers and Ellison 1995; Braddock 1980).

5. In this fable, the signifying monkey tricks a lion into unwisely attacking an ele-phant by suggesting that the elephant was speaking poorly of the lion and his family. Upon his return to where he first encountered the monkey, the badly beaten lion is addressed by a taunting and over-celebratory monkey. Realizing the monkey's decep-tion, a relationship of mistrust and disdain between the two was forever solidified.

6. In her 1881 reflection upon the "alienable" status of Native American land rights in the eyes of those crafting American Indian law, Jackson wrote, "The prece-dents of a century's unhindered and profitable robbery have mounted up into a very Gibraltar of defence and shelter to those who care for nothing but safety and gain. That such precedents should be held, and openly avowed as standards, is only one more infamy added to the list. . . . What an opportunity for the Congress of 1880 to cover itself with the lustre of glory, as the first to cut short our nation's record of cruelties and perjuries! The first to redeem the name of the United States from the stain of a century of dishonor!" (Jackson 2003, 30–31.)

7. There seems to be some confusion about the actual date of this battle, with some historians arguing that it actually took place in 1874 rather than 1876. There is also disagreement about the precise name of the battle. Apparently there were two battles involving the name "Bates" within a two-year span; the Battle of Bates Creek in 1876 and Bates Battle in 1874. The former, which Pierce seems to erroneously attribute to the dispute between the Arapaho and Shoshone, seems to actually have been a battle between the US Army and the Northern Cheyenne also

known as "the Dull Knife Fight." This battle is regarded as effectively ending Cheyenne resistance to the frontier and permanently crippling the Cheyenne's ability to wage war. Bates Battle, in contrast, took place on July 4, 1874, and was named for US Army Captain Alfred Bates, the leader of US Army Camp Brown. Bates Battle involved an attack at No Water Creek on a band of Northern Arapaho by the Shoshones and troops from Camp Brown responding to reports of hostile Indians in the region (Stamm 1999). Either way, the Shoshone people were aligned with the US Army, which for its own reasons, served as protector of the Shoshones from raiding Cheyenne, Arapaho, and Sioux.

8. In his book *Racial Healing*, Harlon Dalton (1995) notes that there are distinct downsides to viewing a multicultural world through a lens that only refracts black and white. Of these, Dalton highlights the fact that the black experience in America tends to be the template against which the experiences of all people of color are measured, effectively using blacks as a measuring rod for all people of color. Not all oppressed people have been oppressed in the same fashion, so to use the black experience as the one by which all oppression is judged does a disservice to those who are not similarly situated. Further, this view tends to obscure frictions within and among minority groups. While I generally agree with Dalton's critique of modern-day racial discourse, I view this placement of blacks in the foreground of racial relations as a distinct and crucial advantage for this research because it indicates a strong possibility that African Americans are not only aware of present inequality but also have been exposed to the history of white-on-black racial oppression—something key to a reconsideration of contact theory.

9. In their discussion of selectivity bias in the application of the contact hypothesis, Powers and Ellison (1995, 206) more generally observe, "First, most empirical investigations over the years have been conducted in specific institutional contexts (e.g., interracial housing projects, desegregated schools, the military) or in laboratories. . . . However, most interracial contact does not occur in these specialized, highly monitored settings. Thus, while these studies have contributed to our understanding of intergroup relations, until recently they have left open the question of whether interracial contact results in positive racial attitudes in the general population."

10. While the legal outcomes in *Plessy v. Ferguson* (1896) and *Adarand Constructors v. Pena* (1996) were radically different than the signature case of the Warren Court and the rights revolution, *Brown v. Board of Education* (1954), the Court in each case recognized the inability of legal change to affect social consciousness without other social forces coming into play.

11. "White over black" is a reference to Winthrop Jordan's classic book of the same name. Published in 1968 by the University of North Carolina Press, Jordan's book explores the historical origins of the racist and irrational attitudes of English and American attitudes toward blacks from the mid-sixteenth through the early nineteenth centuries.

12. In an episode of the classic 1990s sitcom *Seinfeld*, the character Elaine feels like she's entered the world of Bizarro Jerry (the title character), where everything seems in reverse and her new boyfriend's friends are complete lookalikes but exact opposites of Jerry and his friends.

13. This transcript analysis stems from the work of James Scott, who in *Domination and the Art of Resistance* (1990, 2) characterizes the "public transcript" as "the open interaction between subordinates and those who dominate" and contrasts this public display with the "hidden transcripts" or the "discourse that takes place 'offstage,' beyond direct observation by powerholders."

4

Playing It Cool, Pushing Back

At least out here [on the basketball court] I know I'm the man.
While I'm playing ball, breaking niggas off, I don't even think about
anything else. They know I'm the man.

—Black Mike

In the world of Southern California pickup basketball as well as in broader displays of black culture, a variety of manifestations of struggle and resistance are presented through the words and everyday actions of the participants. Perhaps the most easily recognized of these presentations involves the assuming of the *cool pose*. In their analysis of black masculinity in America, Richard Majors and Janet Mancini Billson introduced this phrase to describe the aloof, irreverent, and fearless public transcript often put forth by African American males to counterbalance intense feelings of marginality that stem from "living on the edge of society." They go on to contend, "Of all the strategies embraced by black males to cope with oppression and marginality, the creation of the cool pose is perhaps the most unique" (Majors and Mancini Billson, 1993, 8). Ultimately, the function of this pose is twofold. First, it serves as a sanctuary for black male pride, dignity, and respect. Second, it provides an avenue for the expression of the bitterness, anger, and distrust black males often feel toward the dominant society (Majors and Mancini Billson, 1993).

In the early 1980s *Saturday Night Live* skit "Fernando's Hideaway," Billy Crystal portrayed an aged Latin playboy named Fernando. Usually seated in a plush lounge booth sipping a tropical potable and speaking in a stereotypical Latin accent, Fernando would console his troubled weekly visitors with the flippant remark, "it's better to look good than to feel good." In many ways, this idiomatic expression describes the

79

cool pose. The public transcript of black males is one that emphasizes outward confidence and "cool," despite often experiencing inner feelings of inferiority, hopelessness, frustration, and lacking self-worth, or, as Majors and Mancini Billson characterized it, "being psychologically castrated . . . rendered impotent in the economic, political, and social arenas that whites have historically dominated" (Majors and Mancini Billson, 1993, 1). As UCLA professor Robin Kelley wrote about working at McDonald's during his teenage years in Pasadena, California:

> Nothing was sacred, not even the labor process. . . . what I remember most was the way many of us stylized our work. We ignored the films and manuals and turned work into performance. . . . Tossing trash became an opportunity to try out our best Dr. J moves. The brothers who worked the grill (it was only brothers from what I recall) were far more concerned with looking cool than ensuring an equal distribution of onions on each all-beef patty. Just imagine a young black male "gangsta limpin'" between the toaster and the grill, brandishing a spatula like a walking stick or a microphone. . . . The employees at the central Pasadena McDonald's were constantly inventing new ways to rebel, ways rooted in our own peculiar circumstances. (Kelley 1996, 2–3)

Perhaps beyond all else, this public transcript in all of its performative and material brashness masks the black fear captured by Ta-Nehisi Coates in his wonderful memoir, *Between the World and Me*:

> It was always right in front of me. The fear was there in the extravagant boys of my neighborhood, in their large rings and medallions, their big puffy coats and full-length fur-collared leathers, which was their armor against their world. . . . I think back on those boys now and all I see is fear, and all I see is them girding themselves against the ghosts of the bad old days when the Mississippi mob gathered 'round their grandfathers so that the branches of the black body might be torched, then cut away. The fear lived on in their practiced bop, their slouching denim, their big t-shirts, the calculated angle of their baseball caps, a catalog of behaviors and garments enlisted to inspire the belief that these boys were in firm possession of everything they desired. (Coates 2015, 14)

On the blacktops in Southern California, the public transcript acted out among African American males, expressed both verbally and nonverbally, often took this form. The demeanors displayed by many of the ballers on the court—the way they talk, stand, dress, sit on the bench, and play the game—are all indicative of this pose. With regard to style of play, perhaps Gena Dagel Caponi put it best in her introduction to Jeff Greenfield's "The Black and White Truth About Basketball," a chapter in her edited work *Signifyin(g), Sanctifyin', and Slam Dunking: A Reader in African-American Expressive Culture.* Caponi wrote, "The black basketball style is a form of 'electric self-expression,' . . . and yet integral to this style is virtuoso performance that shows no strain" (Caponi 1999, 373). As it relates to other aspects of the cool pose, a distinct aura of detachment, confidence, and an "I don't give a damn" attitude permeates their personal styles and the way in which they play the game. In this context, athletic and creative excellence and style temporarily mitigate the nihilism[1] and self-doubt felt by those historically oppressed. As Cornel West wrote, "The fundamental crisis in black America is twofold: too much poverty and too little self-love" (West 1993, 63). While both of these are consequences of being black in America, neither is caused by being *black*. However, the temporary dominance afforded black Americans by sport in general—and basketball in particular—and accented through this cool pose affords African American youth a sanctuary from pervasive social and economic inequality.

The significance of this cool pose is as much a race matter as it is a social status issue. Blackness is, for most intents and purposes, a master status, overshadowing the various other social positions that African Americans occupy. Before anything else, African Americans are seen as black and received with much of the attendant bias that blackness has historically carried with it in the United States. For this reason, African Americans of the past and present, and across all socioeconomic boundaries, are constantly engaged in what W. E. B. DuBois (1903) identified as a *double life*.

While the cool pose resulting from this double life is perhaps more pronounced and commonplace among black males of lower socioeconomic status in their day-to-day lives, it is clearly something that has the ability to transcend intraracial socioeconomic boundaries. Blacks of varying statuses experience racial, social, and economic tensions in different ways, yet these acts of injustice are all similar in that they stem either directly or indirectly from the American ideology that blacks are innately inferior. Because this denial of recognition is not economically specific, parallel senses of animosity toward the establishment triggered by their collective sense of political impotence causes many African American males to assume behaviors that appear to mock and defy dominant social institutions. This is the case despite individual and class-based differences in their experiences with discrimination based on their socioeconomic status—while anti-black racism is ubiquitous regardless of class, middle-class blacks are often contextually shielded by class privilege and do not always experience racism in the same way or with the same intensity as blacks in the lower socioeconomic classes. Further, this mockery often takes the form of the cool pose and these behaviors are most often carried out in places of relative sanctuary, away from direct threats of reprisal like the semi-structured environment of the pickup basketball court.

Sagging basketball shorts, oversized shirts, baseball caps cocked sideways, and expensive shoes are all material elements of the culture of cool. These items subtly, yet directly, speak against dominant notions of how people are expected to dress. A loping gait, *jive* talk, slightly slouched posture, machismo, bravado, and an overall "I don't care" attitude expressed primarily through body language are all nonmaterial elements of the cool pose, with a similar effect to that of the material elements. These figments of nonmaterial culture publicly reject the demeanor that is expected and necessary in other aspects of social life.

To be sure, many mistake these cultural symbols for "natural" or innate elements of black culture. And, on the surface, this pose might appear natural in that it is presented with an ease that seems organic and unrehearsed. However, for many younger black males much of this pose, both in its physical display and in the accompanying demeanor, is indeed rehearsed and typically displayed to offer a momentary sense of asylum. To borrow from Boots Riley of the 1990s rap group The Coup:

> In this land I can't stand or sit
> And not get shit thrown up in my face
> A brother never gets his props
> I'm doing bellyflops at the department of waste
> And every day I pulls a front so nobody pulls my card
> I got a mirror in my pocket and I practice looking hard[2]

Culver City's Black Mike[3] looks fluid and casual while executing his flawless crossover dribble at near full-speed. And after his opponent is literally rendered motionless by the smoothness with which Mike feigns right only to actually maneuver to his left, his cavalier attitude about the embarrassment he had just imposed on his defender speaks nothing of the countless hours he spends in the relative seclusion of the local YMCA or his nearby high school gymnasium perfecting his "handles" so that he may make it look easy. The way that he shrugs off the cheers and accolades bestowed upon him by other players and spectators for "taking that boy's manhood" are also responses learned and practiced through hours of competitive play and social interaction.

While his ability and the response to his prowess appear natural, they are in fact well-practiced choreography.

Despite Black Mike's basketball prowess, at five-feet-nine and already sixteen years old, his dreams of a basketball career are a near impossibility. While he also had dreams of going to college and carried a grade-point average of over 3.0 throughout high school, he could not afford tuition and fees at even the state schools, and his SAT scores prohibited him from securing an academic scholarship. As his Division I basketball dreams and visions of college attendance were becoming increasingly remote possibilities, he turned even more to basketball to mask the inadequacy and uncertainty he felt. As he said to me one afternoon while I was giving him a ride from the courts back to the one-bedroom apartment he shared with his mother: "At least out here [on the basketball court] I know I'm the man. While I'm playing ball, breaking niggas off, I don't even think about anything else. They know I'm the man."

Similar to Mike's pose, another one of the regular ballers, Gene, looks as if his gravity-defying slam dunks are effortless. At slightly less than six feet tall, he is commonly known to dunk over much larger opponents. On one such occasion in Encino, Gene and two of his teammates ran a three-on-one fast-break. Felton—a six-foot-five former Division I college player—was the lone opposing player on defense. Doing as any coach would recommend, Felton held back in the middle of the key and defended the ball as Gene led the break. That is to say that he (Gene) was the offensive player traveling down the middle of the court with possession of the ball. His teammates were in proper position, running the court slightly ahead of Gene and off to either side. But instead of *dishing* (passing) the ball to one of his less impeded teammates, and in spite of Felton's position in the middle of the key, completely obstructing Gene's pathway to the basket, Gene opted to keep the ball to himself. Reminiscent of Julius Erving's famed dunk during the 1976 American Basketball Association All-Star Game in which Dr. J (as Erving was more famously known) took off from the free-throw line dunk, Gene leapt from slightly inside the foul line. And, equally reminiscent of six-foot-six NBA all-star Vince Carter's infamous leap over a seven-foot French opponent during the 2000 Olympic Games in Sydney, Gene proceeded to soar over Felton's head and slammed the ball through the basket.

Gene's teammates and the small gallery of players awaiting the next game erupted equally in celebration of Gene's incredibly athletic feat and in ridicule of Felton being "posterized"[4]—situationally embarrassed by the athletic accomplishment of an opponent in the field of play. The mixture of praise and ridicule that made up the ovation was riddled with commentaries on how Gene embarrassed the defender and "took Felton's manhood." One of the more memorable and vivid responses came from Marcus, a lean, light-skinned, regular baller, who exploded hysterically, "Oh shit Felton! He left nut prints on your forehead!" Living up to his end of the cool pose ritual, Felton acted as if the dunk over him and the subsequent jeers didn't faze him, the chorus ultimately died down, and the game resumed.

Gene performed these gravity-defying blacktop heroics on a regular basis, and to the layperson it may have appeared as though he was just a naturally gifted athlete. While genetics certainly played a part in Gene's athletic ability, he too spent hours during the week at a local gym working on his "hops," perfecting his timing, and polishing his presentation. It was all part of his performance and his perpetuation of cool. Not dissimilar to a gymnast who spends hours perfecting the technique and presentation of a floor routine, Gene and other ballers spent hours on both the technical aspects of their game and, just as much, on their performance aesthetic. The simple point is that while all of this bravado and athleticism is presented by the ballers as easy and natural, these skills are honed through hours of court time, weight training, and competition. Perhaps more important, their cultural and ethnic identities are in many ways maintained by these contrived expressions and nonchalance, which serve to gain them recognition and enhance the cool pose.

This last point of cultural recognition is essential in fully understanding the functionality of the cool pose, for, rather than being an accurate depiction of black male self-perception, the cool pose is fundamentally a coping mechanism for feelings of oppression and marginality. That is to say that the cool pose is often little more than a public transcript put forth to downplay the feelings of inadequacy, impotency, and uncertainty experienced by black males. Or, again referencing Coates as he reflected upon the pose embodied by young black men in his native Baltimore, "The crews walked the blocks of their neighborhood, loud and rude, because it was only through their loud rudeness that they might feel any sense of security and power" (Coates 2015, 22).

Willis, a New York City native from a working-class background, moved to a predominantly white area in Southern California to play Division I college basketball. Unlike some of his teammates, he was not an academic risk. Instead, Willis was an intuitive young man and performed well academically. But, shortly after arriving at the university, it became clear to him that the university valued him far more as a point guard than it did as a student, and he routinely offered examples of being exoticized by his fellow students and coaches and dismissed as a serious student by his professors and other students. Initially, he worked hard to counter these reactions to his presence and to play down his "blackness." He focused on academic achievement; put forth an enthusiastic and can-do attitude during practice; routinely code-switched and in the presence of coaches and other white authority figures, spoke without using slang and played down his New York accent; and kept his hair closely cropped.

Willis kept at this routine of positive resistance against being made to feel marginal and, like the Mandingo stereotype, only valued for his athletic ability, for almost a year. But, as his first summer in Southern California approached, I noticed that Willis began letting his hair grow and it had now taken on a short "afro" style. After playing pickup with him and some of his teammates in the university's practice gym one afternoon, I bantered to Willis, "Your wig is looking a little raggedy, son." Since both of us were from the East Coast, we often joked with each other in regional slang, and I was essentially asking him about the noticeable change in his hairstyle. Willis laughed but then became more serious, explaining to me that he was frustrated with what he perceived as constant disrespect and not being taken seriously, at least beyond the basketball court. He then said he would no longer feign excitement and enthusiasm in response to coaches, boosters, and other university authority figures: "I tried that, and I'm not doing it anymore." Finally, he explained that he was taking this statement further and that his afro was just a transitional phase to full-on cornrows—a traditional black hairstyle where the hair is braided very close to the scalp, which had become increasingly controversial and politicized as black consciousness increased in the latter part of the twentieth century.

In another instance of the cool pose masking feelings of marginalization, frustration, and hopelessness, one rare rainy afternoon in Van Nuys several of the area ballers had congregated to play basketball indoors at the local YMCA. Many of the players were of high school age, were relatively impoverished, and didn't have cars, so spending money on public transportation typically meant going without something else. I had interacted with A. J. in pickup games at both the YMCA and the court in Encino for several months, and on this day he approached me and asked if he could catch a ride to the Van Nuys apartment in which he resided with his mother several miles away. Along the way, knowing from previous conversations that I was affiliated with a university and had worked with college-level student athletes, A. J. asked me questions about college and my assessment of his ability to play college basketball.

> I'm thinking about transferring schools but I can't decide. I go to Van Nuys [High School] but am thinking about going over to Cleveland [High School] because their basketball program is tighter. They got more exposure so college coaches might be more likely to see me play and offer me a scholarship. That's the only way I'm going to be able to go to college because my mom can't afford to send me.

A. J. was about an inch shy of six feet tall with outstanding ball-handling ability. I went on to tell A. J. what both a Division I university athletic director and head basketball coach had told me about the new wave of college basketball players. According to the athletic director and the coach, respectively:

> Six-foot guards are a dime a dozen. You've got to have more going for you these days than great handles [dribbling ability] and a nice jumper. You've got to have something special for us to want to take a serious look at you. If you're under six-five and even questionable academically, we're not even going to take a look at you.
>
> I look for attitude and kids that I can work with. Nowadays, you've got so many kids under six-foot-six that can play the game that you have to look for distinguishing qualities off the court.

Based on these insights, I recommended to A. J. that he choose the school with the better academic program and let the basketball take care of itself.

While on the court, A. J. was the embodiment of cool. But off the court and in the relative seclusion of my car, his cool veneer dropped to expose the fallacy of his public transcript of indifference. Ultimately, the impression of the cavalier and indifferent black male that is subtly perpetuated through mainstream depictions of urban black culture, as well as that public self asserted by many African American men, is often inaccurate or at least incomplete.

My interaction with A. J. also illustrates the networks of interdependence and the sense of trust and solidarity forged among certain members of the blacktop community. As Mitchell Duneier (1992, 20) points out in *Slim's Table*, his study of race and masculinity in Chicago:

> At [the cafeteria], Slim and his sitting buddies demonstrate an inner strength characterized by self-control and willpower that is seldom, if ever, attributed to the black male in social scientific and journalistic reports.

Though black men are usually portrayed as so consumed with maintaining a cool pose that they are unable to "let their guard down and show affection," these black men had created a caring community.

I Never Knew It Was so Sweet to Hit a White Man

On many occasions the same feelings of political impotence and denial of honor that inspired the cool pose would trigger more overtly resistive behavior in some of the ballers. In these instances, the simple mocking and subtle defiance of mainstream social conventions were replaced by more overt, aggressive statements of discontent and more direct insistence for recognition of honor—the presupposition that, despite social class or race, each individual deserves "intersubjective recognition"[5] of their humanity, existence, and worth and this recognition then serves as the foundation of moral consciousness. In his discussion of the value of intersubjective recognition in contemporary societies, Axel Honneth (1995, 130) notes the prerequisite of "symmetrical esteem" and defines this condition as one in which "every subject is free from being collectively denigrated, so that one is given the chance to experience oneself to be recognized, in light of one's own accomplishments and abilities, as valuable for society." As evidenced in the earlier discussion of Willis, it is certainly true that the shared sentiment of many black Americans reflects an awareness of the absence of symmetrical social esteem in their daily interpersonal and institutional encounters with the dominant culture, and that this asymmetry is one that has privileged the accomplishments of white Americans while simultaneously demeaning those of blacks.

The on-the-court aggressive statements and behavioral displays that correspond with, or perhaps are consequences of, this denial of intersubjective recognition can perhaps be best described as expressive rather than instrumental, as their objective appears primarily as a demonstration of one's own integrity and an appeal for the recognition of value. Again, like the cool pose, these acts have their roots in lifelong experiences of being insufficiently recognized as individual personalities and instead treated simply as members of a larger social group—something common to the experience of many black men.

On multiple occasions, black men would directly confront and challenge white men and other representatives of formal authority who they felt had overstepped the bounds on the African American dominated blacktop. More often than not, the rationale for this confrontational defiance seemed to be a direct response to the previously mentioned idea of a double life. For example, during an interview with a baller in Culver City whom I knew to be a college graduate and employed in regional sales for a major security alarm company, I asked why his demeanor was so openly hostile toward the few white men who ventured to play in the Culver City pickup games. His response suggested that his behavior was a challenge to the attitude of white male privilege that he saw as commonplace in corporate America.

> Fuck these white assholes. I ain't got shit for 'em. They think that, just because they run everything else, they can come out here and run shit. I have to put up with their bullshit all day and all week at work. I'll be damned if I'm going to put up with it here.

His emotion also highlighted a proprietary conflict and recurring tension that underscored local politics in Culver City. The white residents laid claim to the park based upon its proximity to the homes that they owned. However, black and Latino residents asserted similar claim to the park based, in large part, on their residence in local rental properties. As I discuss later in this section, the interests of the white homeowners seemingly prevailed as their influence shaped local policy, including park regulations.

This sentiment was one that was echoed on several other occasions in Culver City and elsewhere, and was seemingly directed at white men because they were emblematic of not simply institutional oppression but of the forced cultural compromise black men (not to mention women and other minorities) were expected to endure if they wanted to succeed in mainstream America, or to more simply stay out of trouble. In short, African American men in the white-collar world are encouraged to forgo their blackness in order to succeed materially. Similarly, outside of the workplace, African American males at large are required to downplay both material and nonmaterial symbols of blackness if they wish to avoid heightened scrutiny from formal agents of authority.

On another occasion in Van Nuys, five other people and I were playing in a three-on-three pickup game at a local YMCA. Five of us were black males, and the sixth player was a white man in what appeared to be his late thirties or early forties wearing a T-shirt that read "reading jogs the mind." Darrell—a sixteen-year-old baller who played regularly in both Van Nuys and Encino—and the white man were on the same team. During the early part of the game, Darrell was guarding me. Because I had a distinct size advantage on Darrell, I was able to score a couple of easy baskets by backing him down in the post. The white man, who was taller and heavier than Darrell, closer to my size, suggested that he and Darrell switch defensive assignments. Visibly irritated by this suggestion, Darrell's seemingly unprovoked response was a venomous "Fuck you! He's not scoring. CJ's [another player on my team] doing all the scoring. Why don't you guard him!"

The white man persisted, and Darrell became even more hostile and argumentative. Their conflict continued until, finally, Darrell allowed the man to guard me. On our next possession—perhaps driven by a subconscious desire to validate Darrell—I called for the ball in the post and worked particularly hard to score a basket on the new defender. This prompted another immediate verbal attack from Darrell. "What'd you wanna guard him for? He's fucking you up . . . talking all that shit and you didn't stop him."

Clearly, Darrell was not showing the degree of respect and deference that would have most likely been afforded the white man, or most others for that matter, in a different social setting. After the game, Darrell was still brooding. I walked over to him and asked if everything was alright. Darrell's response was consistent with that of many others with whom I spoke over the course of my time on the courts—"I hate when old white motherfuckers come in here thinking they can tell me how to play *my* game."

Darrell's reaction was not directed at the man simply because his suggestion of a defensive switch challenged Darrell's identity as a basketball player. These sorts of propositions were commonplace during all-black pickup games and were often much more insulting in their intent. Yet, almost never did these evoke the sort of response given by Darrell when offered by a fellow African American. Instead, Darrell's hostility was directed at this particular man clearly because he was white, and it was also clear Darrell viewed his suggestion as congruent to the patronage he and those similarly situated were subjected to on a routine basis by white Americans and white American institutions.

Denials of recognition like these are viewed by the offended as violations to the integrity of the person as a whole, which is why Darrell felt so insulted when the white man told him how to play on "his court." Like Nathan McCall described of a brutal beating he and his childhood friends dispensed upon an unknown "white boy" who naively "came pedaling a bicycle casually through the neighborhood," I often observed disdain directed toward white players whom members of the black court majority felt were "definitely in the wrong place to be doing the tourist bit" (McCall 1994, 3). This also adds insight and context to the baller in Culver City who took a particularly hostile stance toward white pickup players in general. Reflecting upon similar feelings, one evening I was chatting with George, a black man in his late forties who worked as a technician for a municipal utility company. I had known George for a couple of years, and he would often begin our conversations by lamenting about work, specifically inferior treatment by his white supervisors. In spite of what he described as higher levels of competence and productivity than his white coworkers, George believed that because of his blackness he was consistently evaluated more harshly than his white peers and routinely passed over for promotion. In addition to his race, George was one of the few people at the company outside of management with a college degree (one that he earned while working full-time), which he determined added an additional level of intimidation.

On this particular evening, George had just come from work and was frustrated because his supervisor had written him up for having "a bad attitude." As George explained it, his supervisor ordered him to complete a meter installation that George had finished earlier in the day. His supervisor insisted that the installation had not been completed, and it wasn't until George went to his company truck and retrieved a completed work order that the supervisor backed down from his insistence. Instead of offering an apology, the supervisor wrote George up for using an insubordinate tone with him. George was visibly irritated, saying, "He never treats the white boys that way!" George continued, saying that he was so annoyed that he began shaking and had to restrain himself from assaulting his supervisor. George, who I knew had been practicing martial arts for several years, then turned to me and said:

> Have you ever hit a white man? About a year ago, I was in my first karate tournament and I was facing this white guy. You know karate, it's sort of like boxing. You dance around on the mat looking for a chance to strike. So we were dancing around, and I realize I'm afraid to hit this guy. Could you believe that? If he was black, I wouldn't have thought twice about it. But, my whole life, I never would have dared to hit a white man, and here I was. But then I thought about work, and how all the white guys treat me like they're better than I am. . . . I broke his nose with my first punch. Let me tell you, I never knew how sweet it was to hit a white man.

The game becomes much more than a game; it has the potential to transform into an opposing hemisphere where interracial aggression flows in reverse. Whether or not these subtle reminders of inequality take place on the basketball court, as was the case with Darrell; in the workplace, as was the case with the other baller in Culver City; in a karate dojo; or in some other social sphere, given the relative security afforded by the recreational basketball court, the blacktop can become a theater for resistant expression. It is one of the few zones in the social life of the black man where there is no immediate privilege associated with whiteness because it's largely dictated by black man's rules; therefore, there is no direct consequence for oppositional behavior.

To be sure, aggressive behavior on the basketball court is not exclusively or even primarily directed from black to white. But hostile attitudes and outbursts certainly seemed to be more predictably focused at a specific target when there was a white person who challenged the court authority of a black player. That understood, most of the acts of aggression observed on the blacktop were between minority group members, typically black on black. For example, one afternoon during an ordinary pickup game in Culver City, an altercation erupted between Jacques and another occasional player.

I was waiting to play next when a conflict between Jacques and the occasional player, also black, seemed to flash up out of nowhere at the opposite end of the court. As best I could tell, the occasional player mildly ridiculed Jacques while disputing a foul call Jacques made on him. Without hesitation, rather than argue his case for the foul as typical protocol would dictate, Jacques violently lashed out at the other larger player, clutching him by the throat, bloodying his face, and dropping him to the ground with one brutal punch. Jacques was poised to continue the assault, but I had run over and very deferentially attempted to restrain him. For reasons I never fully understood, but certainly not related to him fearing me, Jacques seemed to respect me and was generally less aggressive toward me than he was to most other people on the court. He therefore allowed me to guide him to the other end of the court while others helped the dazed and bloodied player to his feet and quickly escorted him away from the courts and out of Jacques's view. Violent outbursts like this were not typical, but they did occur from time to time and can be contextualized as more extreme manifestations of the typically hypermasculine and aggressive undercurrent of the court culture.

The Basketball Element

While evident at virtually every Southern California pickup basketball site visited over the years I spent working on this book, this aggressive expressionism was particularly common on the courts of Culver City. The physical location of the basketball courts, as well as the demographics (both described earlier) and socioeconomic status of the majority of players, contributed significantly to this open hostility. On the most active days, the courts at Veterans Park would draw a couple of dozen players from Culver City and surrounding neighborhoods like Palms and Mar Vista, communities where apartment homes were more common than the single-family residences that characterized Culver City's largely middle-class neighborhoods. In actuality, even most of the regular players who lived within Culver City's boundaries resided blocks away in the more densely populated low-rise apartment buildings lining the city's northern corridor.

On weekdays, shortly after local schools released for the day, the basketball courts at Veterans Park would begin coming to life when primarily black and a handful of Latino teenagers would arrive for some after-school pickup and to otherwise congregate near the basketball courts. Most weekdays during the spring and summer months, when the days were longer and the sun kept the courts illuminated into the evening hours, older players, almost all of whom were African American, would begin to arrive a couple of hours after the teens appeared. These players were a combination of working adults in their twenties and early thirties looking to get in a good run and reconnect with their friends after work, and younger men of spotty or questionable employment for whom the pickup game was a part of their daily ritual. Among this second category of older players were a fair number of former area high school basketball standouts who either never made it to the college level or whose grades or conduct cut their college playing careers short. Conspicuously absent from this mix of players were "typical" residents of the adjacent Park West neighborhood. In fact, in the several years I spent visiting the park, only a handful of Culver City's majority-white residents ventured onto the basketball courts during prime time at Veterans Park.

On the weekends and in the evenings, the tennis courts were filled with almost exclusively white players; the baseball and softball diamonds were crowded with almost all-white recreational league players; and the streets of Park West were filled with predominantly white homeowners playing with their children, washing their cars, and tending to their lawns. This contrast was not lost on the park's neighbors, whose discontent with the strong minority presence on the basketball courts was well articulated in a conversation with Kevin, a white Culver City Department of Parks and Recreation employee in his early twenties. Kevin was somewhat of a jack of all trades at Veterans Park: he served as the park equipment manager, laying out bases for baseball and softball games; he served as the park code enforcer, stopping mostly kids from misusing park facilities and otherwise breaking park rules; and perhaps most important, he served as the eyes of the surrounding community and de facto enforcer of community preferences and standards. Kevin had a small office behind the tennis courts that doubled as an equipment and tool shed, and he and I would often chat near there or as he sat and watched the pickup games.

During one of our conversations, Kevin noted that the basketball courts at Veterans Park were a particular sore spot for white community members who felt that the "basketball element" was undesirable and a likely threat to community safety. Or, as Franklin Foer more succinctly offered in his discussion of soccer's contrasting appeal to suburban yuppie parents as the preferred sport for protecting and promoting middle-class values, basketball "still had the taint of the ghetto" (Foer 2004, 237).[6] Clearly, the residents of Park West did not want this taint to infect their otherwise idyllic slice of Southern California suburbia. *Basketball element* and *ghetto* are, of course, "colorblind" terms that, along with numerous others, are increasingly used as referents to particular racial and ethnic minority groups—in this case African Americans and to a lesser extent Latinos. In his book exploring the National Basketball Association's attempt to tamp down and control the increasingly demonstrative blackness of professional basketball, David Leonard appropriately asserts, "The prominence of colorblindness and the use of implicitly racial language appear to reflect the newest form of an old system by which white privilege has long been maintained through the ideological/institutional justifications of white supremacy" (Leonard 2012, 4).

Consistent with this "new racism" approach and in response to these community concerns, city officials directed more frequent police patrols around the park during peak basketball hours. On more than one occasion, Culver City police officers pulled up to the curb nearest the court, stopped the game in progress, and patted down select players they said fit the description of a robbery suspect or someone else believed to have committed a crime nearby. Their cavalier gait as they approached the courts and the lack of any emergency vehicle sirens in the area would, of course, betray to all of us that they more likely were conducting a routine rousting in an attempt appease the neighborhood's residents and remind the "basketball element" of their status in the park's social hierarchy.

However, this did not quiet the more affluent and influential Park West residents, and they successfully pressured the city to take increasingly significant measures to deter the presence of exclusively basketball players during times when the white and middle-class residents were most likely to be home and would be most interested in using park facilities. For example, when in use, both the softball field and tennis courts at the park remained lighted until approximately 10:00 p.m. In contrast, the two basketball courts had no lights at all. This absence of lighting didn't completely deter local ballers from playing well beyond what would be reasonably considered adequate daylight. As John Edgar Wideman wrote of the pickup game in Philadelphia:

> If you keep playing, the failing light is no problem. Your eyes adjust and the streetlamps come on and they help some. People pass by think you're crazy playing basketball in the dark, but if you stay in the game you can see enough. . . . Part of the game is anticipating, knowing who's on the court with you and what they're likely to do. . . . You could be blind and play if the game's being played right. (Wideman 1990, 39)

In the case of the basketball courts at Veterans Park, the only light cast near the courts came from dim streetlamps on Coombs Avenue, and though the basketball courts were adjacent to both the tennis courts and softball field, a pass that's unseen until it strikes a player in the face or a dislocated finger from misjudging the location of the ball proved that basketball play was impossible after true nightfall due to lack of lighting.

In the most overt and drastic attempt to keep the "basketball element" away from the courts, the Department of Parks and Recreation began suspending basketball play at 5:00 p.m. on weekends. Since the basketball courts were unfenced, park employees, typically Kevin, would be required to halt any game in progress and place a fixed metal bracket over the top of each of the four basketball goals. If you were to look at the rim from directly below, it appeared like a circle with a thick diameter line through it. The eight-foot-long handle of the bracket was then inserted into a hole in the post of the goal and padlocked. While the courts remained physically open, the brackets made it so that a basketball was unable to pass through the rim, relegating the courts to mere slabs of asphalt. Occasionally on weekends, the city would host community fairs and other permitted events in the grassy infield of the park. On those days, while the tennis courts remained open to the public and while the blacktop was not in use for any fair-related purpose, the basketball courts would again be bracketed in what can reasonably be interpreted as an effort to deter the "basketball element." In each of these cases, the law and social policy were used to suppress public expressions of blackness at the times when they might have the most symbolic influence—when the majority of people of all races are unencumbered by work, school, and other daily preoccupations. But of particular interest was the openness with which these restrictive practices were justified. In fact, park employees were forthright in telling me that local homeowners viewed pickup basketball culture as synonymous with dangerous categories of people, principally poorer minorities, and the city government always erred to the side of homeowner interests.

This affirmative response to the predominantly white homeowners by city and park officials is not surprising. As Mike Davis revealed in his literary excavation of Southern California, *City of Quartz*, the region has a local history of middle-class interest formation around home ownership that effectively results in "bastions of white privilege" (Davis 1990, 159). Unlike Northern California, where the interests of rental tenants have historically been taken into consideration during the local political decision-making process, occupants of medium-density multifamily apartment dwellings go largely ignored and play little to no role in similar processes in Southern California. Therefore, as was the case in both Culver City and Encino, tenant interests usually took a far backseat to middle-class political subjectivity and their concerns went largely unaddressed unless they were also consistent with homeowner interests.

It is also worth pointing out that the "basketball element" concept can just as easily be transposed to sports that are associated with other groups of "undesirables," and similar exertions of local political pressure can be used to keep these groups out of ostensibly public spaces. For example, in his extraordinary account of the struggles faced by a youth soccer team comprised solely of refugees relocated from war-torn Eastern European, Middle Eastern, and African countries to the Atlanta, Georgia, suburb of Clarkston, Warren St. John reveals how prejudice, relative economic advantage, and local politics can function to keep "undesirable" populations disenfranchised. Because of its proximity to downtown Atlanta, available public transportation, and cheap housing in the form of run-down apartment complexes, Clarkston became "a textbook example of a community ripe for refugee resettlement" (St. John 2009, 35). The United Nations, World Relief, the International Rescue Commission, and the agglomerate of nonprofit agencies charged with resettling the tens of thousands of refugees accepted into the United States each year took full advantage of Clarkston's appeal. In a matter of just a few decades, refugee resettlement and urban expansion transformed Clarkston from a "sleepy little" traditional conservative white Southern town into a still relatively small but amazingly diverse municipality with a foreign-born population of greater than 43 percent in

2011. By way of comparison, the state of Georgia as a whole had a non-native-born population of less than 10 percent that same year.

The rapid social change experienced by Clarkston and most conspicuously signified by the increase in the city's ethnic and foreign-born population prompted resistance similar to that directed toward the "basketball element" in Culver City. Only, in the case of Clarkston, since the "Fugees" came from places where basketball was largely unknown or inaccessible, the conflict revolved around fields rather than courts and became known locally as the "soccer problem." In a newspaper interview regarding the city's legislation of xenophobia by banning soccer play on public fields, Clarkston mayor Lee Swaney said, "There will be nothing but baseball down [at the city's only general use field] there as long as I'm mayor" (St. John 2009, 9). To be sure, as St. John correctly observed, "Soccer, perhaps more than ever, had become a conspicuous symbol of cultural change" (St. John 2009, 92), a transformation that did not sit well with a globalization-phobic white American public made increasingly jittery by growing and more visible minority and immigrant populations.

Since the 1980s, there is perhaps no place in the United States where this discomfort was more profoundly intertwined with the law and social policy than California, particularly as the Latino population continued to proliferate over the latter half of the twentieth century and into the first decade of the twenty-first. Seemingly overnight, California shifted from having a comfortably white non-Hispanic majority of greater than 75 percent with a mere 12 percent Hispanic population though the 1960s, to earning a present-day status as a "majority-minority" state. According to US Census Bureau data, California's Hispanic population eclipsed 38 percent in 2014, while its white non-Hispanic population continued to decline to less than 40 percent of the state's population during that same year. In Southern California, where the state's physical and cultural connection with neighboring Mexico is more cogent and unmistakable, this ethnic and cultural shift becomes even starker. For example, Los Angeles County's Latino population neared 50 percent as the white non-Hispanic population dwindled to less than 27 percent in 2014.

But, as seen in the aforementioned case of Clarkston, while the cultural texture of California changed, so did the intensity of both overt and more subtle forms of anti-Mexican and antiminority rhetoric. Most blatantly, in 1994 republican state assemblyman Dick Mountjoy introduced Proposition 187, also known as the "Save Our State" (SOS) initiative, to the state legislature. Nearly 60 percent of California voters approved the referendum item establishing a state-run citizenship screening system and barring undocumented Californians from access to publicly funded health care, education, and other social services. While these conspicuous and highly politicized public statements of obstinate resistance to diversity were undoubtedly significant, perhaps more important in the day-to-day lives of minority group members was the constant drumbeat of low-grade hostility and microaggressions like the absence of lights and the suspension of basketball play on weekends in Culver City.

The clear intent to relegate principally black pickup basketball participants to spaces out of sight and away from the dominant culture was not lost on the pickup regulars. In fact, many members of the baller community in Culver City saw this homeowner privilege in the form of basketball prohibition as a direct attack on their honor and integrity. The outcome was that even greater resentment was directed toward white people, of the immediate community or otherwise, who ventured onto the courts. These acts of hostility did not go unnoticed by the nonblack participants. Nonetheless, almost always, they went unchallenged. For example, Ron—an older Jewish player and one of the few white men who regularly participated in games at Veterans Park—was frequently ignored or disrespected by some of the regulars who viewed him as a representative of the surrounding community that sought to hyper-regulate the minority presence in Park West. Some of the ballers would refuse to pass the ball to Ron, even if he was wide-open for a layup; any good play he made at either end of the court would routinely go unacknowledged by court regulars; ballers would refuse to "pick him up" for their team if they had the next game; and some would go so far as to not even speak with him. After a game one evening, while standing near the handball wall behind the main of the basketball court, I asked Ron why he continued to play at Veterans when he knew he would have to endure derision.

> I know I get fucked with because I'm a white guy. But I've been living in Culver City for thirty years, long before most of these guys were born. This is as much my park as it is theirs. They might kick my ass one day, but there's no way I'm going to stop playing up here.

I knew Ron felt like he belonged in Culver City. It was his home, after all. And he certainly wanted to be respected on the court; he played hard on both offense and defense and was unselfish with the basketball. But Ron's lack of external reaction was typical of race politics on the blacktops. For the most part, with only a few exceptions, white players at diverse public courts like Veterans or Encino either passively tolerated aggression or coldness directed their way, or they found other "less street" places to play. Brent was one of these players who ultimately chose to seek games away from the more diverse and potentially confrontational blacktops. Brent was a six-foot-four white man in his early twenties who had played one year of Division II college basketball before giving up his competitive basketball dreams. He was now an aspiring actor who had done a little commercial work and background spots on several sports-related situation comedies. He also regularly participated in indoor pickup games at the Van Nuys YMCA. Van Nuys is a nine-square-mile, densely populated, largely working-class, ethnically diverse, and predominantly Hispanic district in Los Angeles's San Fernando Valley. The membership at the Van Nuys YMCA was certainly diverse, but not as much so as the surrounding neighborhood, and the tenor of the pickup games was far calmer and less turbulent than what could be found at area outdoor courts or public gyms.

One afternoon while shooting around, Brent and I were discussing other Los Angeles venues with fairly competitive pickup games. I mentioned to him that I regularly participated in outdoor games at Encino Park in Encino, a predominantly affluent section of the San Fernando Valley. Brent's response was typical of those expressed by several other white basketball players that I encountered at indoor playing facilities and in corporate league play.[7]

> I don't play too much in those kinds of games. Like, I went down to Venice the other day and after watching for a few minutes, decided not to play. You know, those kind of pickup games are too street. Everyone is hot-dogging, showboating, and arguing all the time. I just want to play ball.

Despite the fact that the Van Nuys YMCA was located in a predominantly minority and lower-income neighborhood, when I initially began working out and playing basketball at this gym, there was a relatively even balance between minority and white gym members, both on and off the basketball court. Over the course of the three years that I was a member at Van Nuys, however, I noticed a distinct change in the racial composition of its membership,[8] particularly on the basketball court. There was an increasing number of black, Latino, and Eastern European immigrant players participating in the pickup games. Similar to the "tipping phenomenon" experienced in residential housing, as the number of minority gym members increased, so did white flight. White gym members became increasingly scarce, joining other gyms, transferring their membership to other (less minority) YMCAs, or coming to the gym earlier in the day, when fewer minorities were present.

Brent was one of the white members and basketball players whose absence I had especially noticed. He was a particularly good and affable player against whom I looked forward to competing. In the earlier months of my membership, Brent was a classic "gym rat," seeming to spend all of his free time working out at the gym. However, apparently correlated to a rise in the gym's minority membership, Brent's presence became scarcer. Because I had afternoon appointments in Orange County, about an hour south of Van Nuys, one morning, I decided to take in an early workout rather than do my typical late afternoon session. To my surprise, Brent was in the free-weight room, training. After greeting one another, I asked him where he had been for the past month or so. Once again, he brought up the "street" reference in explaining why he no longer participated in pickup games at the YMCA.

> I've been working out in the mornings lately instead of the afternoons and I've been playing ball over in Santa Monica mostly. There were starting to be too many kids up here playing and the game was getting too street.[9] So now, I come and lift here in the mornings and go play basketball at the Santa Monica Y in the afternoons. Lots of the guys that used to play up here play over there in the afternoons now.

Brent's comments and those made by other white basketball players that I spoke and played with illustrate two ideas. First, they emphasize the effect that pickup basketball politics has on shaping the behavior of the white basketball community, particularly the aggressive and bombastic behavior that is often associated with the "black" style of play. Second, they demonstrate the relatively passive manner in which white men typically react to these subtle and overt challenges to their traditional authority, at least in the very limited context of sports and basketball.

It's worth mentioning that the court culture's ability to jaundice attitudes toward certain pickup games was not exclusive to white players. For example, even though Venice Beach was fewer than fifteen minutes from Culver City and romanticized as one of Los Angeles's premier places to play pickup, I rarely ventured there to play. This was especially true on weekends, when I found the style of play to be tedious because of the excessive showboating, trash talking, and arguing that characterized the court culture. Zach—a black former Division I shooting guard born and raised in predominantly white and more conservative Orange County—expressed even broader disparagement for the "street game" and what he felt it conveyed to white people about African Americans. Consistent with the Mandingo syndrome, Zach found that people he encountered expected him to play and act a specific way even though he was far more comfortable with the higher-status dialect than he was with what people typically expected of him as a black male basketball player.

Next

One of the unspoken covenants of the pickup game is the calling of "next." The particulars of "next" may vary from court to court, but the basic principle is always the same. If a game is in progress and other people are waiting to play, someone among the waiting will publicly call out "next" to indicate that he (and the four other players of his choosing) will be playing in the following game. If there are more than five people waiting to play on a particular court, someone among those waiting and who has not already secured a spot with the next five players publicly calls out "last"—indicating that he claims the last "next." While "next" is a rule of pickup etiquette that is honored on every pickup court, who calls "next" first often becomes the source of controversy. To alleviate this problem and confrontations that often emerge as a result, many indoor courts post sign-up sheets to more clearly determine who indeed has "next." But this is almost never the case at outdoor courts.

One summer afternoon at Encino Park, a pickup game had just ended. When the following game was about to begin, Eddie—a member of the winning team and one of Encino's regular black ballers—pointed out that the "next" team had six players, one more man than it needed on the court. Five of the six players waiting to play next were black, and the other was a white man in his early twenties whose name I did not know but who I had seen on several other occasions at the park. The de facto captain of the challenging team briefly surveyed his squad, turned toward the lone white player on the court, and told him that he was not a member of his team and would have to play next. Even though the white player had been waiting just as long as, if not longer than, the other players about to take the court, he was effectively fired from the squad.

On the most active days, players would sometimes wait over an hour just for the opportunity to get on the court for a game, and this was one of those days. As an arguably reasonable reaction to his being cut from the team, the dismissed player took immediate offense, and an argument ensued between the two challenging players. After several minutes of debate between the two players, Eddie abruptly interceded, commanding the white player to leave the court. Indignant, the late-comer continued his protest and refused to leave, to which Eddie responded, "Punk, you'd better get your ass off this court before I come over there and make you get off the court. Better yet, don't just get off the court. Take your sorry ass home and get out of my park. You're making me sick."

Other members of the group began jocularly remarking at Eddie's outburst and taunting the ejected white player with emasculating comments like "He just took your manhood,"[10] and goading him with "You're going to let him talk to you like that?" Clearly frustrated and angered, the white player scanned the court as if to weigh his options or perhaps find an ally among the overwhelmingly black basketball crowd on the basketball court. Seeing no alternatives or supporters, after a moment's pause and with a look of dejection, he slowly walked off of the court toward his car, parked nearby on Genesta. As he headed off the court angrily muttering to himself, Eddie got in a final jab: "And don't let me see your ass up here again." Once again, the other players erupted with laughter. This episode had a particular significance because it took place in Encino, a predominantly white and disproportionately affluent section of San Fernando Valley. Encino lies immediately west of the 405 freeway, and most of the neighborhood is tucked away "south of the boulevard," a realtor reference to the valley's prime housing areas that lie south of famed Ventura Boulevard—the valley's primary east-west surface thoroughfare—ascending the hillsides of the Santa Monica Mountains. In stark contrast to the 43 percent majority Latino population of the greater San Fernando Valley, Encino's population is over 80 percent non-Hispanic white and only 8.5 percent Latino. The median annual household income for area residents is about $80,000, some $15,000 more per year than the valley as a whole; and nearly 25 percent of Encino households report a median income greater than $125,000 per year. Therefore, the disrespected player was seemingly more representative of the area than anyone else on the court that day.

How one of the valley's better and most consistent pickup games ended up in Encino, I haven't a clue. Nonetheless, even in places like Encino, blacktop politics were primarily governed by the black ballers and "black man's rules," at least when black men were present. On the surface it may seem like Eddie's reaction was a neutral response to a breech in pickup protocol. After all, he had "next," it was his squad, and he was therefore entitled to play with whomever he chose. However, the transcript underlying this incident speaks to two related issues. First, Eddie was in many ways expressing black male contempt for the sense of entitlement—or "enwhitelement," as a black colleague of mine is prone to say—and ownership that many white people (men in particular) seem to feel when it comes to public spaces.[11] Second, the white player's reluctant but unquestionable adherence to Eddie's directive was consistent with the deference white players afforded black players on the pickup courts, but a deference that exists almost no place else in American society.

White Chocolate

Only rarely did I witness white basketball players successfully challenging what they perceived to be disrespect from a black player or black players. In each such instance, these white players had earned their stripes; they had been around this particular pickup game and these particular players long enough to earn a higher level of respect. Not coincidentally, one example of this white challenge to black basketball authority took place in Encino, where the overall demeanor of African American players, while still loaded with cool pose but perhaps tempered by the serene aesthetic of the surrounding area, was generally less openly hostile toward white players. Reflective of the community at large, the African American players in Encino tended to be somewhat more educated and of higher socioeconomic status than those who played in Culver City, Westwood, Venice, and the other public courts that served as the Los Angeles backdrop for this book. In fact, several of the regular black ballers and other players in Encino were relatively successful recording artists, C-list actors, and other people involved in the entertainment industry.

In this particular instance of white defiance of black authority, Marshall, the white player who was challenged, frequently played in Encino and was well known by many of the other regular players. He was less than six feet tall with a wiry build, very good ball-handling skills and speed, and a smooth jump shot that clearly came from years of formal coaching and practice. The black player challenging Marshall was what could best be described as a peripheral player—someone relatively new to the Encino scene with no significant ties to the local basketball community. On one trip down the court, Marshall took a fairly hasty shot on the basket that some might characterize as selfish, particularly since he had teammates open for higher-percentage uncontested shots. The peripheral player was one of Marshall's by-passed teammates, and in response he shouted, "Man, pass the motherfucking ball," immediately and publicly challenging not just the wisdom of Marshall's poor shot selection but also his status at the park. Without a moment's pause, Marshall lashed back at the new player, saying, "This is my motherfucking court. If you don't like how I play, take your ass somewhere else." While Marshall was not a physically intimidating player and his behavior was most certainly atypical with regard to the usual race-based power dynamics displayed on the pickup courts, it was readily apparent that the other ballers present were at best (as far as the transient was concerned) neutral when it came to Marshall and very well might support Marshall had a more serious confrontation erupted. Seeming a little stunned by Marshall's reaction, but also recognizing this lack of support from the court's black regulars, the peripheral player chose not to respond to Marshall's assault and meekly left the court after the game.

Even though Marshall was a regular player in Encino, this acceptance of him by the other ballers was atypical. Generally, regardless of frequency of participation, white players were not as openly embraced by the black ballers. In fact, white players were often hard to come by at some of the more competitive courts, even in predominantly white areas. Mentioned previously, many white pickup players opted to play at these same parks when black participants were less likely to be around, or they would play in area gyms that they paid to reserve. Like Marshall, nearly all of the white players who ventured onto these more competitive courts had "game" and often a little bit of "swagger." For example, Marshall spoke with a little bit of black slang and would nonchalantly describe his reason for playing so hard in cavalier terms like, "I'm just trying to run some of this chronic out of my system." Atlanta-based baller Clark shared similar reflections on the rarity and ability of white players who braved the predominantly black pickup scene:

> The only time a white guy comes on the court, he can play. I haven't really run into too many just cornball white dudes that's just going come out to a competitive game and then can't play. Almost 90 percent of the time, this guy can play. That's what's interesting. You'll see a bad black guy come onto a court before a bad white dude. Because . . . a white dude . . . if he's going to be the minority out there, he's going to be able to at least go a little bit. Most of the time . . . if they're there, they can play.

One other exception to this general rule of acceptance was Randy, another white player who frequented Encino. Randy stood about six-feet-two and had an easy way about him. While he might be characterized as athletically oafish relative to most of the other court regulars, he was a solid mid-range and perimeter shooter who knew the game's fundamentals well. The nucleus of Encino's ballers group appeared to enjoy Randy's company, and his place in the court community, at least insofar as his whiteness was concerned, was never challenged. Still, a clean jump shot and affable demeanor did not seem to adequately explain Randy's universal acceptance by the ballers. But, after arriving early one afternoon to shoot around a bit before the afternoon's games began, I observed another dimension to Randy's potential appeal and approval. It seemed Randy supplied many of the ballers with marijuana before the afternoon games in Encino, not as a dealer but as a sharer. After taking notice this first time, I witnessed the same ritual on numerous other occasions. Prior to the tip-off of the regular afternoon game, several of the ballers would gather around Randy's late-model convertible Corvette and pass around marijuana joints that Randy provided. Certainly, weed supply did not fully explain Randy's acceptance, but it seemed to be a protective factor insulating him from some of the hostility directed toward other white players who chose to play in these largely black pickup contests.

Nonetheless, Randy and Marshall were allowances to the general culture of racial division and "black man's rules" on the pickup courts. But to this imperative, there was one significant caveat. It was not simply to *whiteness* that this occasional hostility and aggression by some of the African American pickup participants was a reaction. Rather, a notable distinction was made between foreign European white people and white Americans. The occasional white player of foreign descent who happened to venture onto the courts seemed to have an easier time with gaining social acceptance, or at least tolerance, from the black players. While it would be a stretch to say that they were received with open arms by black players, the attitude toward them was one of relative indifference, almost as if they or their perceived racial attributes were invisible. This was even the case at Veterans Park, where the most aggressive displays of animosity toward white men took place. Presumably, these immigrant whites— distinguished by their foreign accents, polished and less aggressive style of play, and other aspects of their nonmaterial culture, such as demeanor[12]—were seen as less of a threat, thus less representative of perceived American repression of racial minorities.

Sebastian was one of a handful of these non-American white players who frequented the pickup games at Veterans Park. For two consecutive summers, he visited California from his native Germany to better learn American language and culture. He was renting a shabby one-bedroom apartment in nearby Mar Vista—a community designation adjacent to Culver City—and happened upon the park one afternoon while driving around to get a feel for his new surroundings. Presuming that the basketball court would be a good place to meet Americans and work on his English, and having played organized recreational basketball for years in Europe, he became somewhat of a park regular. Sebastian was a sturdy six-foot-three, physically fit, broad-shouldered, long-armed southpaw with a solid jump shot and great touch around the basket. He was not as physical on the court as his body would suggest he could be, but that was a common trait among the European players I would meet; their game involved far less contact and more finesse than what was typical of American basketball.

In spite of the fact that it is very public, the pickup basketball court can be a curiously isolating space for an outsider, and this is particularly true for people of oppositional racial or ethnic identities. For prospective players who are new to a particular court, there is often a bit of a feeling-out phase where everything from the style of play and skill level to court politics, social structure, and hierarchy are assessed at a distance before an actual attempt to commit to the court is made. In part, this process is driven by a player's desire not to get in over his head by attempting to play in a game that is too competitive or, conversely, not to waste his time or risk injury in a game that is too far below his skill level. But the politics of the particular court, often perceptible from a distance, are also critically important. The fact that these contests are carried out on public courts notwithstanding, similar to a private golf club where admission requires that you be a member or an invited guest, some games are in effect closed to outsiders. On several occasions at different parks in Los Angeles, I observed newcomers waiting in frustrating vain to get into one of these closed games, only to be repeatedly passed over for other players or ignored entirely.

When I first noticed Sebastian's conspicuous presence at Veterans Park, and as I would later hear from him, he had already gauged the game's skill level from the safety and seclusion of his car, parked at the ground's western wall on Coombs Avenue. Comfortable that he had the skill set to compete in the afternoon pickup game, he then approached the courts to complete the more social part of the assessment and to ultimately attempt to get into the game. There was one other white person at the courts that day, Ron, a long-time Culver City resident in his early thirties whom I mentioned earlier. Ron was interesting in that in spite of not garnering much respect from the local baller community—he would routinely get passed-over for games, disregarded by his teammates in the games that he played, and have his foul calls ignored—he was steadfast in his determination to play at the park. Ron was waiting to get into a game, noticed Sebastian's arrival, and approached him in what looked like an attempt at racial (not racist) solidarity or perhaps empathy. But seemingly aware that Ron was not going to serve as an effective gatekeeper to court access and acceptance, Sebastian politely acknowledged Ron's gesture while maintaining a bit of a standoffish posture as he moved closer to the court's action.

Size matters, at least in the world of pickup basketball, and Sebastian's relative tallness coupled with a comparatively low player turnout that afternoon meant that he was picked up to run in the next game. What I also speculate worked in Sebastian's favor and reasonably quick invitation to play—well before he uttered a word that any of us would hear betraying his heavy German accent—was that he was clearly foreign and likely European. His shorts and shoes were made for basketball, but his shoes in particular looked style-less and almost utilitarian, unlike the more fashionable styles of basketball shoes popular in the States; he was wearing bulky ankle supports that were different from those commonly seen in American athletics, and the likes of which no one ever wore in outdoor pickup games if for no other reason than they did not look "cool"; and his polite and deferential demeanor also screamed "not American." Ultimately, the fact that he appeared European and was showing up to play pickup basketball in a predominantly black setting suggested that he did not carry the sorts of racial baggage that white Americans might bring to a similar environment. Accordingly, and right away, he got more respect from the ballers than Ron, and after he demonstrated that he could play the game, the basketball community seemed comfortable enough with him sticking around.

Having only recently moved back to Los Angeles from Orange County, this was my first summer in Culver City, and I was still fairly new on the Veterans Park scene. So, when Sebastian approached me after the game in an attempt to strike up a conversation, I reacted to him in almost the same way I had seen him respond to Ron a couple of hours earlier. I was not impolite, but I also was not very accommodating. I was still trying to work my way into the culture of this court and establish myself within the court community, and I subconsciously and perhaps irrationally feared that engaging with him, an outsider, could impugn my status. But, after a week or so of Sebastian showing up at Veterans Park for the afternoon games, contests in which I was often paired against him because of our similarities in size, and his earnest attempts to engage me in conversation, we began to talk more and ultimately developed a friendship.

As Sebastian explained to me toward the end of his first summer in California, he was paradoxically put off and pleased by how he was received in the United States. Prior to making his trip, he was cautioned by friends who had previously visited that significant racial tensions between blacks and whites existed in the States, strains that had become even more visible in Los Angeles in the decade or so after the riots that erupted following the acquittals of white Los Angeles police officers videotaped brutally beating unarmed black motorist Rodney King. Beyond deep-seated black-white tensions were escalating political and social conflicts between Los Angeles's blacks and the rapidly growing Latino population. Sebastian was reassured to find that he was generally not greeted with overt hostility by black and Mexican Americans, particularly once they found that he was European. In fact, his insistent presence in Culver City and the regularity with which he played at the park ultimately earned him the affectionately descriptive nickname "Germs" from the ballers. He was nevertheless dismayed by what he perceived to be a racially based barrier that prevented him from significantly bonding with most of the Veterans Park regulars. Sebastian's feeling was that he was not disrespected but was kept at a bit of a distance because he was white, albeit of a culturally different German stripe, and the court was a definitively black space. He also acknowledged treatment from the baller community that was noticeably more respectful and less hostile than that directed toward Ron and the handful of other white American men who frequented the courts.

Peripheral Players

Independent baller communities served as the core for most of the pickup games I experienced throughout Southern California. Every court seemed to have its own constituent community of players who more or less dictated the culture and tempo for each of these public spaces. Interestingly, some of the better pickup games often followed particular groups of ballers as they migrated from park to park for an array of reasons ranging from community tension, like that experienced at Veterans Park; to interpersonal conflicts and fallings-out between particular key players at a given court; to word of a good competitive game elsewhere. However, in spite of the centrality of the ballers, the games often would not take place but for the participation of peripheral players—somewhat regular players at a specific court who have a principally recreational interest in playing but who do not have significant influence over the court's culture. Many, but certainly not all, of these players did not reside in the immediate community in which the court was located. Rather, they traveled to the courts from surrounding areas specifically because the level of competition suited their needs. Furthermore, the socioeconomic status of peripheral players often appeared to exceed that of the less mobile resident ballers.

Despite their relative economic privilege, many of these peripheral players as well as ballers of higher socioeconomic standing embraced the cool pose, directing their aggression toward reclaiming a black identity necessarily obscured through the course of their white-collar, white-dominated work experience. For these players, the court seemed to play a vital role in restoring the self-confidence and identity that has been diminished by the conflict woven into their double lives as black professionals.

Doc was one such peripheral player of relatively high social status who clearly embraced the cool pose. The first time we played together was on a warm summer evening in Culver City. During the game, Doc embodied much of what could be considered stereotypical "black" basketball behavior. His demeanor was defiant, he spoke in the street slang common for the courts, and he played a particularly aggressive style of basketball. He often publicly chastised teammates who missed shots, barking at them, "If you can't shoot, pass the fucking ball!" He similarly berated teammates who passed up seemingly easy shots, growling, "Take the damn shot or get off the court!" After our first day of playing together, Doc and I cooled down next to each other on a rusty shaded bench at the west end of the court. This was a common evening ritual after the day's final game had been played. Players would sit around, stretch out a bit, recap the games' highlights and lowlights, and those who knew each other off the court would discuss plans for later, and otherwise casually socialize.

Doc and I just happened to be seated next to each other and a little away from the other remaining players. He introduced himself to me, I complimented him on his shooting (which was exceptionally accurate), and over the course of our discussion he somewhat quietly revealed that he was a cardiologist at a local hospital. I tried to hide my surprise: absolutely nothing in his on-court behavior would have led me to guess that he was well-educated and of relatively high social status. As I said, his behavior on the court could best be described as *street*. But it then occurred to me that most of the regular players at Culver City knew little about me outside of my on-court identity except that I was originally from Washington, D.C.

In a 2012 *Vanity Fair* article titled "Obama's Way," journalist Michael Lewis offered a related observation of President Obama and the veil that can be cast by a player's on-the-court persona:

> Martin Nesbitt, C.E.O. of an airport-parking company, met Obama before Obama ever ran for public office, playing pickup basketball with him in Chicago. Well into their friendship he knew next to nothing of Obama's achievements. Obama had neglected to inform him that he had gone to Harvard Law School, for example, or been editor of its Law Review, or really anything that would convey his status off the basketball court.

While Lewis does not specifically mention race, multiple accounts of our first "basketball president's" style of play reference trash talking, an aggressive style, and a "swagger" all consistent with the cool pose and the use of the court as an arena to affirm black identity (Lewis 2012).

Similar to Doc was Paul, an eighth-grade English teacher who lived in Culver City and taught in Compton. On the court, Paul too was the embodiment of the cool pose. He trash-talked, played aggressively, and spoke in slang. What I found was that Doc, Paul, and the handful of other professionals who existed at the periphery of the baller community used the pickup game to assert, reaffirm, and reclaim an ethnic identity denied them in the course of their daily professional lives. By comingling with younger, poorer street kids, they were able to embrace a part of their cultural identity that they were forced to forgo when occupying their professional roles and interacting among their professional peers. As Paul Gilroy (1993) discusses in his study of modernity and double consciousness, *The Black Atlantic*, publicly occupying a space between the ethnically absolutist discourses of, in this case, urban black culture and professional white culture is often viewed as insubordination. But, as Douglas Hartmann argues, "this bifocal vision" suggests "a sense of critical possibility and promise, a lens onto alternative visions of race and the larger, mainstream society" (2006, 322).

Despite popular rhetoric to the contrary, the modern workplace generally continues to frown on anything beyond symbolic diversity. As a result of increases in educational attainment and legislation outlawing overt racial discrimination in the workplace, there are now a greater number of female faces and faces of color in the white-collar workforce. However, the culture that dominates is distinctively white and male. In her discussion of differential language use between men and women, Robin Lackoff "emphasizes that the history of male dominance has meant that women increasingly use men's language—imitating the higher status dialect—while the reverse is rarely the case" (quoted in Scott 1990, 30). The same can be said for the history of racial dominance by Anglo Americans. Black males who have been increasingly permitted to enter the white-collar workforce in the post–civil rights act era have necessarily had to conform to white male standards of appropriate behavior, dress, and even grooming in order to not only succeed but survive.

While the pickup basketball courts are not completely freed from these constraints as they remain situated in the broader social context of the outside world, the "white man's rules" that govern behavior in other social settings are suspended to a noticeable degree and replaced by sets of behavioral expectations consistent with "black man's rules." In the world of pickup basketball, public expressions of blackness are not simply tolerated—they are often expected. It is one sphere in which those who are forced to adhere to dominant cultural mandates for the majority of their day can shed their metaphorical shackles and publicly embrace a position of blackness that may more authentically articulate their true feelings about their place in society, or at a minimum serve as an outlet for daily frustrations. These expressions of blackness are not simply what would come out in the workplace if allowed, but rather what come out on the court as a reaction against that which is not allowed.

Freedom Songs and Stealing Home

Discussing the works of theologian James Cone, bell hooks wrote, "The politics of racial domination have necessarily created a black reality that is distinctly different from that of whites, and from that location has emerged a distinctly different black culture" (hooks 1992, 12). Similarly, in his discussion of the distinctive cultures that have emerged from the social and political struggles undertaken by black people, Paul Gilroy notes, "The cultures of the diaspora blacks can be profitably interpreted as expressions of and commentaries upon ambivalences generated by modernity and their locations within it" (Gilroy 1993, 117). Related to this notion of black cultural distinctiveness and as discussed in earlier chapters, the social, structural, and legal barriers that served as hallmarks of postslavery American society unintentionally established pathways toward the formation of subcultures of political opposition among black Americans, who bore the brunt of (but certainly did not have a monopoly on) late nineteenth- and early twentieth-century racial hostility in the United States. Coupled with these barriers, America's inability or refusal to regard blacks as the equal yet merely darker part of the American family facilitated the continuation of black double consciousness[13] and a parallel black American reality "distinctly different from that of whites" but one that simultaneously still exists directly alongside and often in opposition to dominant white culture.

Because of this history of denied opportunity and oppression, these oppositional realities routinely emerged in nontraditional and expressive spheres rather than within more conventional and overtly political arenas. Sports and music are two prominent examples of these resistive spheres. Again borrowing Gilroy's words, "The power and significance of music within the black Atlantic have grown in inverse proportion to the limited expressive power of language" (1993, 74). Even when looking at, for example, what was arguably the zenith of black American politics during the civil rights era, music played a critical role in organization and galvanization, as well as in maintaining morale in the period's most challenging times. During the 1961 Albany Movement, Martin Luther King Jr. said of black music, "The freedom songs are playing a strong and vital role in our struggle. They give the people new courage and a sense of unity. I think they keep alive a faith, a radiant hope, in the future, particularly in our most trying hours."[14]

The genesis of American hip-hop culture and the accompanying musical genre that continues to serve as the primary marker of young urban black existence in the United States can similarly be traced to structural transformations and the unfulfilled promises of the civil rights movement. As white Americans continued their post–World War II exodus from urban centers and into racially exclusive suburban communities, increasingly poorer blacks and a growing Latino population were left behind in decaying cities. Black American poverty rates have always been high, particularly when compared to other racial and ethnic groups in the United States. However, the plight of black Americans substantially worsened in the late 1970s and early 1980s. During the waning years of the Carter administration (1977–1980) and most profoundly during the early years of the Reagan administration (1981–1988) the proportion of US blacks living in poverty skyrocketed nearly 36 percent, the highest proportion of blacks living in poverty since 1967. This time frame is remarkable because, per Reagan administration directives, it directly coincided with the legislative and judicial repeal of government-sponsored attempts to remedy past legal and social discrimination against black Americans, a trend of reversal that continues well into the new millennium. While other apolitical forms of "party rap" had already begun gaining in popularity among urban teenagers, with this abrupt end of the American civil rights movement as its backdrop, "message rap"—hip-hop music with an overtly political message, as exemplified by groups like Grand Master Flash and the Furious Five—emerged as a sufferers' response to these deteriorating social and economic conditions in black America and a statement against institutions of inequality and oppression.

As French sociologist Loïc Wacquant said of the centrality of sport as a means of cultural expression in poor urban black communities, the black rap music that emerged during this era "acquires its full social meaning only in regard to the structure of life chances offered—or denied—by the local system of instruments of social reproduction and mobility" (Wacquant 2002,17–18). Poor schools; the decimation of skilled labor markets that served as the primary catalyst of black migration out of the rural south and fueled the establishment of an American black middle class; the birth of the US prison industrial complex, which increasingly housed a disproportionate number of black Americans; and social policies that served to disjoint the black family all proved markers of a society hostile to black upward social mobility. Beneath the beat's "boom-bop," hip-hop rose as a virtual call to arms for black urban youth, demanding that they examine their plight as residents of a nation that had yet to fulfill its obligation to them as citizens.

Making a similar point about reggae music's role in developing unconventional structures of opposition within black diasporic cultures, Delta State University communication professor and musical historian Stephen A. King attests, "The Jamaican masses use music to counteract oppression and degradation. In fact, music is one of the few avenues for the Jamaican poor both to create a distinctly black Jamaican identity and to vent 'years of pent-up suffering, dehumanization and frustration under the white man's hegemony'" (King 2002, xii–xiii).

Turning the lens to sport as a form of resistive expression, in a 2007 essay on racial justice in America, Robert Justin Lipkin—recently deceased distinguished professor of law at Pennsylvania's Widener University—mused, "Which had a greater significance in extirpating American apartheid? *Brown* [*v. Board of Education*] or Jackie Robinson and Branch Rickey's concerted effort to desegregate baseball?" Making a point not to be dismissive of *Brown*'s tremendous impact, the conclusion reached by Lipkin and one shared by many other civil rights scholars was, "Jackie Robinson . . . and the scores of blacks and whites who resisted the idea that equality and segregation could coexist in a just society deserve more credit than the courts" (Lipkin 2007). Had it not been for the initial softening of America's color barrier in sports and the more subtle political statements made through sports-related avenues during the pre-*Brown* and civil rights era United States, it is fully conceivable that the nation would still be grappling with some of the most basic advancements made in formal legal racial equality and that *Brown v. the Board of Education* would have been a socially unacceptable impossibility.

Certainly, postslavery America was not always prepared to accept the Negro in sports as ambassador to racial equality, particularly when the Negro in question refused to let his athleticism speak as the sole voice of protest. Early twentieth-century heavyweight boxing champion Jack Johnson epitomized the backlash that might occur when "the advancement of the blacks . . . becomes a menace to the whites" (Roberts 1983, 6). During his era, even for demure black leaders but certainly more so for the immodest, gains by blacks were often perceived as a zero-sum game in which white society stood to lose advantage and "as steps toward a final collision between the races" (Roberts 1983, 6). In his biography of Johnson, Randy Roberts summarized:

> More than any other black of his generation, Johnson gave flesh to the whites' jeremiads. . . . Other black leaders, such as Booker T. Washington and even W. E. B. DuBois, spoke cautiously. Johnson, however, moved boldly. . . . He would live by his own rules or not at all. In doing so, Johnson threatened order. He embodied the white man's nightmare of racial chaos. (Roberts 1983, 6).

Unfortunately for black athletes and for black American sports fans hoping to see images of themselves in sports heroes, the "threat to order" posed by Johnson and other early twentieth-century black athletes who refused to abide by this racialized double standard came at a cost. The threat of blacks competing against whites, in general, was enough to upset the surface tranquility of American racial folkways, particularly in the South. During an 1897 interracial boxing match arranged by the Mississippi Pleasure Company and stopped shortly after the fight began, Henry Long (the "loyal Southerner" who stopped the fight) said, "The idea of niggers fighting white men. Why, if that darned scoundrel would beat that white boy the niggers would never stop gloating over it, and, as it is, we have enough trouble with them" (Roberts 1983, 17).

Beyond segregation in sports and in broader society, boisterous successful blacks like Johnson were routinely subjected to intense and biased scrutiny from sport-sanctioning bodies, political figures, and of course the criminal justice system. In 1913, because of his fame and in reaction to his notoriety for consorting with white women, Johnson was questionably convicted by an all-white jury in federal district court for transporting a white prostitute from Pennsylvania to Illinois, an alleged violation of the Mann Act. Also known as the White Slave Traffic Act, the Mann Act (named for its author, Illinois congressman James Robert Mann) made it illegal to "transport any woman or girl" across state lines "for the purpose of prostitution or debauchery, or for any other immoral purpose." Supposedly targeted at protecting innocent girls from being seduced into prostitution, the law was quickly abused to prosecute consensual acts committed by "undesirables" who were otherwise law-abiding citizens. Johnson's prosecution and conviction under the Mann Act is largely understood to be in response to his seven marriages to white women.

Ultimately, in an effort to restore the racial order placed in jeopardy by the "white man's nightmare" and to make emerging professional sports more "respectable," black athletes were forced to sit out of professional sports for the better part of the twentieth century's first half. But economic interests, coupled with institutionalized forms of racial inequality that were increasingly exposed as incongruous with the pro-American democratic rhetoric characteristic of the escalating Cold War, put chinks in the armor of segregation in sports and ultimately made the practice untenable. And at the risk of oversimplification, as went sports, so went the nation.

During a 1997 address to the American Bar Association Forum on the Entertainment and Sports Industries, reminiscent of Tom Cruise's epiphanic speech in the film *Jerry Maguire*,[15] attorney and sports agent Clark C. Griffith questioned the role of contemporary agents in promoting civil rights in sports. In his speech, Griffith discussed the centrality of sport in promoting social change while reflecting upon the broader social impact brought about by the Dodgers' signing of Jackie Robinson:

> The signing of a baseball player in Brooklyn was the pivotal civil rights event of the era. Its significance, great in its own right, was magnified because it was baseball that did it. This event was followed by the integration of the armed forces a year later. The parallel universes had ended and it was baseball that broke the color barrier in America, not just in the Major Leagues. . . . It was the baseball event that had the social impact. I think this is because baseball is like life. It is undeniably real. It is played by real people, some of which are 5'6" and weigh 160 pounds and others are 6"10". It is played in real time, not by the clock. It's over when it's over. (Griffith 1997)

Baseball in Robinson's age was indeed like life in that his mere presence on the field, reserved and quiet as he may have been, made a statement of resistance that rippled across America and inspired a generation of black children and young adults to transform their previously written bodies into writing bodies[16] and, in the process of redefining their existence as Americans, use whatever means available to them to gain access to America's unfulfilled promise of equality. To this day, my mother, who was a ten-year-old black girl in segregated Washington, D.C., when Robinson first took the field, is a fan of the Dodgers not because she cares about baseball but because of the swell of pride she felt in herself and her community when a black man finally had the opportunity to participate in the professionalized form of America's pastime. Even more closely aligned with Robinson's example, the New Negro archetype characterized by this freshly formulated idea of proud, assertive, resistive, and cool blackness became increasingly articulated through and manifest in the marketplace of sports. As I observed and experienced throughout the course of this research, that legacy is still very much apparent in sports today.

Final Thoughts

Over the course of America's curious racial history, African Americans organically established a double-consciousness or sense of "two-ness" in order to achieve social mobility or, in many cases, to merely withstand racism and survive in American society. However, historically rigid racial constructs and continued social and economic exclusion for a wide swath of black Americans have also spawned subcultures of political opposition that often depend upon alternative and nonconventional forms of resistance and expression. These subcultures and the attendant black cultural expressive forms, like music and the pose articulated in black-dominated sports, rightfully serve as "black commentary" and are an ongoing reminder of a hard row to hoe in the nation's journey to become a truly postracial society.

Day-to-day interactions of the type described here—including those appearing purely recreational—that bring together people of different statuses, races, and cultures are governed by rules about language, gesture, demeanor, and attire. These interactions do not passively occur; rather, the aforementioned rules and corresponding protocols are designed to underline and reinforce cultural difference and distinctness. In his historically situated novel *A Little Yellow Dog*, Walter Mosley wrote, "White people like to keep their eyes peeled on blacks, and vice versa. We lie to each other so much that often the only hope is to see some look or gesture that betrays the truth" (Mosley 1996, 58).

It is in these momentary betrayals that the real significance of the intermediate transcript can be found. On the surface, the behavior of African American youth on a basketball court appears to be little more than recreation peppered with episodes of unbridled bravado. And, in fact, when confronted by men of other races, the cool pose and degree of "blackness" portrayed is often escalated. But it would be a mistake to assume that this swagger is an accurate indicator of black-and-white leisure-time relations, as representatives of both groups often "lie to each other" by presenting a multifaceted façade of confidence, deference, and racial harmony. However, it is arguable that this façade is more complex for black males than their white counterparts, as, for most other interactions between the two races, whiteness is the normative standard to which blacks are expected to conform and aspire if they expect to maintain in a mainstream environment.

While black participants in the pickup arena might sometimes be of similar economic status to white participants or even above whites' socioeconomic status— as was often the case in Encino, where many of the ballers were relatively well-compensated entertainment industry workers—the fact remains that blacks are expected to conform to white standards of behavior and etiquette in most other facets of life. As bell hooks suggested, black people "acting black" is often perceived as a threat to the status quo and social harmony and therefore carries with it the potential for alienation and other social consequences. When basketball was successfully claimed as the black man's game, the court became one of the few spaces in American society where embracing "blackness" was socially permissible. Even then, however, the true sentiment and meaning behind the black commentary expressed on these courts remains relegated to the intraracial discourse that occurs offstage in the realm of the hidden transcript or, less often, covertly exposed during the relatively rare times in which the intermediate transcript is displayed. With that said, as James Scott noted, demonstrations of everyday resistance that fail to contest dominant norms on a broader and more visible stage "leaves the dominant in command of the public stage . . . and leaves dominant structures intact" (Scott 1985, 57). But, Scott continued, "If the perceived relationship of power" that in this case would extend beyond the sanctuary offered by the court "shifts in favor of subordinate groups, everyday resistance may well become a direct and open political challenge and surreptitious or disguised symbolic dissent may become a public renunciation of domination" (Scott 1985, 58). Perhaps the revolution could be about basketball after all.

Notes

1. In *Race Matters*, Cornel West (1993, 13) identifies nihilism—"the lived experience of coping with a life of horrifying meaninglessness, hopelessness, and (most important) lovelessness"—as a fundamental threat to black America.

2. Permission to reprint granted by Boots Riley.

3. In Culver City, there were two well-known ballers named Mike—"Black Mike" and "Big Mike." When discussing elements of their game in their absence, other ballers referred to Black Mike as such because he was the darker-skinned and shorter of the two.

4. According to *Urban Dictionary*, posterization occurs when someone makes "a play so picturesque that it may appear on a poster." In basketball, no defender ever wants to be on the receiving end of one of these plays. In the NBA, a defensive player will occasionally be seen deliberately rushing out of "frame" so that his victimization will not be captured in another player's highlight.

5. The idea of intersubjective recognition, at least insofar as I am aware, comes from the work of Axel Honneth and his Theory of Recognition (1995). As Honneth wrote in chapter 5 of his book *The Struggle for Recognition*: "In modern societies, therefore, social relations of symmetrical esteem between individualized (and autonomous) subjects represent a pre-requisite for solidarity. In this sense, to esteem one another symmetrically means to view one another in light of values that allow the abilities and traits of the other to appear significant for shared praxis. Relationships of this sort can be said to be cases of 'solidarity', because they inspire not just passive tolerance but felt concern for what is individual and particular about the other person. For only to the degree to which I actively care about the development of the other's characteristics (which seem foreign to me) can our shared goals be realized. The fact that 'symmetrical' cannot mean here that we esteem each other to the same degree is already clear from the essential openness to interpretation of every societal value-horizon. It is simply impossible to imagine a set of collective goals that could be fixed quantitatively in such a way that it would allow for an exact comparison of the value of individual contributions; 'symmetrical' must mean instead that every subject is free from being collectively denigrated, so that one is given the chance to experience oneself to be recognized, in light of one's own accomplishments and abilities, as valuable for society. For this reason too, the social relations that we have conceived of here in terms of the concept of 'solidarity' open up, for the first time, the horizon within which individual competition for social esteem can then acquire a form free from pain, that is, a form not marred by experiences of disrespect." Ted Fleming (2011) summarizes Honneth's ideas on the subject in the following way: "For people to achieve a productive relationship with themselves, that is a full sense of identity, they require an intersubjective recognition of their abilities and achievements. . . . Intersubjective recognition is the foundation of moral consciousness and one develops one's moral understanding of the world through the reactions, both positive and negative that one receives from other persons in both the private and public spheres. This is part of what Honneth terms 'the struggle for recognition'

through which we develop our ideas of what are the necessary preconditions for a flourishing life and our conceptions of justice."

6. Foer also notes the unique status soccer has in the United States relative to nearly everywhere else in the world where the sport is played and reigns supreme. Everywhere but in America, soccer "is the province of the working class" (Foer 2004, 238).The United States "inverts the class structure of the game," where the sport is largely ignored by the football- and basketball-obsessed working classes and, aside from Latino immigrants, is disproportionately played by professional class youth.

7. The significance of these indoor facilities and the role that they play in maintaining de facto segregation in recreational basketball is revisited later in my discussion of the Aerotech league. Regarding corporate leagues, several larger corporations in Los Angeles sponsored employee basketball teams that compete against one another. These leagues are noticeably different in racial and ethnic composition and in style of play from the noncorporate recreational leagues in the area.

8. This change in racial composition was not coincidental. About a year into my membership at this YMCA, a new director was hired. One of her primary objectives was to improve community outreach and increase the gym's overall membership by drawing more members from the rather diverse surrounding Van Nuys community. Therefore, the representation of racial minorities increased.

9. While more common among white players, this "too street" idea was not limited to white basketball players. For example, a black former college basketball player who regularly participated in Orange County pickup games echoed Brent's sentiment, saying that he did not play in places like Venice because the game was "too street and too thuggish."

10. Effeminizing comments like these were common insults on the basketball courts, underscoring the relationship between basketball prowess and perceived masculinity.

11. Another example of this sense of entitlement came while I was playing one-on-one at an upscale gym in Columbia, Maryland. The one-on-one courts at this gym doubled as racquetball courts and were issued to gym members in hour-long blocks. Attached to each basket was an overhead crank device used to raise the basket when the area was being used for racquetball. Since there were no clocks in this particular section of the gym, a friend (also a black male) and I were unaware that our hour had ended and that two other individuals (both white men) had checked the court out for racquetball. Instead of informing us that our time had expired, one of the men simply began cranking up the basket. When we looked up to the balcony area where the crank was located, the man looked down at us, tapped his watch, and gestured for us to leave the court.

12. With regard to on-court behavior, European basketball—presumably, as dictated by European culture in general—is more "polite." By this I mean that there is less contact, more focus on basketball fundamentals, and less argument over calls and roles. Unlike most of the ballers, European players would also commonly call fouls that they committed against another player. Off-court, the demeanor of the European participants paralleled that of their on-court behavior—relatively polite and nonconfrontational.

13. This phrasing was borrowed from DuBois and his self-defined efforts to study "the history of the darker part of the human family," as quoted by Gilroy (1993, 111). In *The Souls of Black Folk* (1903, 2), DuBois describes double consciousness as "this sense of always looking at one's self through the eyes of others, of measuring one's soul by the tape of a world that looks on in amused contempt

and pity. One ever feels his two-ness—an American, a Negro; two souls, two thoughts, two unreconciled strivings."

14. King made this reflection in 1962. In terms of measurable outcomes, the Albany Movement (named for the town of Albany, Georgia) was not among the more successful protests King was involved in, a problem he attributed to its broad focus on segregation rather than one particular facet of the institution. King's quote regarding music may be found at http://myloc.gov/exhibitions/hopeforamerica /causesandcontroversies/politicalsongs/Pages/default.aspx (last accessed August 3, 2013).

15. *Jerry Maguire* is a 1996 comedic film that revolves around a sports agent played by Tom Cruise who has a moral epiphany critical of his industry. He shares his revelation at the industry's largest gathering and is fired for expressing it.

16. In her essay "Edwidge Danticat's Kitchen History," Valérie Loichot (2004, 93–94) introduced the idea that cooking and writing need to be viewed as "interconnected forms" of female resistance. She argues that by establishing this association, "women's previously written bodies graduate to writing bodies."

5

The Mandingo Syndrome

Black men are natural athletes, but black men also do actually work hard and practice to become elite players. We all know that you can't just wake up one day and become an elite basketball player. Things like that take time for any race, including black men.

—Hank

In his 1951 essay titled "Many Thousands Gone," James Baldwin instructed, "What it means to be a Negro in America can perhaps be suggested by an examination of the myths we perpetuate about him" (Baldwin 1998, 21). Some of these myths iconically captured by the likes of Aunt Jemima and Uncle Tom, Baldwin maintains, "are dead." Or in my view, they have at least had their places taken by more aesthetically refined myth propagators. Notwithstanding the gradual shift away from more offensive caricatures of blackness that began in the 1960s as "darkies began to dream," Aunt Jemima and the Mammy[1] image she was intended to symbolize still exist despite, as rapper Big Daddy Kane once sang, "even if now she got a perm."[2] The same can be said for numerous other stereotypical images of American blackness, particularly those revolving around black masculinity, athleticism, and sexuality.

On my first day as a graduate student in Southern California, another member of the entering cohort, a white man named Brett, approached me—the only black student in our incoming class of thirty women and men—and asked if I was interested in joining his intramural three-on-three basketball team. I declined his offer. At the time, I was still negotiating my new surroundings and, as I described earlier, unsure of my basketball skills. Brett persisted and, time and time again, I politely said no. Finally, he was convinced that I was not interested in

121

playing and threw in the towel. Walking away he said, "Well, if you change your mind, we could really use you."

At the time Brett approached me I was conversing with Luis, a Mexican classmate and one of only two other minorities (the other being an Asian woman) in our class. Interestingly, Brett only directed his basketball invitation to me, all but ignoring Luis. As best I could tell, Brett also did not ask any of the other twenty-seven incoming students, about ten of whom were men, if they were interested in joining his team. I never asked him why he overlooked the others in favor of me or why, even after my refusal, he didn't attempt to draft another member of the group. In Brett's defense, I was the tallest person in our cohort. But, what was also true is that Brett never asked me if I knew how to play basketball. Instead, he assumed that I played and that I had enough "game" to be an asset to his team.

As the first few months of graduate school went by, I became more comfortable with my new surroundings and, more important, with my fellow students. I got to know Brett better and grew confident that his proposition did not come from a place of overt prejudice. He was a genuine and accepting guy with fairly varied tastes in food, music, and other hallmarks of diverse cultures. But with that understood, his presupposition that I—the lone African American male in our class—would complement his basketball team originated from the same social processes that produce the more invidious forms of prejudice people tend to directly correlate with discriminatory acts. Throughout my personal life as well as my professional time spent researching the use of sport by black American males as a mechanism of resistance against cultural hegemony, I experienced countless episodes like that one with Brett. What's more is that I don't know a single black person who has not had similar experiences. I have subsequently ascertained that these comments, assumptions, and attitudes result from what I have labeled the *Mandingo syndrome*—the conscious or unconscious formation of ideas that are rooted in and reinforce stereotypes of, in this case, innate black male athleticism.[3] Beyond suppositions of athletic ability, the Mandingo syndrome also comprises notions of black male promiscuity, sexuality, and sexual prowess.

Mandingo Contextualized

Mandingo is a referent to a West African ethnic group whose population contributed significantly to the transatlantic slave trade. Also known as the Mandinka people, during the thirteenth century this group established an empire that spanned much of present-day West Africa. As a consequence of regional conflict in the eighteenth century, as many as one-third of the Mandingo people were sold into slavery in the Americas. Legend has it that the Mandingo men and women were physically superior to other West African populations of the slave trading era, and they were therefore coveted as bondsmen and bondswomen.

In 1957, Denlinger's Publishers released Kyle Onstott's novel titled *Mandigo*, which became Denlinger's most successful publication, selling over 5 million copies. In this lurid account of 1830s patriarchy and plantation life, the plantation owner's son, Hammond Maxwell, purchases a "top of the line" Mandingo "fightin' nigger" named Mede, with the hopes of bringing in money to the struggling Alabama plantation by training Mede to fight other slaves. However, the introduction of Mede to the plantation incites a saga filled with miscegenation and infidelity as Hammond's wife finds the new "buck" sexually irresistible and makes him the object of her attempt to seek vengeance against her unfaithful husband. In addition to the best-selling book, *Mandingo* was made into a blacksploitation era movie, released in 1975 and starring heavyweight boxing champion Ken Norton.

Mandingo's focus is on the mythology of innate black male sexuality and physical strength. It is important to recognize that the racial and cultural stereotyping presented in the book and film and the social processes that fuel them are not limited to black males. As Ian Haney Lopez has argued, "Social renditions of masculinity and femininity often carry with them racial overtones, just as racial stereotypes invariably embody some elements of sexual identity" (Lopez 1995, 198). Nonetheless, in the spheres of athletics and sexuality in America, the intersection of black and male has arguably been (and continues to be) more impacted by these particular types of stereotypes than any other intersection between race and gender, or any singular racial or ethnic group.[4] Corroborating this position, in her discussion of the ways in which different racial experiences with the law influence conflicting interpretations of the law and legal outcomes, Mary Frances Berry noted that the resulting narratives "reinforced white visions of the violent, sexually consumed black man" (Berry 1999, 7). Accordingly, the stereotypes consistent with the Mandingo syndrome embody attitudes directed toward a particular and sex-specific group of people—black American males.

It has frequently been suggested to me primarily by white friends and colleagues (but sometimes by black and other minority-group colleagues) that encounters like the one I had with Brett and the assumptions rooted in this intersection of black and male are relatively benign and not indicative of broader social threads. In a more casual conversation with a colleague about the current state of US race relations, he suggested that stereotypes presupposing athletic ability or sexual prowess are innocuous and more complimentary than derogatory. "I don't think it's a big deal; I wouldn't be offended," he said. "I think I'd be flattered if people presumed that kind of stuff about me. I'd feel like a stud if people thought that just by looking at me." It is true that many people might find being on the receiving end of "positive prejudice" built around athletic and sexual stereotypes superficially flattering. And playing off of these stereotypes very well may provide black men with a certain degree of social competence that enables them to more effectively deal with a social environment that is generally hostile and dismissive toward black men.[5] However, in the long run, these blanket categorizations do more harm than good as so-called benign prejudice stems from the same place of ignorance that produces the litany of other less-than-flattering and derogatory assumptions based on race, gender, and their intersection.

As a point of comparison, the social processes that produce these ideas are not dissimilar to those that prompted legislators after the Civil War to impose harsher criminal penalties for black men accused of raping white women.[6] These processes are also not significantly different from those that historically and currently generate institutional and public support for racial profiling, racially motivated pretextual stops[7], stop-and-frisk practices,[8] and other law enforcement practices disproportionately steered toward racial and ethnic minority-group members. Finally, the social processes motivating Mandingo are also not markedly different from those acts of stealth racism[9] that prompt women to clutch their purses as a black man approaches or those that cause motorists to suddenly feel an urge to lock their car doors as a black man crosses the street in front of their vehicle. President Obama spoke to this reality in his remarks following the acquittal of George Zimmerman for the 2012 shooting homicide of unarmed black teenager Trayvon Martin in Sanford, Florida:

> You know, when Trayvon Martin was first shot I said that this could have been my son. Another way of saying that is Trayvon Martin could have been me 35 years ago. And when you think about why, in the African American community at least, there's a lot of pain around what happened here, I think it's important to recognize that the African American community is looking at this issue through a set of experiences and a history

that doesn't go away. There are very few African American men in this country who haven't had the experience of being followed when they were shopping in a department store. That includes me. There are very few African American men who haven't had the experience of walking across the street and hearing the locks click on the doors of cars. That happens to me—at least before I was a senator. There are very few African Americans who haven't had the experience of getting on an elevator and a woman clutching her purse nervously and holding her breath until she had a chance to get off. That happens often. And I don't want to exaggerate this, but those sets of experiences inform how the African American community interprets what happened one night in Florida.

Over the course of my exploration of race, masculinity, and resistance articulated through sport, multiple manifestations of the Mandingo syndrome were observed in sporting environments as well as analyzed in other social and media outlets such as film and television. Perhaps the most interesting dynamic of this phenomenon was the numerous instances where black American males seemed to embrace these stereotypes themselves and use them to their personal advantage in the negotiation of day-to-day politics. Embodying these stereotypical personas seemed to serve as what Richard Majors and Janet Mancini Billson characterized as "an important strategy that some black males have developed for dealing creatively with the realities of everyday life" (Majors and Mancini Billson 1993, 37). This "cool pose" routinely seemed to function as "a tool for hammering masculinity out of the bronze of their" daily reality (Majors and Mancini Billson 1993, 2). An extension of this position, then, suggests that this manipulation of the Mandingo stereotype can function as a useful tool for young adult black males in temporarily altering the balance of power that governs their everyday lives—a balance that, more often than not, tips in their disfavor.

For example, I found utilizing the stereotyping of black men as brutes to capitalize on whites' fear of blackness were routine tools of intimidation during mixed-race pickup basketball games. On numerous occasions, I observed black male ballers behaving more aggressively toward white players than they did to other blacks. Whenever I asked them about what I witnessed, more often than not they contextualized their behavior as a legitimate response to their daily struggles with inequality and encounters with racism and discrimination. The net effect of this behavior was a general air of white deference to black men on the basketball court. For example, almost never in these mixed-race pickup games did unestablished white men challenge a foul call made by a black baller, whereas the black players, established or not, would routinely challenge calls they thought unfair. Similarly, when white players acted out in an impulsive way toward black players, they frequently followed their outbursts with an immediate apology. On one such occasion I was playing in a predominantly white indoor pickup game held on a university campus. Despite my best efforts to stop him, an opposing player who was white secured an offensive rebound over me and put the ball back up to score an easy basket. Typical of the bravado expressed during basketball contests, he boasted, "Yeah, in your face, bitch." As he began to trot back to the other end of the court to play defense, he glanced over his shoulder seeing that it was me—the only black player on the opposing team— whom he was attempting to emasculate through his "bitch" reference. At that point, his demeanor changed; he stopped and said, "Sorry, man. I was just pumped up. I didn't mean anything by it."

This embrace of negative imagery and stereotype is one of the instruments that these young black men have been relegated to accepting in carving a collective identity out of the unforgiving landscapes that have come to characterize postindustrial urban America. But publicly embracing the stereotype and the corresponding cool pose for temporary advantages presents a paradoxical array of negative effects that are arguably more damaging in the aggregate. The posture simultaneously protects self-image and contributes to black masculine identity while running the risk of perpetuating cultural ignorance and becoming habitually ingrained in black men to the point of "self-deception" (Majors and Mancini Billson 1993, 40) "like maybe they'd taken in too many of those popular sneaker commercials that feed America's myths about their super ball-playing skills" (McCall 2002, 110). The attitudes and habits associated with the pose can also permanently lock black males out of the mainstream, socially and economically, as they run counter to conventional codes of conduct. Finally, Majors and Mancini Billson note that intraracially, the preoccupation with coolness among young black men can damage relationships between black males and black males, and relationships between black males and black females.

What follows is a sampling of the many accounts of the Mandingo syndrome I experienced while working on this book. Episodes of Mandingo were observed on a near-daily basis, but I have chosen only a few examples that, in my view, typify the syndrome. In order to frame and add context and understanding to this discussion, I will begin with a brief dissection from somewhat older popular cinema, the analytical elements of which were first brought to my attention by the work of bell hooks and Margaret M. Russell.

Soul Brother Number One

In the 1986 film *Soul Man*, Mark Watson, an upper-class white man played by actor C. Thomas Howell, has the good fortune of being admitted to Harvard Law School. Unfortunately for Watson, his well-off parents decide to buy a time-share condominium in Barbados rather than subsidize his law school education. Reluctant to incur the expense of attendance on his own, Watson resigns himself to never realizing his dream of being a Harvard-trained lawyer. In the eleventh hour, Watson learns that a full scholarship to Harvard Law has gone unclaimed and that he meets all the scholarship criteria except one important condition—the color of his skin; the funds are specifically earmarked for a black student. Rather than accumulate personal debt or seek employment to offset the cost of tuition, Watson opts to assume a "black" identity. Through a combination of melanin pills and tanning lotions, Watson undergoes a transformation similar to that of John Howard Griffin's metamorphosis from white to black in his 1960s gaze-altering nonfiction account, *Black Like Me*. This racial shift, for all intents and purposes, renders Watson black (on the outside) and allows him to claim the scholarship.

During his self-indulgent journey into blackness, Watson is confronted with a variety of stereotypes based on black masculinity to which he otherwise, as his white self, would not have been subjected but with which he was certainly familiar. In one scene, Watson and a friend decide to participate in a game of pickup basketball with other law students. Given that the game was taking place at Harvard, an institution not historically renowned for its African American representation in the student body or faculty, there was only one "other" black participant. In seeing Watson arrive in athletic attire, the white players began quibbling among themselves about which team Watson would play on. The screenwriter's point here is clear: in this limited setting, and specifically because of his apparent blackness, Watson was viewed by the other participants as a natural basketball player and therefore a commodity. The irony was, as the other players were soon to find, that Watson was a player pathetic beyond all imagination.

In another of the film's scenes, Watson becomes the object of Whitney's affection—a white female neighbor—presumably largely because of his blackness rather than other attributes. Consistent with the Mandingo theme, Whitney's desires were fueled by stereotypes of black male sexuality and sexual prowess. This is a point that the filmmakers present rather clearly, as, among other things, this particular woman knew Watson in his white state and displayed no interest in him. After some short-lived resistance, Watson ultimately succumbs to Whitney's advances and indulges her "chocolate" fantasy.

I first saw this movie as a teenager and, at that time, just thought it was entertaining. But, as hooks and others observed in their more mature contemplation, without question this film is worthy of criticism for its gimmicky use of race to advance a formulaic Hollywood storyline. It is also flawed in its telling of the black experience through a dominant white gaze.[10] However, in four important ways, the use of this gaze in the aforementioned scenes is instrumental in exposing the race-based dialect that sits at the core of the Mandingo syndrome. First, and most obviously, the basketball scene highlights the existence of America's (both white and black) presumption of innate black athleticism. Second, the existence of the unclaimed scholarship specifically earmarked for African American students evokes thoughts of "reverse discrimination" and preferential treatment for minorities while simultaneously insinuating that, in spite of this lowered bar, Harvard still could not find a black student who could make the cut. Third, the African American student who, it was revealed later in the film, should have received the scholarship Watson transformed himself to steal was the stereotyped black single mother.

Fourth and more subtly, the white male gaze through which the film was produced, directed, and ultimately told, in actuality served to further perpetuate this stereotypical set of assumptions in noticeable ways. In the basketball scene, Watson is an absolutely lousy basketball player, seemingly mocking or even chiding the white players' presupposition that the unknown black player would be a better athlete than available white players, thus challenging the Mandingo stereotype. But, in the same scene, the only actual black person, whose character is curiously named Leon, has superior athletic ability and completely dominates the pickup game, thus promoting this idea that *real* black people are still innately superior athletes and that Watson's ineptness on the court stemmed from his masked whiteness. Further, with the exception of the black single mother whose scholarship Watson appropriated and one professor played by the iconic black actor James Earl Jones, the relative absence of black Americans in the film among the Harvard student body is indicative of the clichéd intellectual inferiority of African Americans.

The scene in which Watson finally succumbs to the sexual advances of his neighbor produces a similar dichotomous effect. After consummating their relationship and fulfilling the neighbor's lust for a black man, Watson's partner was left satiated but also questioning some of her other sexual presuppositions of *black* Watson:

> It was like you could really feel 400 years of anger and oppression in every pelvic thrust. I hope you don't mind if I use bits of this interlude in a short story I'm working on. It's called "Shades of Gray." Because, you know, I really don't feel there is any black and white; only shades of gray. Well, like the stereotypes about black men. Some of them are true, like the breast thing. And, you really are very dynamic sexually. But, then of course some of the stereotypes are completely untrue, like the one about penis size.

Again, the subtext in this scene does nothing to challenge the stereotype of black sexuality itself. Rather, in a way it affirms the Mandingo stereotype because Whitney's puzzlement with Watson's endowment appears to stem primarily from the fact that she believes that he is black. This notion is reinforced when, toward the film's end, as Watson is unmasked as white, Whitney nods in epiphanic understanding, saying "no wonder."

It could be argued that these examples are simply the result of cinematic license and therefore are not truly reflective of actual race relations. However, as I found over the course of working on this book, race- and sex-based stereotypes of this nature are commonplace. For example, during one afternoon of pickup ball, James—an average height, average build, African American baller—gave the following account of his high school transfer from a mixed-race suburb of Washington, D.C., to a predominantly white suburb of Albany, New York:

> The first day that I got there, every coach came up and asked me to play their sport. They wanted me to play basketball, football, run track, everything. They would stop me in the halls and say things like, "Hey, are you interested in doing a little running?" They would be waiting for me after class saying, "Have you thought about playing football for us?" They were even calling me at home trying to get me to play everything. Everything except golf, that is.

As James quickly realized, he was one of the very few black males in his otherwise all-white junior class and was perceived as an instant athletic commodity. Aside from a few years in Pop Warner football and Little League baseball, he had never played organized sports. Still, based solely on his blackness and maleness, coaches representing every sport in which blacks are traditionally overrepresented sought his participation.

Hoopin' It Up, Aerotech Style

During consecutive summers as a graduate student, I worked editing electronic codes in corporate tax forms for the Los Angeles offices of a "big four" accounting firm. With an office staff of over 100 people, I was one of four black employees at the firm—three men and one woman. One of the other two men was a heavy-set African immigrant, and the other was of similar physical stature but of Jamaican descent. I bring up their physical and ethnic backgrounds simply to point out that neither of the men was what would traditionally be described as athletic or African American. Further, while most people in the United States would not hesitate to identify either of my coworkers as black, neither saw themselves as such. In fact, both made it a point to accentuate their national and ethnic identity and distance themselves from American blacks. This is not an uncommon phenomenon among "black" immigrants, the root of which was captured well by May Akabogu-Collins in her essay titled "Coming to Black America," in which she writes:

> Growing up in Africa, my impression of the black American was of a lazy, uneducated, ghetto-dwelling, dependent, disruptive and accomplished criminal. Upon arriving in America in 1980, I was surprised to find black American students on a college campus. Racial preferences, I thought, and distanced myself from them. . . . I'm not exactly sure where or how I got this stereotype of black Americans, though I'm certain the movies had something to do with it. As did my parents. When I left Nigeria for grad school, my dad told me: "If you look for racism in America, you'll find it. But prove to them that you are a tribal African, not one of those addlebrained former slaves. And do steer away from them; they're nothing but trouble." When my mother came to visit, she made us cross the road upon spotting a black man approaching. . . . In grad school, I collaborated in my own discrimination. A Korean classmate was equally surprised to find me—a black doctoral student. She had grown up in Korea to believe that black people were "lazy and dumb . . . only dance and crime." I concurred but with a slight modification: "only black Americans, not black Africans." I had assumed that to get respect in America, I needed to distinguish myself from those blacks. (Akabogu-Collins 2004, 1-2)

Shortly after I began my employment with the firm, Bill, a white coworker to whom I had never been formally introduced, approached me at my desk. During the ensuing exchange, and oddly reminiscent of my first day in graduate school, he asked, "Me and some guys I used to work with play in this basketball league on Monday nights and need another player on our team. You think you might want to play?"

Over the course of my graduate studies, basketball had become my escape, and the court began to function as one of the only spaces where I could shed my anxiety over dissertation deadlines, grading term papers, relationship woes, the scramble for continued funding, and the other things that tend to preoccupy graduate students. I had also become increasingly interested in the politics and personalities that defined pickup basketball in varied settings. Therefore, unlike my first day of graduate school when I rejected Brett's offer, I accepted Bill's invitation and began to play in the league on a team sponsored by Aerotech Enterprises—a defense industry technologies firm. I also began participating in a regularly scheduled pickup game with some of the other players in the league.

By that time, both pickup games and league basketball had become my passion, and I was happy to join another league. I was already playing in two fairly competitive Los Angeles area leagues, and Bill's somewhat-less-competitive group seemed like a good opportunity to just play ball and work on shortcomings in my game. But, with that said and in spite of my willingness to participate in the Aerotech league, it seemed clear that Bill's motivation for approaching me as a candidate to fill the empty roster position was consistent with the Mandingo theme. As an aside, every other adult basketball league in which I have played has been overwhelmingly African American, and requests for my participation have come only after my level of basketball ability had been observed by other players on the respective teams. In this case, not only was I the only black player on my team, I was one of six or seven black participants in this league of seventy-two players. Given that this took place in a corporate environment, aside from presumptions fueled by my physical appearance, there was nothing that could have reasonably indicated to my coworker that I would be an asset to his team. Outside of the workplace and apart from the one black American female employee of the company, whom I had known prior to taking the job, I had never had any contact with the people at this firm. So, similar to my first day in graduate school, they could not have known for a fact that I enjoyed playing basketball or that I had any reasonable basketball skills.

Furthermore, when others in the office found that I was participating in the league with Bill, none acted with surprise. Like Nathan McCall wrote in *Makes Me Wanna Holler*, his autobiographical account of growing up black in America, "Black men are generally the last ones selected for crucial project teams yet are the first to be chosen during company picnics, when it's time to relax outdoors, drink some beer, and shoot some hoops" (McCall 2002, 112). But, interestingly, when many of these same people discovered that I had gone on a golf outing with one of the firm's managers, the reaction was quite different. It seems that as an African American male, I was expected to play basketball; after all, "Abraham Lincoln freed the slaves so they could play basketball" (McCall 2002, 112). But golf, a sport from which blacks have been traditionally excluded and one in which blacks remain underrepresented, struck a different chord among my coworkers. Perhaps the firm's managing partner, Todd—a late-thirties white man—captured the overall sentiment best when he said of me, "Golf? He doesn't look like he'd play golf." I genuinely liked Todd and know that he had no malign intent behind his comment. Nonetheless, not dissimilar to white golfer Fuzzy Zoeller's suggestion that black golfer Tiger Woods might order a victory dinner of fried chicken and collard greens after winning the Masters Tournament,[11] Todd's comments were driven by a stereotype of black males being better suited for physical sports requiring brutish and unrefined athletic ability rather than sports more dependent upon strategy or technique.

Like everyone else with whom I worked at the firm, my attire was business-casual—khaki pants, collared shirts, and appropriate shoes. Further, like all "code switchers," my speech around members of the firm was always professional and never what could be considered "street" dialect. Finally, aside from Bill, one other office accountant, and myself, there were no other players on this team who worked in our office. Therefore, the sole inference I can draw with regard to my coworker's proposition and Todd's statement is that their presumptions were based on this stereotype of black male athleticism, one that also encompassed types of sports that black people were "supposed" to play.

The pickup basketball game that coincided with playing on the Aerotech team was held on Friday afternoons around our corporate lunch hour on a secluded basketball court located to the back of Aerotech Enterprises' sprawling San Fernando Valley campus. Aerotech sponsored two of the six basketball teams participating in the league and, aside from Bill (a former Aerotech employee) and me, everyone who played in this particular pickup game worked for Aerotech. During the pickup game one afternoon after his squad suffered a league loss to our team the night before, Dennis—a tall, thin white man in his late thirties and a member of the other Aerotech-based team in our league—began boasting about a new player that they had added to their roster. According to Dennis: "The only reason you guys won last night was because our new guy, Chaka, couldn't make it. If he was there, there's no way you guys would've won. Wait 'till you see this guy. He's a freakin' house. He's a six-foot-five, 230-pound black guy. He's unstoppable. He's a monster."

On several occasions after that day, Dennis bragged about the size and ability of Chaka, stressing his six-foot-five frame and his dominating presence. Thanks to comments like "he's huge," "he dominates," and "just wait until you see him the next time we play," I was expecting the second coming of Charles Barkley. Because I was among the tallest players on our team and was our team's most physical defender, I figured that I would be the one to match up against Chaka the next time our two teams met. Therefore, I decided to linger after our next game to scout the most recent addition to Dennis's roster. Much to my surprise, the "unstoppable" six-foot-five Chaka was only about six feet tall, nearly two inches shorter than I. Even more shocking was his basketball ability; aside from being a formidable rebounder, his game could best be described as average. He was not able to handle the ball very well and, apart from layups (which no league player is expected to miss), he was a poor shooter, frequently missing long and short range jump shot attempts. When we finally met Dennis's Chaka-improved team in a game, we beat them as handily as we had during the pre-Chaka pickup game.

I bring up this account of Chaka to once again highlight that, not unlike Brett in graduate school, Bill and the Aerotech invitation, and Todd's thoughts on me as a golfer, Dennis's assessment of Chaka seemed fueled more by Chaka's skin color and the stereotypes associated with black athleticism than any rational appraisal of his size or ability. Certainly, aware of Dennis's disposition by this time, I should have known that his remarks might have been deliberately hyperbolic or an attempt to intimidate his opponents by providing us with an exaggerated impression of Chaka.

But it is also worth noting that Dennis's bravado seemed more sincere than jest and was likely rooted in "positive" prejudicial beliefs for two obvious reasons. First, even a cursory assessment of Chaka's size and skill would immediately betray to anyone not deluded by his blackness that he was not what Dennis had indicated. Second, given that Dennis had other players on his team with far superior basketball ability to that of Chaka, his touting of Chaka rather than the better players had to be partially based on Chaka's status as the only African American player on the squad and one of the few in the league, and therefore rooted in stereotypes of black male athleticism. In fact, when playing in the Aerotech league and in other predominantly white settings (usually indoor gymnasiums at area colleges), this white male weighting as extraordinary of relatively normal feats of athleticism by black males was commonplace.

General Hospital

Another experience with the Mandingo syndrome came during a period when I participated in pickup basketball games around Southern California approximately three to four days per week. As a consequence of playing as much basketball as I could find the time for, I sustained the first of what would be a number of sports-related injuries, including a chronic pain that had developed in both of my knees that I later found to be patellar tendinitis. As the discomfort intensified, I made an appointment to see an orthopedist. On the morning of my initial examination, a medical intern was shadowing the doctor, the latter a white man who appeared to be in his early forties. The intern was also white and male, and younger. I explained my symptoms to the doctor and noted that they were likely related to basketball, although, I went on to explain, I had also recently begun playing tennis recreationally.

Reuben A. May wrote in his exploration of high school basketball and the American dream, "The extent to which Americans use race as a proxy for athletic ability cannot be overstated" (May 2009, 81). Consistent with this assertion, as the orthopedist began to evaluate my condition, he glanced up at me and began the following exchange.

"You have pretty good hops, don't you?" he asked. I knew to what he was referring but I was a little taken aback by his suddenly cavalier demeanor. I replied, "Excuse me?" He repeated, "Hops? You've got pretty good hops, right? You can get up there when you're playing ball, right?" "I can jump OK but I'm no Jordan," I responded. And, in fact, my leaping ability was only average. At six-foot-two and 185 pounds, I could dunk a basketball with some effort, but I certainly was not going to win any awards for style. And my few-and-far between dunks were anything but the seemingly effortless dunks of some of the more high-flying ballers with whom I routinely played. Oblivious to my self-assessment, my doctor then turned to the intern and, as if attempting to indoctrinate him into medical justifications for stereotypes, said, "You see the lean and high calf muscles. That's how I could tell that he had good jumping ability. He's a natural leaper."

Interestingly, as I later learned, while developed calf and other leg muscles likely play a role in leaping ability, the length and stiffness of the Achilles tendon is believed to be a critical factor in determining whether a person is a "high-riser." As David Epstein writes in his book examining the science of athletic performance, *The Sports Gene*: "A longer Achilles tendon allows an athlete to get more power from what's called the 'stretch shortening cycle,' basically the compression and subsequent decompression of the springlike tendon. The more power that is stored in the spring when it is compressed, the more you get when it's released" (Epstein 2013, 32–33).

In his examination and lesson to the intern, my doctor never glanced at my Achilles tendon, and he certainly never made mention of the tendon's relationship to jumping ability. Instead, like other presumptions of innate racial attributes, the orthopedist's medical scientific justification seemed generally crafted around an existing (but false) postulation of racial characteristics—my skinny black calves.

On an earlier occasion while still a graduate student, I sustained a shoulder injury while lifting weights. After several days the pain failed to subside, so I sought medical attention at the university's student health center. After an initial examination, the doctor referred me to the radiology department for x-rays. The x-ray technician, a white woman who appeared to be in her late forties or early fifties, asked, "What sport do you play?" Not having played organized sports since early in high school, I replied, "I don't." Seemingly stunned or confused by my answer, she asked again, "No, I mean, what sport do you play here at the university?" "Nothing," I replied. "I don't play any sports here. I'm a graduate student." Still somewhat puzzled, she looked at my medical chart and asked, "A graduate student? They have athletic scholarships for graduate students?" "They might," I replied. "But I wouldn't know. I don't play any sports for the university. I am *just* a graduate student," I said again. She persisted, "Well what sport did you play as an undergraduate?" Once again, not having played any organized sports in college, "Nothing. I didn't play any sport as an undergraduate either." In apparent disbelief, her last comment on this subject was, "You didn't play basketball or football in college? Humph."

What struck me as significant about these two experiences was the extent to which their respective comments seemed shaped by the Mandingo syndrome rather than by any objective examination or even my own words. In the case of the orthopedist, it was presumed from the moment that he and the intern walked into the examination room that I had some innate athletic and basketball ability. Certainly, at the time, I played a good bit of basketball and he knew that my examination was the result of a basketball-related injury. But, I think it is safe to assume that a large percentage of his patients came under his care for sports-related injuries, including basketball injuries. In the instance involving the radiologist, it was presumed that athletic ability was the most plausible gateway by which I could have accessed my college and graduate education. But, as I noted earlier, I am not, nor have I ever been, a natural leaper. And, prior to my foray into daily basketball games and the conditioning that necessarily came as a result of running and jumping for a couple of hours each day, my "hops" were even less noteworthy. Similarly, despite my assurance to the contrary, the x-ray technician had difficulty understanding that I was not currently a scholarship athlete at the university, nor had I ever been a scholarship athlete at any university. As with the orthopedist, her opinion of me seemed based on superficial racial criteria formed when she saw me as she entered the room and prior to her examination.

In our increasingly intercultural marketplace, prejudice in exchanges like those just described and others routinely experienced by minority group members often must be inferred from the subtext of encounters rather than from what is said literally. That is, in the post–civil rights movement era, overt prejudice of most sorts has been increasingly replaced by more subtle presumptions and stereotypes that remain rooted in the greater politics of race. Whether it be that the actors are unaware of their prejudices or that they mask them in ways that are more socially palatable, for the most part comments and behaviors that may reasonably be construed as prejudiced are not couched in explicitly prejudicial language. A possible explanation for this deference to African American sensibilities is that the world of pickup basketball is largely dominated by black males. Accordingly, political correctness, the fear of physical violence stemming from an actual or perceived racist remark, and the fear of being labeled a racist likely generate restraint in openly expressing prejudice.

On some occasions, however, encounters occur with individuals who are more forthright or uncoded with their race-based assumptions. For example, one afternoon in Culver City, Jurgis and I were waiting to play next. As explained earlier, "next" literally means that yours is the game to be played immediately after the ongoing game is completed. Next always involves a public declaration of a player's intention to play.

This practice is not without controversy and often results in arguments as more meek players are bullied out of their "next" position by those who are more outspoken or aggressive. Further, race politics often play a role in these arguments. For example, I occasionally observed some ballers deliberately ignoring white players' claims of next. In one instance in Encino, a baller named "D" stole next from a white player who had clearly been waiting longer than he. When the white player voiced his discontent and refused to leave the court, similar to Eddie's earlier-mentioned rebuke of a white player who challenged his dismissal from an overstocked team waiting to play next, D stepped up into his face, saying, "You'd better get your dumb white ass off this court before you get carried off. And don't come back up here again either!" Clearly disturbed but also clearly unnerved, the white player left the court and went to sit in his car parked along the street. Ultimately he drove off and, per D's directive, did not return.

Back to Culver City: Jurgis was a nineteen-year-old white male born in Eastern Europe and raised primarily in Los Angeles. He stood about five-foot-ten and had a slim build, solid basketball fundamentals, and was good-natured and generally well-liked in the court community. Over the year that I had known Jurgis, we had come to get along relatively well and had a relationship characterized by greater candor than most of the more interstitial relationships people on the courts had with one another. He was also one of the few regulars who knew about my educational background, information I did not hide when asked but also did not volunteer because of the social distance it might artificially create. Accordingly, we would frequently chat about courses he was taking at the local community college and what he should do academically to make his goal of transferring to UCLA materialize.

On this particular day, Jurgis and I were chatting about nothing particularly noteworthy when our conversation drifted into a discussion on race and sports. At one point during the conversation, he stated: "Black guys are just better athletes. . . . It's the truth. I've got to work harder than black guys just to be able to compete. I don't know what it is, genetics or whatever. But, black guys are just better in sports than white guys."

Jurgis's frankness with his racial presumptions was certainly the exception rather than the rule on the courts, particularly when having conversations with the relatively few white players. In fact, many white players, especially the younger players, were reluctant to engage in any conversation of race politics at all. This was the case even when I attempted to initiate a conversation on the subject. It was if they felt a sense of tenuousness in their court status, and that they would be further alienated from the baller community, face other reprisal, or merely be unmasked as white if they opened up to talk about race.

Mandingo's Message

As I have noted, relationships in the world of pickup basketball are often transient and interstitially limited to the intervening space carved out of everyday life that the game offers. Therefore, games are often necessarily played with others that you know only in the context of the court, whose basketball personality and skills you have no prior assessment of. Accordingly, teams are typically selected based on superficial characteristics and physical attributes; apparent athleticism, height, clothing, and other visible traits all play important roles in selecting teammates at the start of a pickup contest. However, because of the apparent "blackness" of basketball and football, the belief that race is the first criterion in determining athletic competence—as well as the primary contribution black Americans have to offer US society—has extended beyond the field of play into other aspects of life. Essentially, as was the case in *Soul Man*, in spite of significant achievements by black people in every other aspect of social and economic life in America, black men remain largely viewed through the prism of Mandingo.

Over the course of my research, there were countless interactions— well beyond the few documented here—where the Mandingo syndrome seemed manifest. While each incident was significant in its own way, they collectively bespeak the pervasive and deep-seated nature of race- and gender-based stereotypes in America, at least as they relate to black men. These beliefs and assumptions associated with the Mandingo syndrome, whether held consciously or subconsciously, are inextricably linked to a broader and long-held collection of black male stereotypes related to sports, physicality, intellectual ability, and sexuality. They also further highlight the extent to which these sentiments are not fully offset by factors like age, contact, or education. Collectively, these exchanges and observations illustrate an underlying consciousness of race and race relations that generally resides just beneath the surface of our typically more superficial race politics; a consciousness that often seems to serve as self-fulfilling prophecies for whites and blacks in black-and-white interracial encounters.

It is challenging to distill the Mandingo syndrome into a set of simple words, but maybe Ta-Nehisi Coates managed this feat when he wrote, "And it is true that there is something particular about how the Americans who think they are white regard us—something sexual and obscene" (Coates 2015, 127). The beliefs serving as the foundation for the Mandingo syndrome are connected to the same sets of ideas that contribute to the ongoing formal and informal educational tracking that holds back blacks in schools, ultimately stymieing economic advancement for large segments of the African American population. They serve as an apology for the continuing de facto redlining and more recent "reverse redlining"[12] practices in home-lending based on the idea that blacks are less credit-worthy than nonblacks, a toll (in the context of the recent housing crisis) that led legal scholars Charles L. Nier III and Maureen R. St. Cyr to conclude, "The impact of the financial crisis is nothing short of the preeminent civil rights issue of our time, erasing, as it has, a generation of hard fought wealth accumulation among African Americans" (Nier and St. Cyr 2011, 942). Described earlier in this book, Mandingo-based assumptions and the accompanying perceptions of black male criminality and violence serve as the catalyst to send blacks to prisons at alarmingly higher rates than members of other racial and ethnic groups. They lend credibility to provably ineffective and destabilizing policing practices like stop-and-frisk. They permit demonstrably false statements supporting these "law and order" tactics, such as those offered by then-candidate Donald Trump, to go largely unchecked. "Now, whether or not in a place like Chicago you do stop and frisk, which worked very well in New York. It brought the crime rate way down," Trump said (Shabad, 2016). Ultimately, the Mandingo tradition and its other accompanying inequalities serve as ongoing impediments to meaningful black American progress and significantly improved minority-majority relations.

The Mobilization of Bias

At least as damaging as these more discreet demonstrations of ongoing racial prejudice is the internalization of these cues by black Americans and the role these racially coded signals play in cultivating a narcissistic, hedonistic, and discretely self-loathing mentality among younger black males. Similar to theories of social strain[13] and Elijah Anderson's (1999) "code of the street," the far too frequent consequence of this mindset is the development by young black men of a social posture and set of superficial values that are incompatible with attaining success through conventional means. As Anderson wrote in his book describing "the code," "The despair is pervasive enough to have spawned an oppositional culture, that of 'the streets,' whose norms are often consciously opposed to those of mainstream society" (Anderson 1999, 32—33). When coupled with all-too-real hindering forces embedded in American institutional racism, those young black males who internalize popular stereotypes of black maleness like those encoded in the Mandingo image may find themselves ensnared in a negatively synergistic cycle in which the cultural adaptation resulting in their street posture "can be traced to the profound sense of alienation from mainstream society" (Anderson 1999, 34). However, the adaptation also compounds the disadvantages associated with structural inequalities rooted in racial prejudice and simultaneously offers a justification of sorts for ongoing racial inequality by keeping the public lens trained on "Mandingo" and away from the inadequacies of an unfair social structure that makes the internalization of the Mandingo stereotype seem like a reasonable posture for so many young black men.

At the root of the problem of internalized unconstructive stereotypes is the fact that African Americans have historically lacked the power to shape their own public images. And, as bell hooks attests, black people and other people of color are routinely "bombarded by a powerful colonizing whiteness that seduces us away from ourselves, that negates that there is beauty to be found in any form of blackness that is not imitation whiteness" (hooks 1996, 218). This distorted socialization is clearly visible in the media, where whiteness is commonly presented "as a status to be achieved, a way of life to emulate, with homogeneity as the goal," whereas minority groups are typically cast as "the objectified other, created and controlled through practices of exclusion, expulsion, and violence" (Sutherland and Feltey 2010, 65). But the media serves as only one vehicle through which ideologies of inequality are constructed and maintained. Throughout history and today, common perceptions of blacks and other members of the racial and ethnic subaltern continue to be formed through overtly and discretely racist ideologies perpetuated and reinforced by the totality of American political, social, and economic institutions. Sociologist Alfredo Mirandé labels this process "the mobilization of bias" and defines it as "the manipulation of symbols in such a way that they perpetuate myths about the inferiority of the group." Speaking of Chicanos but transposed easily to the African American experience, Mirandé argues, because they "lack power over the schools, the media, and other agents of socialization, most prevalent images of them are externally induced" (Mirandé 1987, 23).

Therefore, through the manipulation of common socialization mechanisms like the media, criminal justice, education, and sport, the most prevalent and accessible images of African Americans have been those that either perpetuate myths of black inferiority or relegate black merit to the ghettoes of physicality and other nonintellectual accomplishments.

This mobilization of bias has not only propagated the image of black men as little more than athletes and entertainers, but also triggered recent generations of black male youths to embrace these sporting and entertainment images while concurrently shunning career pursuits far more likely to garner economic and social stability. With no irony intended, Harlem-based rapper Big L's 1995 underground classic "Street Struck" perfectly captured this aspirational paradox: "And yo, it's not even funny. I've seen a lot of my peers give up their careers for some fast money. They could've been boxers, ballplayers, or rap singers. Instead they bank robbers and crack slingers." A dozen years earlier on the 1983 Grand Master Flash and the Furious Five hip-hop classic "New York New York," emcee Melle Mel versed parallel lyrics that still seem to hold true today: "Staring at a skyscraper reaching into Heaven when over in the ghetto I'm living in hell. Just play ball or be an entertainer, 'cause niggas like me can't read too well." Similar to Big L's and Melle Mel's rhymes, in telling the story of black high school basketball players, sociologist Rueben May explains, "The young men believe and make choices about their lives based on the view that sports enhances mobility rather than from the perspective that sport impedes mobility . . . a waste of time and energy that detracts from efforts they could put forth in alternative pursuits to mobility" (May 2008, 3). Again, in Mirandé's words, "When they began to internalize and espouse such negative images, the mobilization of bias has come full circle" (Mirandé 1987, 24).

Certainly, aspirations toward goals of athletic excellence are not, in and of themselves, self-destructive or otherwise negative. In fact, it was the athletic successes of African Americans like Muhammad Ali, Jackie Robinson, Bill Russell, John Carlos, and Tommie Smith that offered them the platform to publicly campaign for social equality. It is also true that sports can be beneficial to young men and women in a variety of social and physical respects. However, the mobilization of bias as constructed around black athleticism and participation in sports simultaneously devalues intellectual contributions of African Americans and deemphasizes the images most likely to lead to self-empowerment and economic achievement. While talking with me about the impact of race and sports in her all-black neighborhood in northern Jacksonville, Florida, college basketball player and former high school player of the year Ice Lady noted:

> Where I'm from [Jacksonville's black side], everybody was athletic. Our schools were run off of that—our athletic program. Now that I'm older I

see that they didn't put as much money, and time, and attention into academic programs. My school was an "F" school, but our basketball team and our football team were top 5 in the nation. A boy came from New York just because he heard about our football team. Like, moved from New York to Jacksonville to play football at our high school. Our boys were going to colleges, a lot of them.

Referring to a high school classmate who received a Division I football scholarship at a major SEC school, she continued:

ICE LADY: I had, like, six classes with this boy and I've never seen him turn in not one homework assignment. I'd hardly seen him in class. How'd he get to [that university]? I don't know.

ARM: What happens when they come home? I presume most of them don't make it to the pros.

ICE LADY: They all come home and then they join the [drug] game. There's not really many jobs you can have where I'm from. You play sports. You can play basketball. You can rap. You can sell drugs. You would think they would come home with a degree. They're majoring in something that they can't even use, like . . . crazy stuff. . . . They're taking these small classes just to keep their GPA up and be eligible and they come home and they can't use it. So, there's nothing much you can really do. . . . In the minds of the people that I'm around, they see it like, "OK, I'll go to college. I'll be on TV. I'll be on ESPN. I'll live the life. If I don't go to the NFL, I'll just come home." . . . They see other people riding around in nice cars; rimmed out, painted out. And they're like, "well, if that fails" . . . because these people have nice houses, nice cars, a lot of money, they dress really nice. To a twenty-year-old mind, that's like . . . "that's what I want." If football doesn't work out, you've got a backup plan—the [drug] game.

It is unfortunate that through their everyday interactions with white America, some black males begin to adopt these views of themselves as little more than athletes, entertainers, and the increasingly popular thug. Many young black males see these pursuits as the only avenues to push upward against the pressures created by economic stratification and social inequality, therefore making these activities their life's ambition.

In doing this, they not only invest in the fallacy of innate black athletic superiority but also play into the misconception that athletics, entertainment, or crime are their most likely means of upward social mobility. In truth, only slightly more than 3 percent of high school athletes go on to play NCAA college sports, and fewer than 2 percent of all NCAA student-athletes will ever compete professionally in their sport.[14] Along these lines, stepping away from the historical fiction for which he is most commonly known, Walter Mosley wrote:

> Of all the constraints placed upon us, two of the most powerful are those of spectacle and illusion. Chains are expensive, as are surveillance tools and armed guards. The best way to keep a worker working is to bedazzle her or him. Sublimation is the best remedy for rebellion. Give them something inconsequential to think about or a dream that leads nowhere. Organized sports are perfect for these ends. Ferdinand Marcos distracted a whole revolutionary movement in the Philippines by hosting the Thrilla in Manila, the battle royal between Joe Frazier and Muhammad Ali. (Mosley 2000, 25)

Looking back on the role that basketball played in his life choices over the course of his teens and twenties, baller Clark reflected, "Primarily, man, every decision in my life has been basketball-based. I didn't know what I wanted to do; I just know I wanted to play basketball." And, as Van Nuys baller Tony shrieked through pain-clenched teeth immediately after suffering a particularly bad ankle sprain in a pickup game, "There goes my career!" Or, as then-eighteen-year-old New York playground legend Ed "Booger" Smith said in the 1997 basketball documentary *Soul in the Hole*, "If I don't make it to the NBA? Then I'm going to be a drug dealer. Some way I'm going to get me a Lexus." In a 2009 follow-up interview, Smith reflected on his life after dropping out of high school in a failed attempt to pursue basketball full-time and then spending four years in prison on drugs and weapons charges, "I think that when I said that if I didn't make the NBA I'd be a drug dealer, people got scared of that. But it was a real story. I mean, that's what I was going to do. Did they want me to lie and say I was going to be an architect or something? I don't regret saying it. She [the interviewer] just told me to be myself" (Dhani 2009).

To be sure, not everyone, black or white, fully accepts the notion of innate black athleticism. In fact, most scientific literature on the subject remains consistent with David Hunter's conclusions from two decades ago that "discussion of racial variations in sport performance should be set within both a biological and social context. . . . It seems more likely that physiological function is only one slice of the pie to explain performance and participation discrepancies" (Hunter 1997, 36). Along those same lines, Malcolm Gladwell concluded, "African populations seem to create more of these genetic outliers than white populations do, and this is what underpins the claim that blacks are better athletes than whites. But that's all the claim amounts to. It doesn't say anything at all about the rest of us, of all races, muddling around in the genetic middle" (Gladwell 1997, 50).[15] But even in rejecting the premise of white intellectual superiority hidden in the Mandingo myth, many of the ballers I encountered still seemed to at least partially assign black athletic achievement to racial attributes. Baller Hank captured this reality well during one of our conversations:

> If white men can't jump, meaning their athletic achievements and skills do not come naturally, then the implication is that they become good athletes as a result of hard work, discipline, and a level of intelligence. They practice, they learn, while black men, the "natural athletes," simply play. I feel a certain type of way because people actually do believe this. Black men are natural athletes, but black men also do actually work hard and practice to become elite players. We all know that you can't just wake up one day and become an elite basketball player. Things like that take time for any race, including black men.

Conclusion

The relatively recent prominence of the National Basketball Association—ushered in by the league's coerced acceptance of a more street-ball inspired on-the-court swagger[16]—and the National Football League and the financial success and celebrity these leagues have bestowed upon black athletes from humble beginnings has only served to accelerate a process of misdirected ambition. Almost every black playground baller interviewed over the course of this research expressed to me some aspiration of a career in professional sports or, particularly for the older ballers, some lost dream of becoming a college or NBA star—a dream to which they devoted an unreasonable amount of their youthful physical and intellectual resources. Even ballers like Bobby in Culver City, who clearly lacked the skills or size to play Division I college basketball (let alone professional basketball), clung to unrealistic dreams of this sort. Like Booger Smith, marijuana sales and basketball were the only two pathways toward success that Bobby could see for himself. When I asked the eighteen-year-old

Angeleno what he would do if neither of these options panned out, telling him, "I bet you don't know many old drug dealers, and the odds of making the NBA are slim to none," he simply shrugged his shoulders and mumbled, "Don't know."

The mobilization of bias also impacts those who have no realistic expectations of a career in professional sports but who are still confronted with daily images of black inferiority in other walks of life, and it therefore speaks to "the ways that inequality and race help systematically structure the kinds of choices young black men make" (May 2008, xvi). For example, one afternoon at Encino Park in Encino, I arrived about a half-hour before the afternoon pickup game usually began and observed two white men playing a game of one-on-one basketball. As I often did, I sat in my car, waiting for the regular afternoon ballers to arrive. Among the first to show up was Eddie, someone I had come to know in the limited context of the court. He was in his late twenties or early thirties, black, and college educated. Seeing Eddie, I exited my car and walked over to say hello and to ensure that my spot in the afternoon's first game was claimed. As he and I chatted casually and stretched, two other black men in their mid-twenties arrived for the afternoon run. It was clear from stolen glances in our direction that the white men were aware of and discomforted by our presence on the court. A few moments later, another pair of the park's black regular ballers made their way to the court. Seeming to reach a tipping point, the visitors' level of uneasiness became more apparent and they hastily headed off the far end of the court and toward their car.

Mind you, this took place in predominantly white, predominantly upscale Encino in broad daylight. To my knowledge, none of us had even acknowledged the presence of the two white men, yet they seemed visibly intimidated by our presence. As they walked away, Eddie offered a snarky comment on the impetus for their hasty retreat, and I asked him if it made him angry or upset that white people often reacted that way to the presence of blacks. His response highlighted another dimension of the mobilization of bias, that being the use of these largely negative images of black men by black men for the purpose of temporary empowerment. As Eddie said:

> It used to bother me when shit like that happened. Now, I kind of dig it. I like it when the white boys fear me when I walk on the court or walk down the street. I finally have some power over them. Man, it was really cool after the [1992] riots. I got respect from white people that I never got before.

In *Weapons of the Weak: Everyday Forms of Peasant Resistance*,"
James C. Scott contends that the success of any resistance "is contin-
gent on relationships of power" (Scott 1985, 41). It stands to reason,
then, that in the context of the court, embodying the Mandingo image
for the purposes of momentary retaliation or situational gain amounts to
some form of modest success. But the fact that these articulations are
inherently limited in scope and are not as commonly expressed in the
more plentiful public spaces where black people remain largely disenfranchised means that these forms of everyday resistance are largely
"expunged from the official record." And rather than be widely recognized statements of still-tenuous race relations in the United States,
these resistive acts become overshadowed by a "public record of compliance and deference" revealing "only half of the double life that W. E.
B. DuBois understood all subordinate groups were obliged to lead"
(Scott 1985, 50). As Mirandé (1987) warned of the mobilization of bias
traveling full-circle, since these labels help carry on the Mandingo
mythology, the internalized stereotypes that serve to protect black masculinity in the context of the court also may function as an impediment
to individual and collective black progress.

Notes

1. Deborah Gray White describes the black plantation-era Mammy character as
"the woman who could do anything, and do it better than anyone else. Because of
her expertise in all domestic matters, she was the premier house servant and all others were her subordinates. . . . Mammy is especially remembered for her love of her
young white charges" (White 1999, 47).
2. This verse appears in the Public Enemy song "Burn Hollywood Burn" from
the hip-hop group's 1990 *Fear of a Black Planet* album.
3. To be sure, mine is not the first attempt to apply the language of Mandingo
to stereotypical concepts of blackness.
4. Historically, black women have also been mired by similar stereotyping, particularly as it pertains to sexuality. In her chapter on mythology and female slavery,
Deborah Gray White describes one such image of antebellum blackness, the
Jezebel, as a bondswoman governed almost entirely by her libido, who serves as
"the counterimage of the mid-nineteenth-century ideal of the Victorian lady" (White
1999, 29). But White notes that black women on the plantation were also, and
sometimes interchangeably, stereotyped as a polar opposite Mammy character—an
almost asexual black woman in complete control of the household and more concerned with the well-being of her white charges than that of her own family. While
neither stereotypical image is particularly flattering of black women, black men in
plantation societies were generally not afforded a similarly contrasting image to the
"black buck" as a counterbalance.
5. See Majors and Mancini Billson (1993). A specific discussion of "social
competence" begins on p. 38.

6. Stereotypes based on black male sexuality, as well as a schizophrenic fear of creating a "mongrel breed of citizen," resulted in laws requiring the castration of black men accused of raping white women. I refer to this fear as *schizophrenic* because the rape of slave women by white men was an everyday tragedy of plantation life. Under these same codes, a white male convicted of the same crime faced a maximum sentence of five years. See Burns (1998).

7. Pretextual stops occur when officers use racial or ethnic minority status as the primary criterion in the formation of the requisite reasonable suspicion for traffic stops. The US Supreme Court upheld the constitutionality of these practices in *Whren v. US* (1996), concluding that if a police officer has a valid basis for making a traffic stop (even if the interest in making that stop was motivated by some other subjective purpose), the stop is valid.

8. Stop-and-frisk policies give a police officer who is suspicious of an individual the right to detain and "pat down" the individual in an effort to prevent a crime from taking place. In 2013, New York City's stop-and-frisk practices came under scrutiny as potentially racially biased and a US District Court judge ruled that policing strategy amounted to "indirect racial profiling" and was therefore in violation of the Fourth and Fourteenth Amendments. The New York Police Department's own data confirm that in 2012, over 500,000 New Yorkers were stopped by police, and 87 percent of those stopped were either black or Latino. In 2003 the NYPD began collecting racial and ethnic data for those stopped by police, and the percentage of minorities stopped has consistently hovered around this 85 percent mark each year. Overall, between 2002 and 2013, nearly 4 million New Yorkers were subjected to stop-and-frisk practices; 87 percent were either black or Latino, and 90 percent resulted in either no arrest or no conviction. In total, only 3 percent of stop-and-frisk arrests led to a conviction. In vowing to veto two 2013 bills by the New York City Council requiring an inspector to monitor the NYPD's stop-and-frisk practices for possible racial bias, Mayor Michael Bloomberg said "Nobody racially profiles." In continued defense of the practice, Bloomberg acknowledged that a disproportionate percentage of particular racial and ethnic groups are stopped. But, he contended, "It's not a disproportionate percentage of those who witnesses and victims describe as committing the murder. In that case, incidentally, I think we disproportionately stop whites too much and minorities too little" (Chen, 2013).

9. For more on stealth racism, see Eddings (2000).

10. See Margaret M. Russell's article "Race and the Dominant Gaze: Narratives of Law and Inequality in Popular Film" in Delgado (1995).

11. It is customary that the winner of the Masters Tournament—one of golf's most prestigious events—selects the menu for the following year's tournament banquet. After twenty-one-year-old Woods became the first African American in tournament history to win the Masters, Zoeller said before cameras, "He's doing quite well, pretty impressive. That little boy is driving well and he's putting well. He's doing everything it takes to win. So, you know what you guys do when he gets in here? You pat him on the back and say congratulations and enjoy it and tell him not to serve fried chicken next year. . . . or collard greens or whatever the hell they serve" (CNN 1997).

12. Reverse redlining refers to "the practice of extending credit on unfair terms to communities that have been historically denied access to credit, predominantly on the basis of race" (Nier and St. Cyr 2011, 942).

13. The interpretation of social strain that I am suggesting here is most closely aligned with the work of Robert Merton and others his work influenced. Merton's strain theory began with his interest in social deviance and "how social structures

and cultural values exert definite pressures to conform, yet create disjunctions and contradictions which make deviance a necessary outcome. . . . The American value-system creates almost universal striving for success, and specifies a range of normatively approved means of securing this goal, but the structure of economic resources in that society enables only certain privileged groups and classes to succeed" (Scott and Marshall 2005, 19–20).

14. Based on a 2013 NCAA study on the probability of competing in athletics beyond high school. The margin is even smaller for sports dominated by black athletes, where only 1.2 percent of NCAA men's basketball players and 1.6 percent of NCAA football players will be drafted by a professional team.

15. The literature debunking notions of innate black athleticism and locating these myths in a history of scientific and biological racism is far too extensive to list here. Some recent research on the human genome has challenged "the basic assumption that races have no biological basis." Finding "genetic clusters consistent with certain racial classifications, even these studies are reluctant to diminish "the social character of their context, meaning, production, or consequences" (Shiao et al. 2012). For a more specific application of genome research and social context to athletic performance, see Malcolm Gladwell's *Outliers: The Story of Success*, Little, Brown, 2011; and Epstein (2013).

16. In the late 1970s the NBA rival American Basketball Association was forced to merge with the NBA. The ABA's signature was a more flamboyant style of play and greater room for athletic expression. When the ABA was swallowed by the NBA, the bigger league could not afford to lose the fan base drawn by the ABA and some of its featured players. Most notably, the street-ball inspired game of Julius "Dr. J" Erving paved the way for Dominique Wilkins, Michael Jordan, Vince Carter, Allen Iverson, Kobe Bryant, Steph Curry, and many other players who have come to symbolize today's NBA. The style of play in the NBA was radically transformed from a more controlled, below-the-rim style of play into one involving increased physicality, slam dunks, alley-oops, and the crossover dribble.

6

Taking Soul to the Hole

*He simply wishes to make it possible for a man to be both a Negro
and an American, without being cursed and spit upon by his fellows,
without having the doors of Opportunity closed roughly in his face.*
　　　　　　　　—*W. E. B. Du Bois*, The Souls of Black Folk

When my mother was a child growing up in the racially segregated neighborhoods of Washington, D.C., she and her best friend,
Elise, used to sit at the fringe of the school grounds at the end of her
block and watch as white children played basketball on the school's
blacktop. While this school was much closer than the one she and her
black peers attended several blocks away, the shortest route to which
required a perilous journey through unfriendly street-gang territory, she
and anyone who looked like her were forbidden from setting foot on her
neighborhood school's property. Here, literally blocks from the US
Capitol, the White House, and the US Supreme Court, and only a few
miles from the National Archives that house the US Constitution, Declaration of Independence, and all other legitimizing documents of the
great American democracy, my eight-year-old mother was already
painfully aware of the racial inequality that served as the cornerstone of
this country's often hypocritical foundation. In her all-black school, my
mother and her classmates were taught that the United States was a
country built on the principle that "all men are created equal," but the
Jim Crow reality in which they lived told a story of a rather different
history. As Mary Frances Berry wrote in her book on post–Civil War
racism and sexism in the United States, "White Americans have their
own stories, but these do not include African Americans' profoundly
racist and discriminatory experiences with the law" (Berry 1999, 5).

Indeed, throughout her entire childhood, the presence of the white school in their otherwise all-black neighborhood stood as an everyday reminder that she and other African Americans were regarded as second-class citizens by America's white establishment. It was clear to them that not much had changed since the Supreme Court, by a 7-2 majority, reasoned in 1857 that she and others like her were "beings of an inferior order, and altogether unfit to associate with the white race either in social or political relations, and so far inferior that they had no rights which the white man was bound to respect."[1] My mother's experience was not unique for blacks in D.C. at the time of her childhood, or before, or after. Captured in his short story "The Girl Who Raised Pigeons" and set in a 1950s Washington neighborhood eerily like that of my mother's upbringing, Edward P. Jones wrote:

> Myrtle Street was only one long block, running east to west. To the east, preventing the street from going any farther, was a high medieval-like wall of stone across 1st Street, Northeast, and beyond the wall were the railroad tracks. To the west, across North Capitol, preventing Myrtle Street from going any farther in that direction, was the high school Gonzaga, where white boys were taught by white priests. (Jones 2005, 11)

In the tradition of subalterns past, my mother and her friends made the best of their situation and tried not to accept the badges of inferiority placed upon them by dominant sociopolitical institutions, labels, and stigmas consistently reaffirmed by the courts that established and upheld a "separate but equal" society. So, many afternoons after school, my mother, her friend, and other black children would simply sit and watch, sometimes in curiosity, sometimes in anger, sometimes in envy, as the white children played on the blacktop schoolyard that no blacks were permitted on.

There was, however, episodic solace for the black children; on occasion, an errant pass by one of the white boys playing basketball would find its way over the surrounding chain-link fence and off the school grounds. As part of an unspoken ritual, the young black onlookers would swoop down from their hillside perches, snatch up the loose ball, and vanish into the relative safety of their neighborhood. Fulfilling their end of the ritual, the white children would scream and flail their arms in protest, hurling racial epithets at my mother and her friends as they fled. Quite obviously, even at this young age, the white children were also aware of racial inequality—an inequality that, in contrast to the black children, afforded them positions of social, economic, and political advantage, bestowing upon them badges of superiority. Despite their venomous denouncements, not once did the white children give chase beyond the fenced sanctuary provided by the schoolyard. Instead, as the ball bandits disappeared from view, one of the white children would simply venture into the school building, return a few moments later with another basketball, and continue with their afternoon recreation.

To the outsider, the snatching-up of the white children's loose basketballs by the black children probably seemed like little more than youthful deviance. Perhaps, the more cynical onlookers might have reasoned the behavior of the black kids stemmed from jealousy, or verified their prejudicial beliefs that blacks were innately inferior—born thieves with some predisposition toward criminal behavior—thereby justifying the social inequality from which they benefited. However, both of these related propositions escape the deeper context and symbolic meaning behind the behavior of the black children.

My maternal grandmother was a high school math teacher with a master's degree in education from Columbia University, a degree paid for by the state of Maryland, which instead of offering graduate educational opportunities for blacks, opted to pay for qualified black students to attend integrated universities out of state. These "out-of-state scholarships" and similar tactics were commonly used to keep qualified black students from attending state graduate institutions while remaining in compliance with the doctrine of separate but equal.[2] My maternal grandfather was a full-time benefits-based employee of the US Postal Service. Both of these were relatively high-status positions for blacks in a Jim Crow America that legislatively and customarily excluded blacks from more prestigious occupations.

My mother's parents and many others in their neighborhood were middle-class by Negro standards. They were not desperately poor and they had their own basketballs, footballs, and bicycles with which they played—toys and equipment that did not previously belong to white children. Therefore, my mother and her friends did not take the white children's basketballs out of necessity. Instead, to them, their actions embodied a far greater meaning. Their deviance was one of the only means by which they could protest their subaltern status in a country that, yes, even "way back" in the 1940s, claimed equal access to life, liberty, and the pursuit of happiness all while practicing a system of apartheid that was grossly inconsistent with these promises and as psychologically abusive as that carried out in South Africa. Certainly, my mother and her neighbors were not unique in their protests, and one could reasonably imagine that small-scale acts of resistance like these were common among the 13-or-so million black Americans of her era who constantly faced injustice. As James Scott said of seemingly varied events ranging from white defections from the Confederate Army during the US Civil War to the avoidance of agrarian taxes by Malaysian peasants in the 1960s, "Acts which, taken individually may appear trivial, however, may not have trivial consequences when considered cumulatively. . . . The small self-serving acts of thousands of petty producers may deprive a regime of the wherewithal to maintain its ruling coalition" (Scott 1985, 42).

Fifty years later, while browsing the African American Studies section of a Barnes & Noble bookstore in suburban Washington, D.C., not far from where she spent her childhood, my mother selected and purchased a book on the Amistad slave ship revolt. Consistent with the system of primary and secondary education of her youth as well as today, to the extent that the "peculiar institution" of slavery was even discussed, the myth of the "happy slave" was common in curricula, and schoolchildren of all racial stripes were led to believe that black slaves passively accepted their oppression. Reminiscent of a recent "Marriage Vow" signed by 2012 Republican presidential hopefuls Michelle Bachman, Rick Santorum, and numerous other prominent conservatives suggesting conditions under slavery actually benefited the black family relative to today's society, students of my mother's era were led to believe that America's system of chattel slavery actually served to the slaves' advantage.[3] My mother's educational experiences again echoed Mary Frances Berry's reflections on official narratives, specifically that "The stories of the powerful are the only ones that count, and the counting further enhances the power of the tellers in the economic and political arenas" (Berry 1999, 4). Or, as an African proverb says, "Until the lion becomes his own historian, the hunter will always be portrayed as the hero." My mother was taught that slavery, rather than being an ignoble institution worthy of reflective condemnation, did no great harm to anyone involved and actually uplifted black slaves. After all, but for slavery, American blacks would still be locked behind the austere, pagan walls of the "dark continent" and not be able to participate in the splendors of European culture. She learned the same of Native Americans who were liberated by the "superior genius of Europe" and duly compensated for their lost land and lives by "bestowing on them civilization and Christianity."[4] Therefore, because of her formal miseducation, my mother was excited by the late 1990s literary and cinematic acknowledgment that this passive acceptance of enslavement was not the case.

My now sixty-year-old mother was thrilled to find that, just as she and her friends did in their own way as seemingly powerless children in pre–*Brown v. Board of Education*[5] America, stolen Africans destined for New World colonies and those who arrived as black slaves resisted at every step of their capture, during their months-long voyage across the Atlantic, and throughout their enslavement.[6] When she returned home from the bookstore and began browsing through the pages of the latest addition to her growing library of black studies, a "business" card fell out of the book with an emblem reading, "We're still here." The card was from an establishment in South Carolina called *The Redneck Store*. At the bottom, the card read "100% Americanism," and scrawled in ink at the top were the letters KKK.

My mother's Barnes and Noble experience is but one example of what many black people, as well as other ethnic and racial minorities in the United States, realize on a daily basis; prejudice and discrimination based on socially constructed ideas of racial inferiority are still omnipresent in our society and play an enduring role in the day-to-day politics of social interaction. As the "business" card suggested, racism is "100% Americanism."

Back, to the Future

Since the late 1970s, the battle to do away with American racism has progressively moved away from the Jim Crow forms effectively dismantled during the Warren Court's "rights revolution" and toward so-called reverse racism as the most important form of racial discrimination. Indeed, a large number of Americans, with the growing support of dominant sociolegal institutions like the Supreme Court, have comfortably subscribed to the idea that America is now "postracial." Take basketball icon Michael Jordan, who at the height of his career, for many Americans stood as "an illustration of the progress and accomplishments of the post–civil rights era" (Hartmann 2006, 302). Even more profoundly than Jordan's transracial acceptance, postracial proponents point to America twice electing the nation's first black—or at least biracial—president as evidence that traditional forms of racism are, for all intents and purposes, dead. All the while, as anti-black racism has gone away and as a strong majority of working-class white Americans expressed even before Donald Trump won the White House, white Americans are the ones who increasingly bear the disproportionate brunt of discrimination.[7] These racism reformists point to programs where race is used as a criterion in determining occupational or educational eligibility as "benign prejudice" that is, in the words of the Court's lone black Justice, Clarence Thomas, "just as noxious as discrimination inspired by malicious prejudice." Thomas made this argument in a 1995 concurrence to *Adarand v. Pena*, a Supreme Court ruling rejecting federal Department of Transportation minority set-aside contracts. In language eerily similar to that used by the Court's majority in *Plessy v. Ferguson*, the now-debunked late-nineteenth-century ruling that established the doctrine of separate but equal, Thomas went on to reason, "Government cannot make us equal; it can only recognize, respect, and protect us as equal before the law."[8]

In 2012 the Supreme Court agreed to hear *Fisher v. Texas*, a case centered on an extension of this centerpiece to the racism reformist argument. The gist of this argument was that because of programs that privilege minorities over whites, more qualified applicants would have been hired for a given position, admitted to a particular university, or received a government contract but were passed over because of affirmative action policies. In the *Fisher* case, the petitioner was denied admission to the University of Texas' flagship campus in Austin and argued that but for her whiteness she, a presumably superior candidate for admission, would have been accepted to the university. Instead, due to university admissions policies favoring African American and Hispanic applicants,[9] she was denied acceptance and her opportunity to become a Longhorn was handed to an unqualified or underqualified minority.

This is not new terrain for the twenty-first-century Supreme Court. In the spring term of 2003 the Court was asked to review a similar case involving the University of Michigan. In *Gratz et al. v. Bollinger et al.*, two petitioners, both of whom were Michigan residents and white, applied for admission to the University of Michigan's College of Literature, Science, and the Arts (LSA). Although the LSA admissions officers considered both petitioners to be within the qualified range, both were denied acceptance. The university's Office of Undergraduate Admissions utilized written guidelines for each academic year and, in these guidelines, considered a number of factors in making admissions decisions, including high school grades, standardized test scores, high school quality, curriculum strength, geography, alumni relationships, leadership, and race/membership in an underrepresented racial or ethnic group. Under the guidelines contested in this case, a selection method was used in which every applicant from an underrepresented racial or ethnic minority group was automatically awarded 20 points of the 100 needed to guarantee admission. The petitioners filed a class action alleging that the university's use of racial preferences in undergraduate admissions violated the Equal Protection Clause of the Fourteenth Amendment, Title VI of the Civil Rights Act of 1964, and 42 U.S.C. §1981. The Court agreed with the petitioners' claims holding that the university's use of race in its freshman admissions policy was not narrowly tailored to achieve what the university deemed an "interest in diversity" and therefore violated both the Civil Rights Act of 1964 and the Constitution's Equal Protection Clause.

As a professor specializing in issues of law and inequality, I am often asked to weigh in on matters related to race neutrality, this issue of "reverse discrimination," and assertions of minority-on-majority racism intended to mitigate the existence and much longer history of white-on-other racism. Most commonly, this takes the form of a white and typically male student visiting me in my office to point out that he "knows someone who didn't get a job because of affirmative action," or his "friend got rejected from law school because they gave his slot to a minority." Another predictable refrain from these students is that blacks and other minorities can be just as prejudiced as whites. Many will go further and offer as examples incidents in which they were singled out, harassed, taunted, or their opinions devalued by blacks and other minority group members because of their whiteness. As historian Edward Baptist wrote in response to claims that he exaggerated the brutality of slavery in his book, *The Half Has Never Been Told* (Basic Books 2014), the persistence of comments like these reveal "just how many white people remain reluctant to believe black people about the experience of being black" (Parry 2016).

Depending on my mood that day or perhaps more whimsically determined by what I "had for breakfast,"[10] my response to these comments varies. However, it always includes two points. First, race politics are most certainly not unilateral, flowing solely from white to black or other minority. Members of all groups are prejudiced in that they make assumptions about others based on superficial characteristics like racialized physical attributes. And I am certainly not naive enough to espouse what I have heard from other African American scholars who, perhaps not coincidentally, seem most often chosen as spokespersons for the "black community." The scholars to whom I am referring are those who maintain that black people cannot be racist and discriminate because they do not have aggregate power over whites. Certainly, blacks, like members of all racial groups, can be racist in that they can harbor and act on prejudices and stereotypes, and the targets of this racism still certainly feel the sting accompanying these slights. That understood, the power dynamic must be taken into consideration when exploring race relations, just as it should when looking at sexual harassment or any other relationships rooted in similar power inequalities.

The second point that I make revolves around the issue of formal equality. Despite the "level playing field" rhetoric that has dominated affirmative action and racial equity discourses over the past several decades, it is inconceivable that a mere fifty years of formal equality can erase over four centuries of social and legal distinctions based on race that have been used to consistently privilege those identified as white. As I noted previously, the statistical tale of the tape supports this conclusion in a manner too clear for argument. Black Americans, Latinos, Native Americans, other racial minorities, and women continue to disproportionately suffer from race-based and economic discrimination at the hands of American institutions, as well as by individual actors. And, unfortunately, neither the handful of black millionaires in professional sports nor the election of a black president has served as the death knell of racial discrimination and the dawn of a truly postracial America. The current attention paid toward racial profiling, state violence against people of color, or hate crimes, and situations like my mother's bookstore experience highlight more insidious forms of this discrimination. However, I do not know of a single black American who has not encountered some form of racial discrimination, overt or subtle, in the recent past. And, as my mother was already very much aware as a young girl, most racial minorities are savvy enough to understand discrimination, are cognizant of the ongoing existence of white privilege, and are fully conscious of our nation's failure to achieve full equality for its citizens irrespective of race, gender, or class. As black comedian Chris Rock humorously lamented in his HBO special, *Bring the Pain*:

> There isn't a white person in here that would change places with me . . . and I'm rich! There's a white one-legged busboy in here right now who wouldn't trade places with me. He'd say, "nah, I'm just going to roll these white dice and ride this white thing out a little longer."

Of course, this realization of white privilege and disparate outcomes rooted in racial prejudice is not limited to minorities. Author and educator Tim Wise became one of the nation's most prominent speakers against racism through his scholarly and personal acknowledgments of the unearned assets associated with his status as a white man. Peggy McIntosh's 1988 essay examining her own white privilege is widely considered a "classic" and is still required reading in many introductory gender and ethnic studies courses. To a lesser extent, though, and certainly something that has consistently been a mainstay in black cultural art forms, this awareness of an uneven playing field advantaging whiteness is also promulgated in popular media constructed by white artists. For example, white and Jewish satirical hip-hop performer Lil Dicky (David Andrew Burd) raps about the recognition of white and male privilege in his 2013 release "White Dude." Celebrating "livin' life" as a "muthafuckin joy," not having to "worry where the cops at," or about wearing "a fucking bra strap," Burd rhymes "I ain't black or Dominican, not Hispanic or Indian, so imprisonment is not a predicament, I envision." In this song he also makes clear that, in the unlikely event that he is subjected to the type of criminal justice scrutiny that young black men experience on a regular basis, he can easily call upon one of his father's lawyer friends to ensure he only receives a "slap on the wrist." Ultimately, and in likely intentional contrast to the anomalistic "good day" rapper Ice Cube versed about in the early 1990s, Lil Dicky concludes that every day is "a damn good day to be a white dude."[11]

The wiggers and wannabees—idiomatic terms for "white niggers" and "want to be blacks"—of the world show us that American black culture might be cool and even functional at times to emulate. Indicative of a phenomenon I label *reverse emulation*—situations in which nonblack people model aspects of their behavior after what they perceive to be cool "black" behavior, like that seen in pickup basketball culture—as a white colleague once said to me about her fifteen-year-old son's admiration of African American–driven hip-hop culture, "He wants to be black so bad."[12] Like the envelopment of rock-and-roll culture during the 1950s, the hippie culture during the 1960s, or the Seattle grunge culture of the 1980s, acting "black" came into vogue in the 1990s and has persisted into the new millennium. It has done so with so much force that the hip-hop aspect of black culture is now a common means and medium through which suburban white youth in America speak out against their adolescent powerlessness. Indeed, emulating urban blackness has made white musical artists like Eminem,[13] Justin Timberlake, Brother Ali, Macklemore, Robin Thicke, and even Lil Dicky countless millions of dollars and international celebrities.

Imitating black musical styles, even if driven by genuine appreciation of the art form, has also become a successful vehicle for white female artists. For example, Iggy Azalea's 2011 viral video for a rap song unambiguously titled "Pussy" landed her on the cover of America's leading hip-hop magazine, *XXL,* and spawned a rap career that has already resulted in greater than one dozen music award nominations and wins including a 2014 Black Entertainment Television (BET) Awards nomination for "Best Female Hip-Hop Artist." This is, of course, not to take anything away from any artist's legitimate talents or to suggest that musical influence and other forms of expression should be constrained by racial boundaries. Also duly noted is that this generation's hip-hop and blue-eyed soul artists are certainly not the first collective of whites who imitated blacks as a form of artistic expression. However, emulative mimicry aside and in all reality, which of these cultural tourists would really prefer to live in America as a *nigger*?

During his 2016 BET Humanitarian Award acceptance speech, actor and human rights activist Jesse Williams summarized the frustrations he and many other black people experience when bearing witness to reverse emulation, and the ease and fluidity with which some white entertainers as well as noncelebrities appropriate black American culture:

> We've been floating this country on credit for centuries, and we're done watching and waiting while this invention called whiteness uses and abuses us, burying black people out of sight and out of mind while extracting our culture, our dollars, our entertainment like oil—black gold, ghettoizing and demeaning our creations then stealing them, gentrifying our genius and then trying us on like costumes before discarding our bodies like rinds of strange fruit. The thing is, though . . . the thing is that just because we're magic doesn't mean we're not real.

By Any Means Available

As we continue through the relatively new era of formal racial equality and what has already started as the American century of "level playing fields," it is important not to lose sight of the ebbs and flows of subterranean racial politics at play in the United States. This focus is particularly necessary to the extent that these politics revolve around the continued "ordinariness of unfreedom" (Wilder 2013, 45) and a history of minority oppression that has yet to be fully reconciled—#Black Lives Matter and Donald Trump's ascendance as the Republican nominee for president on a recycled race-based "law and order" platform are just a couple of examples. Clearly, as W. E. B. DuBois prophetically said of the twentieth century, the problem of the twenty-first century in America continues at least in substantial part to be the problem of the color line. In examining the color line in a new millennium context, it is also important to highlight the extent to which black Americans and other racially subordinate groups do not passively accept discrimination and persistent disadvantage. Instead, like my mother did as a child and as her ancestors did since the first days of slavery in the Americas and Caribbean, minority group members continue to employ any means available to defend themselves against the predations of racial politics, to make statements of identity, and to challenge the dominant ideology.

Critical race theorist Richard Delgado proposed that "ideology—the received wisdom—makes current social arrangements seem fair and natural. Those in power sleep well at night—their conduct does not seem to them like oppression" (Delgado and Stefancic 1995, 65). On the contrary, as others have said, what seems like oppression to those accustomed to power and privilege is equality. The text that is etched into American blacktops, forged by centuries of inequality, announces a different story from that told by those in positions of power. It speaks a narrative of resistance, discontent, and struggle that seeks to challenge current social arrangements and unsettle those who "sleep well at night" thinking all is OK in the USA. The animated discourse spoken and displayed in these arenas is not principally one of social harmony or consensus. Rather, this is a discourse of resistance and an ongoing struggle for recognition.

While often trivialized as ordinary recreation, the pickup basketball game provides a critical canvas for young black Americans to participate in this discourse on race. For better or for worse, basketball has become an integral part of African American male culture, serving as a temporary form of native reciprocity—situations in which those in positions of power are brought low and the relatively powerless take control. The black street game also serves as a virtual affidavit about what the intersection of young and black and male means in the United States; testimony that goes beyond that which is written but that, as part of the tapestry of expressive traditions characteristic of black diasporic cultures, carries the same significance as more formal accounts. Necessarily, to understand the game in this context requires a certain degree of cultural relativism and an earnest attempt to see through the eyes of the doer and the cultural lenses of those who have come to define it. To view it any other way runs the risk of misconstruing its real meaning. In this sense, the game is a firsthand African American reading of the black experience in America. To echo anthropologist Clifford Geertz (1973) in a statement he made about interpreting Balinese culture by examining their sporting pastimes, the pickup basketball game unveils a story of cumulative knowledge black men tell themselves about themselves.

In the novel *A Little Yellow Dog*, Walter Mosley's protagonist, Easy Rawlins, visits an upscale black nightclub in search of clues to a murder. As Rawlins enters the club, he hears the familiar sounds of trumpeter Lips McGee:

> In the center of that spectacle was a boy-sized man holding on to a silver trumpet. He was playing a high staccato riff that had temporarily damp-ened conversation. . . . Lips brought it up as high as he could and stopped. He licked his lips and took a tight breath, then he hit a note that was somewhere west of the moon. He was a coyote calling up the dead. . . . Lips sat down and wiped his face. The room cheered him. Cheered him for all the years he'd kept us alive in northern apartments living one on top of the other. Cheered him for remembering the pain of police sticks and low pay and no face in the mirror of the times. Cheered him for his assault on the white man's culture; his brash horn the only true heir to the European masters like Bach or and Beethoven. Or maybe they were just applauding a well-made piece of music. (Mosley 1996, 179–180)

Historian Ronald Takaki wrote, "The 'mirror' of history can guide the living and also help us recognize who we have been and hence are . . . but what happens when someone describes our society and you are not in it?" (Takaki 1993, 16). Or, like the Mandingo stereotype, what happens when the mirrors of history as well as the mirror of the times grossly distort the image of some who gaze into it? As I have described throughout this book, in order to recover from the "psychic disequilib-rium" created by invisibility and misrepresentation, many young black men have adopted sport as a vehicle to become seen and to make expressions of resistance.

But, similar to the diversity of responses to Lips McGee's horn sup-posed by Rawlins, most young black men certainly know what it is to exist on the short end of American racial inequality. And, to be sure, far too many have experienced and continue to experience "the pain of police sticks." However, not every young black man on the pickup court is resisting hegemony and inequality through blacktop expressionism. Nor does every black observer celebrate the game for its resistive qual-ities or feel triumphant when bearing witness to the black man's "assault" on what was once the white man's game. Instead, for many, the game is just that—a game. It is a way to escape into an alternative reality in which a regular kid can temporarily be LeBron James, Michael Jordan, Magic Johnson, Allen Iverson, Kevin Durant, Steph

Curry, or anyone but himself. A regular kid is allowed to momentarily entertain a dream of being on a Division I college basketball roster, playing under John Wooden, Dean Smith, Bobby Knight, John Thompson, Mike Krzyzewski, Tom Izzo, or any of the other all-time great college coaches. In this space in time, it is safe for him to imagine living in the athletes' dorm as a Tarheel instead of sleeping in the cramped bedroom he shares with his two younger brothers like many thousands of other Bigger Thomases.

Even those who do take advantage of the relative sanctuary offered by the court to strive against inequality and momentary alter the tilt of the social playing field, to some extent, seek freedom. But, as Orlando Patterson (1982) notes, the concept of freedom is not spontaneous. It arises as a reaction to institutions of oppression—it is *freedom from* something rather than *freedom to* anything. The basketball court affords those without other outlets the opportunity to express resistance and demand recognition, even if these acts of microresistance offer nowhere to go. The basketball court allows for the expression of freedom from the daily oppression that slowly crushes the conscience and distorts the aspirations of many of the inner-city black males with whom I came in contact over the course of this examination of pickup basketball, and before and since. Like Nelson Mandela once said, "Sport can create hope where once there was only despair" (Mandela 2000).

In contrast to what many proponents of the contact hypothesis have observed in arenas where people of different backgrounds overcome their difference by working side-by-side toward a common goal, the display on these slabs of asphalt and concrete is not one of multiethnic bridge building, at least not primarily. To suggest that is to only observe the characters performing in this theater without looking at the more complex story unfolding through their actions. It would be the same as looking at an integrated neighborhood, school, church, workplace, or other public space and suggesting that the mere interracial interaction is evidence of a narrowing racial divide. Simply because ebony and ivory share the same space does not mean that they, as Stevie Wonder and Paul McCartney once crooned, "live together in perfect harmony."

Equally inaccurate is the suggestion that the on-the-court behaviors of pickup ballers are exclusively bravado and showmanship without any greater social meaning or connection to broader social forces. Bill "Bojangles" Robinson smiled as he shuffled alongside Shirley Temple, seemingly embracing the happy-go-lucky black racial stereotypes of the times. Behind the scenes, however, he worked to break down barriers for other black entertainers and cofounded a Negro League baseball team called the New York Black Yankees. Butterfly McQueen seemed perfectly comfortable with her portrayal of the thoughtless and whiny Prissy of *Gone with the Wind*, a part the *Los Angeles Times* said "was a role no black performer could relish—a slave, and a dimwitted one who gets slapped by the heroine."[14] Who, after all, could forget her infamous delivery of the line "Oh, Miss Scarlett, I don't know nuthin' 'bout birthin' babies." This wasn't the only role played by McQueen in which she was cast in the part of a "silly maid"; she played similar characters in the 1945 films *Flame of the Barbary Coast* and *Mildred Pierce*. When *Gone with the Wind* premiered in 1939, McQueen could not attend because the premier was held in Atlanta's "whites-only" Loew's Grand Theater; before the showing, and "A rousing ovation greeted a group of Confederate veterans who were guests of honor."[15] In a 1986 interview McQueen said of the role, "I hated it. The part of Prissy was so backward." Of being cast in similar roles thereafter, "After I did the same thing over and over I resented it. I didn't mind being funny, but I didn't like being stupid."[16]

In the sporting world, Jackie Robinson also appeared content "just playing ball" for the Brooklyn Dodgers during his tenure as "the most savagely booed, ruthlessly libeled player in the game" (Zirin 2005, 49). But behind closed doors at the Dodgers' training camp in segregated Vero Beach, Florida, Robinson would tell his black teammates, Don Newcombe and Roy Campanella, "We're bitter now but one day we're going to change one letter, we're going to change the 'i' to 'e' and things are going to get better. . . . So we're going to have to endure all this, take it because we can't fight back, and just go out and be the best we can be" (Newhan 2008). In the year following his retirement from the Major Leagues, Robinson capitalized on his celebrity to support the NAACP's Fight for Freedom Fund initiative to end racial segregation in the United States. Becoming the NAACP's most requested speaker— even more sought after than Martin Luther King Jr.—Robinson closed his speeches with, "If I had to choose between baseball's Hall of Fame and first-class citizenship I would say first-class citizenship to all of my people" (Zirin 2005, 49).

The proportionally few black luminaries who ventured during the height of their celebrity to more visibly challenge America's racialized status quo tended to be publicly ostracized and suffer other forms of personal hardship. In much the same way that black athleticism, in and of itself, "conspicuously challenged white supremacy," (Wiltse 2007, 125), these more open acts of defiance ran the risk of negatively affecting opportunities for other black entertainers, athletes, and public figures.

For "brandishing his wealth and his disdain for racial rules,"[17] Jack Johnson, the first black American to win the heavyweight boxing title, found himself under constant scrutiny from white America. It's worth noting that some prominent black Americans were also critical of Johnson for fear that "his preference for white women . . . would bring the wrath of whites down on the heads of every black person."[18] He was ultimately convicted for "white slavery" charges because of his romantic relationships with white women, and fled the United States for seven years to avoid serving out his sentence. But on the broader scale, due to resentment over Johnson's success and his "contemptuous posture of defiance,"[19] black fighters seeking a shot at the heavyweight title were effectively blacklisted between 1915 and 1936 (until the "Brown Bomber" Joe Louis got the opportunity against Jimmy Braddock) because of white champion boxers' collective refusal to fight black challengers.

Launching his entertainment career in the early days of the Harlem Renaissance, by World War II Paul Robeson had become the most famous African American entertainer in the world.[20] But his growing frustration with racial segregation and America's mistreatment of blacks prompted Robeson to use his celebrity as a platform to very publicly advocate for civil rights in the United States. Robeson's protests were considered a particular threat to existing race politics because "he often interspersed his performances with comments about race relations in the United States" and "he gave numerous interviews condemning segregation and discrimination in America."[21] But what made Robeson's protests even more noteworthy was the political climate of the time; the Cold War was underway and Robeson very openly brought Soviet disavowals of US racism and discrimination to the attention of the American public. In response, the US Department of State revoked Robeson's passport, thereby crippling his ability to earn a living abroad or to cast a spotlight on America's racial hypocrisy on foreign soil. Even while he was barred from leaving the United States and was being ostracized at home for his political views, "US enemies halfway around the world celebrated Robeson's music and activism" (Frazier 2015, 88). In a 1956 hearing before the House Committee on Un-American Activities ostensibly regarding the status of his passport revocation, Robeson challenged Congress by referring to the hearing as "complete nonsense" and testifying:

> Could I say that the reason that I am here today, you know, from the mouth of the State Department itself, is: I should not be allowed to travel because I have struggled for years for the independence of the colonial peoples of Africa. . . . The other reason that I am here today, again from

the State Department and from the court record of the court of appeals, is that when I am abroad I speak out against the injustices against the Negro people of this land. . . . This is the basis, and I am not being tried for whether I am a Communist, I am being tried for fighting for the rights of my people, who are still second-class citizens in this United States of America. My mother was born in your state, [Committee Chairman Walter], and my mother was a Quaker, and my ancestors in the time of Washington baked bread for George Washington's troops when they crossed the Delaware, and my own father was a slave. I stand here struggling for the rights of my people to be full citizens in this country. And they are not. They are not in Mississippi. And they are not in Montgomery, Alabama. And they are not in Washington. They are nowhere, and that is why I am here today. You want to shut up every Negro who has the courage to stand up and fight for the rights of his people, for the rights of workers, and I have been on many a picket line for the steelworkers too. And that is why I am here today.[22]

Robeson's travel ban remained in effect from 1950 until 1958, when the US Supreme Court ultimately ruled the revocation a deprivation of his due process rights and reinstated his travel privileges. However, the ban brought Robeson's career to a halt; he suffered from several bouts of depression and lived in seclusion from 1963 until his death in 1976.

Perhaps no public figure used his celebrity more effectively and at a greater cost to advocate for racial equality and black unity in America than Muhammad Ali. As sports historian Dave Zirin wrote, "Never has an athlete been more reviled by the mainstream press, more persecuted by the US government, or more defiantly beloved throughout the world than Muhammad Ali" (Zirin 2005, 53). Dozens of books and documentary films have chronicled Ali's career, his personality, and the controversies that followed him as he transformed from the "Louisville Lip" called Cassius Clay to a follower of the Nation of Islam who would simply become known as "The Greatest." Returning from the 1960 Rome Olympic Games with a gold medal for boxing, Ali was refused service at a restaurant in his hometown of Louisville, Kentucky. Already known to speak his mind, this bout with segregation after representing his country abroad served as a catalyst for Ali's greater political awareness. In 1964, the day after defeating Sonny Liston and winning the world heavyweight championship, Ali publicly confirmed that he converted to Islam and one month later announced that he would henceforth be known by his new Muslim name, a proclamation that drew condemnation from whites and mainstream blacks alike. In 1966, as the Vietnam War began heating up, Ali was classified as "fit for service," meaning he was eligible to be drafted. He opposed this designation on religious grounds and asked to be reclassified as a conscientious objector, telling reporters, "I ain't got no quarrel with them Vietcong" and saying later that "no Vietcong ever called me nigger." After being called up for service in 1967, Ali refused his induction and was convicted for draft evasion, receiving a five-year prison sentence, $10,000 fine, and a three-year ban from boxing. Ali stayed out of prison while his case was under appeal, and his conviction was ultimately overturned in 1971 by the US Supreme Court. But, in the meantime and at the height of his career, Ali lost millions of dollars in fight earnings and endorsements, clearly illustrating that "we live in a world that exalts individuality as long as it is superficial and nonthreatening" (Zirin 2005, 99).

These more vocal exceptions notwithstanding, the majority of resistance by black athletes and entertainers to ongoing racial discrimination in America has necessarily been less directly antagonistic. But the historical record clearly shows that, despite their public grins and compliance, despite the smiling and shuffling, each of these individuals was using the opportunities available to them in a centuries-long war of attrition as tools to open doors for other African Americans and to make broader statements about social injustice in a place that has consistently proclaimed itself the land of the free.

The same can be said for everyday actors; simply because they do not have celebrity status and the stage that accompanies this station does not mean that they are incapable of using the more mundane opportunities available to them to voice their opposition to the perpetuation of racial inequality in the United States. Like Paul Gilroy said of the adoption of this antihierarchical analytical position and in reference to the work of C. L. R. James, "Ordinary people do not need an intellectual vanguard to help them to speak or to tell them what to say" (Gilroy 1993, 79). In her book *The Moral Underground*, Lisa Dodson (2009, 288) similarly concluded, "There have been many stands against unfairness in American history, and they were named by these ordinary people who chose to act upon injustices in their midst."

It has been my contention that the pickup game in particular and sports in their ordinary form have created an opening for young black men to "speak" through participation in this tradition of everyday resistance. In the case of using basketball as a vehicle to voice mistrust and frustration, it also is important to recognize that this is just one arena used by African Americans to resist and protest their indisputably unequal social and economic status. There are currently others, and historically there have been others. On plantations in the slaveholding South and in the Caribbean, bondsmen and bondswomen routinely employed strategies of everyday resistance and oppositional tactics, not so much with the goal of freedom in mind but with the objective of, in some way, making their condition more bearable. Certainly, had they their druthers, they would have opted for tactics more revolutionary in scope.[23] However, the New World enslavement of Africans existed as an institution for as long as it did not because of the ignorance or naivety of those held in captivity, but because of despotic and violent rule and "the extent to which white dominance rested on naked force" (Burnard 2004, 3). Beyond violence and terror, in the US South the subordination of blacks as slaves and then as nominally free people was also held intact by support from poor whites (even if they did not materially benefit from the institution) and, more significant, through explicit political support from northern industry and the US government and state governments.[24] As Jeffrey Herbst attests, "The central point is that political power cannot simply be judged in a vacuum by the organizational characteristics of the pressure group but must be assessed in light of the institutional arrangements on the part of the government that the pressure group is trying to influence" (Herbst 1989, 218).

As I commented in the introduction and throughout this book, it is both dismissive and mistaken to suggest that African Americans are not cognizant of ongoing race-based social and economic inequalities. It is an even greater insult to assume that those who are relatively powerless or voiceless passively accept their subordination rather than employ whatever means they have available to challenge the existing structure and alter the present-day terms of engagement. Like the second-generation urban American Jews who dominated basketball and other city sports in the decades prior to the black athletic ascension,[25] the pickup basketball court is simply one of the arenas that has been and remains available to an inordinate number of black male youth. In acknowledgment of contemporary US racial inequalities and through the on-the-court public manipulation of traditional power relations lies a clear statement by young black men on the disjunction between the descriptive "is" and the prescriptive "ought," particularly to the extent that the latter is routinely presented as the former in our contemporary "postracial" politics.

Like Clifford Geertz's (1973) interpretation of the Balinese cockfight, the pickup game in urban America is not the master key to black male life any more than bullfighting is the master key to Spanish life, capoeira is the key to understanding the Brazilian subaltern existence, or youth soccer is the key to understanding white suburban America. However, the interpretations of the symbols and imagery displayed in the context of pickup basketball illustrate that the playground is an integral arena for black youth to construct and reinforce ideas of ethnic strength and identity. As baller Clark summarized, "Your identity is so intertwined with basketball, and it's hard to separate that."

Through their pose, language, and the attitude with which they play, young urban black males are repeatedly telling a counter-story to anyone deemed a representative of the power structure and, just as important to themselves, that all is not well in America, despite what we might think it ought to be. Theirs is a rich text of the political, social, and economic struggle of black men, told by black men. And these resistive displays may offer a critical lens into part of black America's hidden transcript and into the souls of some black folks.

Notes

1. The US Supreme Court's language in *Scott v. Sandford* (1857), 60 U.S. 393. Justice Taney, writing for the Court, reasoned that no person who descended from slaves could ever be a citizen of the United States.

2. In the Jim Crow South, the majority of states did not offer graduate opportunities to blacks in separate accommodations, nor did they permit them into white graduate schools. In attempts to avoid equal protection litigation, several of these states adopted policies like Maryland's, offering "out-of-state scholarships" to pay in full expenses for graduate education outside of the state. Interestingly, neither Maryland nor its flagship university had laws or rules mandating graduate education. Rather, qualified black students were excluded from the University of Maryland as a matter of policy (Pierre 2012). At the Maryland state level (*Murray v. Pearson*, 1936), the Court of Appeals found the practice violated the Fourteenth Amendment's Equal Protection Clause. However, this ruling did not outlaw segregation in education throughout Maryland. Furthermore, even though Maryland's practice of segregating graduate institutions was deemed unconstitutional, it was still permissible to separate black students from white students within institutions. At the federal level, in *Gaines v. Canada* (1938) the US Supreme Court declared these arrangements unconstitutional violations of the "separate but equal" doctrine established in *Plessy v. Ferguson* (1896), effectively ordering states with segregated graduate programs to build equal facilities for blacks or integrate.

3. The pledge was titled "The Marriage Vow—A Declaration of Dependence upon Marriage and Family" and was issued by conservative Christian organization the Family Leader. The most controversial aspect of the pledge argued, "Slavery had a disastrous impact on African-American families, yet sadly a child born into slavery in 1860 was more likely to be raised by his mother and father in a two-parent household than was an African-American baby born after the election of the USA's first African-American President."

4. These quotes in reference to Native Americans are the words of US Supreme Court Chief Justice John Marshall in *Johnson v. McIntosh* (1823), 21 U.S. 543. This

settlers' history is still commonly taught in American schools. For more on curricular distortions and omissions, see James W. Loewen (1995), *Lies My Teacher Told Me: Everything Your American History Textbook Got Wrong*, New York: Touchstone Books.

5. *Brown v. Board of Education* (1954) formally abolished segregation in public schools and helped pave the way for formal equality in other areas of social life for African Americans.

6. As Robert Harms (2002, 269) describes in *The Diligent: A Voyage Through the Worlds of the Slave Trade*, slave ship captains feared revolts on-board from the very moment the ships left West African ports.

7. A June 2016 survey conducted by the Public Religion Research Institute and the Brookings Institute found that Americans are effectively split on the direction of racial discrimination, with 49 percent of all Americans believing that "today discrimination against whites has become as big a problem as discrimination against blacks." This finding was particularly strong (66 percent) among working-class white Americans. See "How Immigration and Concerns About Cultural Changes Are Shaping the 2016 Election," available at http://www.prri.org/wp-content/uploads/2016 /06/PRRI-Brookings-2016-Immigration-survey-report.pdf (last accessed September 13, 2016).

8. Thomas's reasoning as well as his actual choice of words in Adarand is strangely and perhaps unironically similar to that used by the Court 100 years earlier in *Plessy v. Ferguson* (1896), 163 U.S. 537, the very same case that established the doctrine of separate but equal and brought forth the need for the late twentieth-century "affirmative action" programs designed to provide minorities and women access to opportunities previously denied them by the law. In *Plessy*, Justice Brown wrote for the Court's 7-1 majority, "The argument also assumes that social prejudices may be overcome by legislation, and that equal rights cannot be secured to the Negro except by an enforced commingling of the two races. We cannot accept this proposition. If the two races are to meet upon terms of social equality, it must be the result of natural affinities, a mutual appreciation of each other's merits, and a voluntary consent of individuals. As was said by the Court of Appeals of New York in *People v. Gallagher*, 93 N.Y. 438, 448, 'this end can neither be accomplished nor promoted by laws which conflict with the general sentiment of the community upon whom they are designed to operate. When the government, therefore, has secured to each of its citizens equal rights before the law and equal opportunities for improvement and progress, it has accomplished the end for which it was organized, and performed all of the functions respecting social advantages with which it is endowed.' Legislation is powerless to eradicate racial instincts or to abolish distinctions based upon physical differences, and the attempt to do so can only result in accentuating the difficulties of the present situation. If the civil and political rights of both races be equal, one cannot be inferior to the other civilly [p552] or politically. If one race be inferior to the other socially, the Constitution of the United States cannot put them upon the same plane."

9. At the time Fisher was denied admission, the University of Texas automatically admitted Texans who graduated in the top 10 percent of their high school classes. This part of the admissions formula accounted for approximately three-quarters of students accepted to the university. The remaining quarter's acceptance used a different, more subjective "Personal Achievement Index" based on a formula that takes into consideration an applicant's "leadership abilities, awards and honors, work experience, extracurricular activities, and 'special circumstances,'" which may include socioeconomic status, family status, and race and ethnicity. University officials say that this formula was necessary for them to have a student

body representing a broad range of backgrounds and for the campus to have significant minority student representation in most classrooms. In June 2016, with no Justice yet serving in the seat of the recently deceased conservative Justice Antonin Scalia, the Supreme Court ruled, "The race-conscious admissions program in use by the University of Texas at Austin when Abigail Fisher applied to the school in 2008 is lawful under the Equal Protection Clause."

10. This often misinterpreted phrase was classically used to debunk legal interpretation by the courts and the influence of the "legal realist" movement in jurisprudence. The expression appears to have originated with legal philosopher, legal realist, and federal appeals court judge Jerome Frank, who in a rejection of legal positivism said, "A judicial decision might be determined by what the judge had for breakfast."

11. The song concludes with Lil Dicky speaking more than rapping, saying that he appreciates being white because, among other advantages, it means everybody naturally assumes he is a great person, that he can underperform academically and still gain access to highly selective educational institutions and "get a fair shot" at the life he "deserves." In contrast to the cool pose discussed earlier in this book, Burd also notes that his whiteness prevents him from having to fight or otherwise assume a street demeanor "for social purposes."

12. White suburban teens are reported to be the largest retail consumers of rap and hip-hop music. Industry estimates suggest that this demographic is responsible for approximately 70 percent of all hip-hop album purchases.

13. Shortly after its release, Eminem's debut album *The Marshall Mathers LP* became the highest-selling rap album of all time. With more than 10.5 million units sold, it still holds the number-two spot among best-selling hip-hop albums. Atlanta rap duo OutKast's album *Speakerboxx/The Love Below* is hip-hop's best seller, with nearly 11.5 million albums sold.

14. This quote appeared in McQueen's December 23, 1995, obituary in the *Los Angeles Times*. Available at http://articles.latimes.com/1995-12-23/news/mn-17061 _1_butterfly-mcqueen (last accessed July 25, 2014).

15. "Atlanta Premiere of *Gone with the Wind*" in *About North Georgia*. Available at http://www.aboutnorthgeorgia.com/ang/Atlanta_Premiere_of_Gone_With_The_Wind (last accessed July 25, 2014).

16. From McQueen's December 23, 1995, obituary in the *Los Angeles Times*. Available at http://articles.latimes.com/1995-12-23/news/mn-17061_1_butterfly-mcqueen (last accessed July 25, 2014).

17. Dr. Gerald Early highlighted about Jack Johnson's resistance to white rule, "What most bothered whites about Johnson was that he openly had affairs with white women—and even married them—at a time when miscegenation of this sort was not only illegal but was positively dangerous. Johnson did not seem to care what whites thought of him, and this bothered most whites a great deal. He was not humble or diffident with whites." From "Rebel of the Progressive Era," available at http://www.pbs.org/unforgivableblackness/rebel/ (last accessed July 25, 2014).

18. Ibid.

19. John C. Walter, "The Changing Status of the Black Athlete in the 20th Century United States." Available at http://www.americansc.org.uk/Online/walters.htm (last accessed February 23, 2017).

20. It is also worth noting that prior to becoming an entertainer, Robeson received a scholarship to Rutgers University, where he was class valedictorian, and went on to earn a law degree from Columbia University. He left his law career behind because of racial strife within the New York firm where he worked. For more

on Robeson's life, see http://www.pbs.org/wnet/americanmasters/episodes/paul-robeson/about-the-actor/66/ (last accessed February 23, 2017).

21. This quote is from a 1995 History Channel web article titled, "Paul Robeson Loses Appeal over his Passport." Available at http://www.history.com/this-day-in-history/paul-robeson-loses-appeal-over-his-passport (last accessed July 25, 2014).

22. From the transcript of Robeson's testimony before the House Committee on Un-American Activities. Available at http://historymatters.gmu.edu/d/6440 (last accessed July 28, 2014).

23. As indicated by a variety of post-*Amistad* sources and their comments on the frequency of attempted slave ship insurrections and sources documenting the existence of Maroon communities throughout the Caribbean, many slaves did clearly set their sights on goals that were more overtly revolutionary than disruptive.

24. The various clauses in the US Constitution that openly support and extend the institution beyond the colonial period slavery speak to this fact. Also, various interpretations of the Constitution by the courts support this idea as well. See Robert J. Cottrol and Raymond T. Diamond, "The Second Amendment: Toward an Afro-Americanist Reconsideration"; Derrick Bell, "Chronicle of the Space Traders"; Randall Collins, *The Debt*; or Kenneth O'Riley, *Nixon's Piano*, for more examples of the governmental support of racial oppression.

25. Edward Shapiro (1995, 69–70) notes of this era, "During the 1920s and 1930s, the golden age of Jewish athletes, a disproportionate number of America's leading athletes were second-generation Jews. This was particularly true in boxing and basketball, the classic city sports. Eight American Jews held professional boxing titles during the 1920s, and ten more held titles during the 1930s. Of the ninety-one persons who played in the professional American basketball League during the 1937–38 season, forty-five were Jews."

Bibliography

Akabogu-Collins, May. 2004. "Coming to Black America: A Native of Nigeria Confronts Her Own Prejudices About African Americans." *Los Angeles Times*, February 1. Available at http://www.csun.edu/~vcspc00g/301/comingtoblackam-lat .html (last accessed September 4, 2013).

Amichai-Hamburger, Y., and K. Y. A. McKenna. 2006. "The Contact Hypothesis Reconsidered: Interacting via the Internet." *Journal of Computer-Mediated Communication* 11 (3), article 7. http://jcmc.indiana.edu/vol11/issue3/amichai-hamburger.html. Last accessed November 4, 2011.

Anderson, Elijah. 1999. *Code of the Street: Decency, Violence, and the Moral Life of the Inner City*. New York: W. W. Norton.

Anderson, Kathryn Murphy. 1997. Review of the book *Muscular Christianity: Embodying the Victorian Age*, by Donald E. Hall. *College Literature* 24, 3 (October): 190–193.

Austin, Algernon. 2011. "Remembering Martin Luther King and the March for Jobs and Freedom." *The Hill*, http://thehill.com/blogs/congress-blog/civil-rights /178175-remembering-martin-luther-king-and-the-march-for-jobs-and-freedom. Last accessed November 15, 2011.

Axthelm, Pete. 1968. "Boycott Now—Boycott Later?" *Sports Illustrated*, February 26. Available at https://www.si.com/vault/1968/02/26/547303/boycott-nowboycott -later#. Last accessed May 7, 2017.

———. 1999. *The City Game: Basketball from the Gardens to the Playgrounds*. Lincoln: University of Nebraska Press.

Baldwin, James. 1967. "Negroes Are Anti-Semitic Because They're Anti-White." *New York Times*, April 9.

———. 1998. *Collected Essays*. New York: Library of America.

Baum-Snow, Nathaniel. 2007. "Did Highways Cause Suburbanization?" *Quarterly Journal of Economics* 122, 2 (May): 775–805.

Becker, Howard S. 1953. "Becoming a Marihuana User." *American Journal of Sociology* 59, 3: 235–242.

Bell, David V. J. 1973. *Resistance and Revolution*. Boston: Houghton Mifflin Company.

Bendix, R. 1962. *Max Weber, an Intellectual*. Garden City, N.Y.: Doubleday.

Berry, Mary Frances. 1999. *The Pig Farmer's Daughter and Other Tales of American Justice: Episodes of Racism and Sexism in the Courts from 1865 to the Present*. New York: Vintage.

Bouie, Jamelle. 2014. "The Crisis in Black Homeownership: How the Recession Turned Owners into Renters and Obliterated Black American Wealth." *Slate*, July 24. http://www.slate.com/articles/news_and_politics/politics/2014/07/black_homeownership_how_the_recession_turned_owners_into_renters_and_obliterated.html. Last accessed July 28, 2014.

Braddock, Jomills Henry, II. 1980. "The Perpetuation of Segregation Across Levels of Education: A Behavioral Assessment of the Contact-Hypothesis." *Sociology of Education* 53, 3: 178–186.

Brooks, Scott N. 2009. *Black Men Can't Shoot*. Chicago: University of Chicago Press.

Bruchac, Joseph. 2008. *Jim Thorpe: Original All-American*. http://www.nativetelecom.org/files/JimThorpe_viewerguideWEB.pdf. Last accessed October 31, 2011.

Bureau of Labor Statistics. 2010. "Labor Force Characteristics by Race and Ethnicity, 2009." Available at http://stats.bls.gov/cps/cpsrace2009.pdf. Last accessed December 13, 2011.

Burnard, Trevor. 2004. *Mastery, Tyranny, and Desire: Thomas Thistlewood and His Slaves in the Anglo-Jamaican World*. Chapel Hill: University of North Carolina Press.

Burns, Haywood. 1998. "Law and Race in Early America." In David Kairys and Rene Cramer, eds., *The Politics of Law: A Progressive Critique*. 3rd ed. New York: Basic Books.

Calhoun, Donald W. 1987. *Sport, Culture, and Personality*. Champaign, IL: Human Kinetics.

Campbell, Mavis. 1988. *The Maroons of Jamaica, 1655-1796: A History of Resistance, Collaboration and Betrayal*. Santa Barbara, CA: Praeger.

Caponi, Gena Dagel, ed. 1999. *Signifyin(g), Sanctifyin', and Slam Dunking: A Reader in African American Expressive Culture*. Amherst: University of Massachusetts Press.

Carrington, Ben. 2007. "Merely Identity: Cultural Identity and the Politics of Sport." *Sociology of Sport Journal* 24: 49–66.

———. 2015. "Assessing the Sociology of Sport: On Race and Diaspora." *International Review for the Sociology of Sport* 50: 391–396.

Carson, E. Ann. 2014. "Prisoners in 2013." Bureau of Justice Statistics. Available at http://www.bjs.gov/content/pub/pdf/p13.pdf. Last accessed February 6, 2015.

Chen, David W. 2013. "Bloomberg Says Math Backs Police Stops of Minorities." *New York Times*, June 28. Available at http://www.nytimes.com/2013/06/29/nyregion/bloomberg-says-math-backs-police-stops-of-minorities.html. Last accessed May 8, 2017.

Cherner, Reid. 2010. "Eye-Opener: Kids Get Peace Message Through Hoops." *USA Today*, January 14, 3C.

Cleaver, Eldridge. 1968. *Soul on Ice*. San Francisco: Ramparts.

CNN, 1997. "Golfer Says Comments about Woods 'Misconstrued'." April 21. Available at http://www.cnn.com/US/9704/21/fuzzy/. Last accessed May 8, 2017.

Coates, Ta-Nehisi. 2015. *Between the World and Me*. New York: Spiegel and Grau.

Cohn, Bernard. 1989. "Law and the Colonial State in India." In June Starr and Jane F. Collier, eds., *History and Power in the Study of Law: New Directions in Legal Anthropology*. Ithaca: Cornell University Press.

———. 1996. *Colonialism and Its Forms of Knowledge: The British in India*. Princeton, NJ: Princeton University Press.

Colburn, Forrest D. 1989. *Everyday Forms of Peasant Resistance*. Armonk, NY: M. E. Sharpe.

Crouch, Stanley. 1997. *Sports Illustrated*, December 8: 33.

Currie, Elliott. 1993. *Reckoning: Drugs, the Cities, and the American Future*. New York: Hill and Wang.

Curtin, Phillip D. 1969. *The Atlantic Slave Trade: A Census*. Madison: University of Wisconsin Press.

Dalton, Harlon L. 1995. *Racial Healing: Confronting the Fear Between Blacks and Whites*. New York: Doubleday.

Davis, David Brion. 2006. *Inhuman Bondage: The Rise and Fall of Slavery in the New World*. New York: Oxford.

Davis, Mike. 1992. *City of Quartz: Excavating the Future in Los Angeles*. New York: Vintage.

DeLand, Michael. 2013. "Basketball in the Key of Law: The Significance of Disputing in Pickup Basketball." *Law & Society Review* 47, 3: 653-685.

Delgado, Richard, and Jean Stefancic, eds. 1995. *Critical Race Theory: The Cutting Edge*. Philadelphia: Temple University Press.

Demby, Gene. 2015. "On Wyatt Cenac, 'Key & Peele,' and Being the Only One in the Room." Available at http://www.npr.org/sections/codeswitch/2015/07/29/427190143/on-wyatt-cenac-key-peele-and-being-the-only-one-in-the-room. Last accessed May 7, 2017.

Dhani, Josh. 2009. "Drugs, Basketball, A Legend: The Tale of Ed 'Booger' Smith." Available at http://8points9seconds.com/2009/09/06/drugs-basketball-a-legend-the-tale-of-ed-booger-smith/#!bjp0xm. Last accessed July 21, 2014.

Dodson, Lisa. 2009. *The Moral Underground: How Ordinary Americans Subvert an Unfair Economy*. New York: New Press.

Donziger, Steven. 1996. *The Real War on Crime: The Report of the National Criminal Justice Commission*. New York: Harper Perennial.

Downey, Greg. 2010. "Practice Without Theory: A Neuroanthropological Perspective on Embodied Learning." *Journal of the Royal Anthropology Institute*: S22–S40.

DuBois, W. E. B. 1903. *The Souls of Black Folk*. New York: Dover.

Dudziak, Mary L. 1995. "Desegregation as a Cold War Imperative." In Richard Delgado and Jean Stefancic, eds., *Critical Race Theory: The Cutting Edge*. Philadelphia: Temple University Press.

Duneier, Mitchell. 1992. *Slim's Table: Race, Respectability, and Masculinity*. Chicago: University of Chicago Press.

Eddings, Jerelyn. 2000. "The Covert War: Stealth Racism in America." In Robert Lauer and Jeanette C. Lauer, *Troubled Times: Readings in Social Problems*. Los Angeles: Roxbury.

Edwards, Harry. 1973. *Sociology of Sport*. Homewood, Illinois: Dorsey.

Edwards, Harry. 1998. "An End of the Golden Age of Black Participation in Sport?" *Civil Rights Journal* 3 (Fall): 19-24.

Ellison, Ralph. 1947. *Invisible Man*. New York: Vintage.

Epstein, David. 2013. *The Sports Gene: Inside the Science of Extraordinary Athletic Performance*. New York: Current.

Farley, John E. 1995. *Majority-Minority Relations*. 3rd ed. Upper Saddle River, NJ: Prentice Hall.

Federal Bureau of Investigation. 2014. "Crime in the United States 2012." Available at https://www.fbi.gov/about-us/cjis/ucr/crime-in-the-u.s/2014/crime-in-the-u.s.-2014/tables/table-43. Last accessed May 28, 2016.

Feldman, Bruce. 2007. *Meat Market: Inside the Smash-Mouth World of College Football Recruiting*. New York: ESPN Books.

Fisher v. University of Texas at Austin. 2013. No. 11-345, 2013 BL 167358, 118 FEP Case 1459. June 24.

Fleming, Ted. 2011. "The Struggle for Recognition in Hegel, Honneth, and Higher Education: What Non-traditional Students Say." Paper presented at C.A.V.E. Conference on Building the Contemporary University, Trinity College, Dublin. Available at http://www.dsw.edu.pl/fileadmin/www-ranlhe/files/Fleming_Paper .pdf. Last accessed July 7, 2014.

Foer, Franklin. 2004. *How Soccer Explains the World: An Unlikely Theory of Globalization.* New York: HarperCollins.

Frazier, Clyde. 1972. "Between Obedience and Revolution." *Philosophy & Public Affairs* 1, 3 (Spring).

Frazier, Robeson Taj. 2015. *The East Is Black: Cold War China in the Black Radical Imagination.* Durham, NC: Duke University Press.

Frey, Darcy. 2004. *The Last Shot: City Streets, Basketball Dreams.* New York: Mariner.

Friedman, Lawrence. 1994. *Total Justice.* New York: Russell Sage Foundation.

Geertz, Clifford. 1973. *The Interpretation of Cultures: Selected Essays.* New York: Basic Books.

Gilroy, Paul. 1993. *The Black Atlantic: Modernity and Double Consciousness.* Cambridge, MA: Harvard University Press.

Gladwell, Malcolm. 1997. "The Sports Taboo." *New Yorker*, May 19, 50.

Goffman, E. 1959. *The Presentation of Self in Everyday Life.* Garden City, NY: Doubleday.

———. 1961. *Encounters.* Garden City, NY: Doubleday.

Goldblatt, David. 2014. *The Game of Our Lives: The English League and the Making of Modern Britain.* New York: Nation.

Goudsouzian, Aram. 2006. "Bill Russell and the Basketball Revolution." *American Studies*, 47, 3-4 (Fall/Winter): 61-85.

Greenfield, Jeff. 1999. "The Black and White Truth About Basketball." In Gena Dagel Caponi, *Signifyin(g), Sanctifyin', and Slam Dunking: A Reader in African American Expressive Culture.* Amherst, MA: University of Massachusetts Press. Originally published 1975, *Esquire* magazine.

Griffen, John Howard. 1961. *Black Like Me.* Boston: Houghton Mifflin.

Griffith, Clark C. 1997. "Jackie Robinson's Contributions to America." From at the Westin Hotel, Miami, Florida, October 17. Available at https://clarkgriffithblog.com /2013/04/07/jackie-robinsons-contribution-to-america. Last accessed May 8, 2017.

Hall, Donald E. 1994. *Muscular Christianity: Embodying the Victorian Age.* Cambridge: Cambridge University Press.

Hargreaves, John. 1986. *Sport, Power, and Culture: A Social and Historical Analysis of Popular Sports in Britain.* Cambridge: Polity.

Harms, Robert. 2002. *The Diligent: A Voyage Through the Worlds of the Slave Trade.* New York: Basic Books.

Hartmann, Douglas. 2006. "Bound by Blackness or Above It? Michael Jordan and the Paradoxes of Post-Civil Rights American Race Relations." In David K. Wiggins, *Out of the Shadows: A Biographical History of African American Athletes.* Fayetteville: University of Arkansas Press.

Henslin, James M. 1999. *Sociology: A Down to Earth Approach.* 4th ed. Needham Heights, MA: Allyn and Bacon.

Herbst, Jeffrey. 1989. "How the Weak Succeed: Tactics, Political Goods, and Institutions in the Struggle over Land in Zimbabwe." In Forrest D. Colburn, ed., *Everyday Forms of Peasant Resistance.* Armonk, NY: M. E. Sharpe.

Hill, Jane H. 2008. *The Everyday Language of White Racism*. Hoboken, NJ: Wiley.

Hobsbawm, E. J. 1965. *Primitive Rebels: Studies in Archaic Forms of Social Movement in the 19th and 20th Centuries*. New York: W.W. Norton.

Honneth, Axel. 1995. *The Struggle for Recognition: The Moral Grammar of Social Conflicts*. Cambridge, UK: Polity.

Hooks, Bell. 1992. *Black Looks: Race and Representation*. New York: South End.

Horger, Marc. 2005. "A Victim of Reform: Why Basketball Failed at Harvard." New England Quarterly, 78, 1 (March): 49-76.

Hu-DeHart, Evelyn. 1993. "Rethinking America: The Practice and Politics of Multi-culturalism in Higher Education." In B. W. Thompson and S. Tyagi, eds., *Beyond a Dream Deferred: Multicultural Education and the Politics of Excellence*. Minneapolis: University of Minnesota Press.

Huizinga, J. 1950. *Homo Ludens: a Study of the Play Element in Culture*. New York: Roy .

Hunter, David W. 1997. "Race and Athletic Performance: A Physiological Review." *Journal of African American Men* 2, 2/3, Special Issue on Sports (Fall 1996/Winter 1997): 23–38.

Jackson, Helen Hunt. 2003. *A Century of Dishonor: The Classic Expose of the Plight of the Native Americans*. Mineola, NY: Dover .

Jackson, Scoop. 2010. "Obama Victory Raises Social Significance of Basketball." In Gerald Early, ed., *Best African American Essays*. New York: One World Books.

Jones, Edward P. 2005. "The Girl Who Raised Pigeons." In Edward P. Jones, *Lost in the City: Stories*. New York: Amistad/HarperCollins.

Jordan, Winthrop. 2002 [1968]. "The Simultaneous Invention of Slavery and Racism." In David Northrup, ed., *The Atlantic Slave Trade*. 2nd ed. Boston: Houghton Mifflin.

Kampf, Louis. 1977. "A Course on Spectator Sports." *College English* 38, 8: 835–842.

Kelley, Robin. 1996. *Race Rebels: Culture, Politics, and the Black Working Class*. New York: Simon and Schuster.

Kent, Alexander, and Thomas C. Frohlich. 2015. "The 9 Most Segregated Cities in America." *Huffington Post*, August 27. Available at http://www.huffingtonpost.com /entry/the-9-most-segregated-cities-in-america_55df53e9e4b0e7117ba92d7f. Last accessed September 2, 2015.

King, Stephen A. 2002. *Reggae, Rastafari, and the Rhetoric of Social Control*. Jackson, MS: University Press of Mississippi.

LaFraniere, Sharon, and Andrew W. Lehren. 2015. "The Disproportionate Risks of Driving While Black." *New York Times*, October 24. Available at http://www .nytimes.com/2015/10/25/us/racial-disparity-traffic-stops-driving-black.html. Last accessed October 26, 2015.

Leary, Joy DeGruy. 2005. *Post Traumatic Slave Syndrome: America's Legacy of Enduring Injury and Healing*. Milwaukie, OR: Uptone.

LeFeber, Walter. 1999. *Michael Jordan and the New Global Capitalism*. New York: W. W. Norton.

Leonard, David. 2012. *After Artest: The NBA and the Assault on Blackness*. Albany, NY: State University of New York Press.

Lewis, J. Lowell. 1992. *Ring of Liberation: Deceptive Discourse in Brazilian Capoeira*. Chicago: University of Chicago Press.

Lewis, Michael. 2012. "Obama's Way." *Vanity Fair*, October. Available at http:// www.vanityfair.com/news/2012/10/michael-lewis-profile-barack-obama. Last accessed February 18, 2015.

Liebow, Elliot. 1967. *Tally's Corner*. Boston: Little, Brown.

Lipkin, Robert Justin. 2007. "Jackie Robinson's Breaking the Color Line or *Brown v. Board of Education*: Which Did More for Racial Justice in America?" Available at http://essentiallycontestedamerica.org/?p=863. Last accessed August 2, 2013.

Little, Daniel. 1993. Review of *Domination and the Arts of Resistance: Hidden Transcripts*, by James C. Scott. *Political Theory* 21, 1: 153–156.

Loichot, Valérie. 2004. "Edwidge Danticat's Kitchen History." *Meridians* 5, 1: 92–116.

Lomax, Michael. 1999. "The African American Experience in Professional Football." *Journal of Social History* 33, 1 (Autumn): 163–178.

Lopez, Ian Haney. 1995. "The Social Construction of Race." In Richard Delgado and Jean Stefancic, eds. *Critical Race Theory: The Cutting Edge*. Philadelphia: Temple University Press.

Loy, John W., and Gerald S. Kenyon. 1969. *Sport, Culture, and Society: A Reader on the Sociology of Sport*. Toronto: Macmillan.

MacClancy, Jeremy, ed. 1996. *Sport, Identity, and Ethnicity*. Oxford: Berg.

MacFarlane, Leslie J. 1971. *Political Disobedience*. London: MacMillan.

Majors, Richard, and Janet Mancini Billson. 1993. *Cool Pose: The Dilemma of Black Manhood in America*. New York: Simon and Schuster.

Malveaux, Julianne. 2007. "Gladiators, Gazelles, and Groupies: Basketball Love and Loathing." In Margaret L. Anderson and Patricia Hill Collins, *Race, Class, & Gender: An Anthology*, Sixth Edition. Belmont, CA: Thompson-Wadsworth.

Mandela, Nelson. 2000. Transcript of speech at the inaugural Laureus Lifetime Achievement Award, Monaco. Available at http://db.nelsonmandela.org/speeches/pub_view.asp?pg=item&ItemID=NMS1148. Last accessed May 8, 2017.

Maraniss, David. 2012. "President Obama's Basketball Love Affair Has Roots in Hawaii High School Team." *Washington Post*, June 9. Available at https://www.washingtonpost.com/sports/president-obamas-basketball-love-affair-has-roots-in-hawaii-high-school-team/2012/06/09/gJQApU2mQV_story.html?utm_term=.c59dc3a2fe31. Last accessed February 27, 2017.

Martinez, Sylvia C. 2000. "The Housing Act of 1949: Its Place in the Realization of the American Dream of Homeownership." *Housing Policy Debate* 11, 2: 467. Washington, DC: Fannie Mae Foundation.

May, Reuben A. Buford. 2009. *Living Through the Hoop: High School Basketball, Race, and the American Dream*. New York: New York University Press.

McCall, Nathan. 1994. *Makes Me Wanna Holler: A Young Black Man in America*. New York: Vintage.

———. 2002. "The Revolution Is About Basketball." In Joel M. Charon, *Social Problems: Readings with Four Questions*. Belmont, CA: Wadsworth.

McIntosh, Peter. 1987. *Sport in Society*. Thousand Oaks, CA: Sage.

McKernan, Signe-Mary, Caroline Ratcliffe, Eugene Steuerle, and Sisi Zhang. 2013. "Less Than Equal: Racial Disparities in Wealth Accumulation." Urban Institute. Available at http://www.urban.org/UploadedPDF/412802-Less-Than-Equal-Racial-Disparities-in-Wealth-Accumulation.pdf. Last accessed July 28, 2014.

McPherson et al., 1989. *The Social Significance of Sport: An Introduction to the Sociology of Sport*. Champaign, IL: Human Kinetics Publishers.

Mieszkowski, Peter, and Edwin S. Mills. 1993. "The Causes of Metropolitan Suburbanization." *Journal of Economic Perspectives* 7, 3 (Summer): 135–147.

Mirandé, Alfredo. 1987. *Gringo Justice*. Notre Dame, IN: University of Notre Dame Press.

Mohamed, A. Rafik, and Erik D. Fritsvold. 2009. *Dorm Room Dealers: Drugs and the Privileges of Race and Class*. Boulder, CO: Lynne Rienner.

Morrissey, Rick. 1997. "Past Imperfect, Future Intense." *Chicago Tribune*, November 30. Available at http://articles.chicagotribune.com/1997-11-30/sports/9712020327 _1_adolph-rupp-kentucky-tricky/2. Last accessed January 1, 2012.

Mosley, Walter. 1996. *A Little Yellow Dog*. New York: Pocket Books.

———. 2000. *Workin' on the Chain Gang: Shaking Off the Dead Hand of History*. New York: Ballantine.

Mosley, Walter. 2013. *Little Green*. New York: Doubleday.

———. 2002. *Bad Boy Brawly Brown*. Boston: Little, Brown.

Muhammad, Latifah. 2017. "LeBron James Says We Don't Need More Athletes, Encourages Young People to Pursue STEM Careers." *Vibe*, April 1. Available at http://www.vibe.com/2017/04/lebron-james-verizon-stem-careers/. Last accessed May 9, 2017.

Nadel, Joshua. 2014. *Futbol: Why Soccer Matters in Latin America*. Gainesville: University Press of Florida.

Nathan, Daniel A. 1998. Review of "City Dump: The Story of the 1951 CCNY Basketball Scandal." *Journal of American History* 85, 3: 1192–1193.

Newhan, Ross. 2008. "Not Everyone Was a Happy Camper: Newcombe Does not Have Fond Memories of Spring Training at a Time When Baseball Was only Recently Integrated and Florida Was Still Segregated." *Los Angeles Times*, February 10.

Nier Charles L., III, and Maureen R. St. Cyr. 2011. "A Racial Financial Crisis: Rethinking the Theory of Reverse Redlining to Combat Predatory Lending Under the Fair Housing Act." *Temple Law Review* 85, 4 (Summer): 941–978.

Northrup, David, ed. 2002. *The Atlantic Slave Trade*. 2nd ed. Boston: Houghton Mifflin.

Novak, Michael. 1976. *The Joy of Sports*. New York: Basic Books.

Pager, Devah. 2003. "The Mark of a Criminal Record." *American Journal of Sociology* 108, 5: 937–975.

Parry, Marc. 2016. "Shackles and Dollars: Historians and Economists Clash Over Slavery." *The Chronicle Review*, December 16: B6-B9.

Patterson, Orlando. 1982. *Slavery and Social Death: A Comparative Study*. Cambridge, MA: Harvard University Press.

Peterson, R. 1970. *Only the Ball Was White*. Englewood Cliffs, NJ: Prentice-Hall.

Pew Research Center. 2011. "Twenty-to-One: Wealth Gaps Rise to Record Highs Between Whites, Blacks, and Hispanics." July 26. Available at http://www.pewsocialtrends .org/files/2011/07/SDT-Wealth-Report_7-26-11_FINAL.pdf. Last accessed November 24, 2011.

Pierce, Charles P. 1996. "Basketball Nation." *Gentlemen's Quarterly*, February: 56–63.

Pierre, John K. 2012. "History of De Jure Segregation in Public Higher Education in America and the State of Maryland Prior to 1954 and the Equalization Strategy. *Florida A&M University Law Review*, 8, 7 (Fall): 81–109.

Piersen, William D. 1999. "A Resistance too Civilized to Notice." In Gena Dagel Caponi, ed., *Signifyin(g), Sanctifyin', and Slam Dunking: A Reader in African American Expressive Culture*. Amherst: University of Massachusetts Press.

Powers, Daniel A., and Christopher G. Ellison. 1995. "Interracial Contact and Black Racial Attitudes: The Contact Hypothesis and Selectivity Bias." *Social Forces* 74, 1: 205–226.

Price, Richard. 1996. *Maroon Societies: Rebel Slave Communities in the Americas.* 3rd ed. Baltimore: Johns Hopkins University Press.

Price. S.L. 1997. "What Happened to the White Athlete?" Sports Illustrated, December 8. Available at https://www.si.com/vault/1997/12/08/8093391/what-ever-happened -to-the-white-athlete-unsure-of-his-place-in-a-sports-world-dominated-by-blacks -who-are-hungrier-harder-working-and-perhaps-physiologically-superior-the -young-white-male-is-dropping-out-of-the-athletic-mainstr. Last accessed May 8, 2017.

Reese, Renford. 2004. *American Paradox: Young Black Men.* Durham, NC: Carolina Academic Press.

Reily, Suzel Ana. 2010. Review of *The Hidden History of Capoeira: A Collision of Cultures in the Brazilian Battle Dance* by M. Talmon-Chvaicer. *Bulletin of Latin American Research* 29, 2: 259-261.

Reiss, Steven A. 1992. "The Historiography of American Sport." *OAH Magazine of History* 7, 1, History of Sport, Recreation, and Leisure (Summer): 10–14.

Rhoden, William C. 2006. *Forty Million Dollar Slaves: The Rise, Fall, and Redemption of the Black Athlete.* New York: Three Rivers.

Ripley, Amanda. 2013. "The Case Against High-School Sports." *The Atlantic*, October.

Roberts, Randy. 1983. *Papa Jack: Jack Johnson and the Era of White Hopes.* New York: The Free Press.

Rosen, David. 1994. "The Volcano and the Cathedral: Muscular Christianity and the Origins of Primal Manliness." In Donald E. Hall, ed., *Muscular Christianity: Embodying the Victorian Age.* Cambridge: Cambridge University Press.

Rosenblum, Bruce E. 1979. "Discriminatory Purpose and Disproportionate Impact: An Assessment After "Feeney." *Columbia Law Review* 79, 7: 1376–1413.

RTI International. 2016. "Exploring Racial Disproportionality in Traffic Stops Conducted by the Durham Police Department: Report." Available at http://nc-durham .civicplus.com/DocumentCenter/View/9594. Last accessed May 28, 2016.

Russell, Margaret M. 1995. "Narratives of Law and Inequality in Popular Film." In Richard Delgado and Jean Stefancic, eds., *Critical Race Theory: The Cutting Edge.* Philadelphia: Temple University Press.

Schiappa, Edward, Peter B. Gregg, and Dean E. Hewes. 2005. "The Parasocial Contact Hypothesis." *Communication Monographs* 72, 1: 92–115.

Schlesinger, Arthur. 1991. "The Cult of Ethnicity, Good and Bad: A Historian Argues that Multiculturalism Threatens the Ideal that Binds America." *Time*, July 8.

Scott, James C. 1985. *Weapons of the Weak: Everyday Forms of Peasant Resistance.* New Haven, CT: Yale University Press.

———. 1990. *Domination and the Arts of Resistance.* New Haven, CT: Yale University Press.

———. 1992. "Domination, Acting, and Fantasy." In Carolyn Nordstrom and JoAnn Martin, eds., *The Paths to Domination, Resistance, and Terror.* Berkeley: University of California Press.

Scott, John, and Gordon Marshall. 2005. *Oxford Dictionary of Sociology.* New York: Oxford University Press.

Shabad, Rebecca. 2016. "Checking Donald Trump's 'Stop and Frisk' Claims During First Debate." Available at http://www.cbsnews.com/news/exploring-donald -trumps-stop-and-frisk-claims-during-first-general-election-debate-hofstra -2016/. Last accessed May 8, 2017.

Shapiro, Edward. 1995. "*Ellis Island to Ebbets Field: Sport and the American Jewish Experience*, by Peter Levine." *Journal of American Ethnic History* 15, 1: 69–71.

Shiao, Jiannbin Lee, Thomas Bode, Amber Beyer, and Daniel Selvig. 2012. "The Genomic Challenge to the Social Construction of Race." *Sociological Theory* 30, 2 (June): 67–88.

Simmel, Georg. 1980. *Essays on Interpretation in Social Science.* Totowa, NJ: Rowman and Littlefield.

Snyder, Howard N. 2011. "Arrest in the United States, 1980–2009." US Department of Justice, Office of Justice Programs, Bureau of Justice Statistics. Report available at http://bjs.ojp.usdoj.gov/content/pub/pdf/aus8009.pdf. Last accessed December 9, 2011.

Sommers, Dale. 1972. *The Rise of Sport in New Orleans, 1850–1900.* Baton Rouge: Louisiana State University Press.

Sowell, Thomas. 2005. *Black Rednecks and White Liberals.* San Francisco: Encounter Books.

Spivey, Donald. 2006. "Hot Potato: How Washington and New York Gave Birth to Black Basketball and Changed America's Game Forever." *Journal of African American History*, 91, 1 (Winter): 97-99.

Stamm, Henry E. 1999. *People of the Wind River: The Eastern Shoshones 1825– 1900.* Norman: University of Oklahoma Press.

St. John, Warren. 2009. *Outcasts United.* New York: Spiegel & Grau.

Stokes, Martin. 1996. "'Strong as a Turk': Power, Performance, and Representation in Turkish Wrestling." In Jeremy MacClancy, ed., *Sport, Identity, and Ethnicity.* Oxford: Berg.

Stuart, Ozzie. 1996. "Players, Workers, Protestors: Social Change and Soccer in Colonial Zimbabwe." In Jeremy MacClancy, ed., *Sport, Identity, and Ethnicity.* Oxford: Berg.

Sumner, William Graham. 1906. *Folkways: A Study of the Sociological Importance of Usages, Manners, Customs, Mores, and Morals.* Boston: Ginn.

Sussman, Herbert. 1996. Review of *Muscular Christianity: Embodying the Victorian Age*, by Donald E. Hall. *Victorian Studies* 39, 2 (Winter): 290–293.

Sutherland, Jean-Anne and Kathryn Feltey. 2010. *Cinematic Sociology: Social Life in Film.* Lost Angeles: Pine Forge.

Takaki, Ronald I. 1993. *A Different Mirror: A History of Multicultural America.* Boston: Little, Brown.

Telander, Rick. 2009. *Heaven Is a Playground.* Lincoln, NE: University of Nebraska Press.

Trotter, Joe William. 2001. *The African American Experience.* Boston: Houghton Mifflin.

Tucker, Jacob. 2012. "Dreams Ignored: When the Person Gets Lost in the Player." *The Good Men Project*, January 18. Available at http://goodmenproject.com /featured-content/dreams-ignored-when-the-person-gets-lost-in-the-player/. Last accessed February 10, 2014.

USA Today. 2009. "Basketball Teams for Peace." January 26. Available at http://articles .cnn.com/2009-01-26/living/ypwr.evans_1_lapin-social-networking-northern -ireland?_s=PM:LIVING. Last accessed October 30, 2011.

Valenti, John. 1990. *Swee' Pea and Other Playground Legends: Tales of Drugs, Violence, and Basketball.* New York: Michael Kesend.

Veblen, Thorstein. 1899. *The Theory of the Leisure Class.* Available at http://moglen .law.columbia.edu/LCS/theoryleisureclass.pdf. Last accessed May 7, 2017.

Wacquant, Loïc. 2002. "From Slavery to Mass Incarceration: Rethinking the 'Race Question' in the US." *New Left Review* 13 (January-February): 41–60.

Walter, John C. 1996. "The Changing Status of the Black Athlete in the 20th Century United States." Liverpool, UK: Liverpool John Moores University. Available at http://www.americansc.org.uk/Online/walters.htm. Last accessed March 14, 2014.

Weiss, Paul. 1969. *Sport: A Philosophical Inquiry*. Carbondale: Southern Illinois Press.

West, Cornel. 1993. *Race Matters*. Boston: Beacon.

White, Deborah Gray. 1999. *Ar'n't I a Woman: Female Slaves in the Plantation South*. New York: Norton.

Wideman, John Edgar. 1990. *Philadelphia Fire*. New York: Henry Holt.

———. 2001. *Hoop Roots: Playground Basketball, Love, and Race*. New York: Houghton Mifflin.

Wigginton, Russell. 2006. *The Strange Career of the Black Athlete: African Americans and Sports*. Westport, CT: Praeger.

Wilder, Craig Steven. 2013. *Ebony and Ivy: Race, Slavery, and the Troubled History of America's Universities*. New York: Bloomsbury.

Williams, Eric. 2002 [1944]. "Economics, Not Racism, as the Root of Slavery." In David Northrup, ed., *The Atlantic Slave Trade*, 2nd ed. Boston: Houghton Mifflin.

Wilson, William Julius. 1978. *The Declining Significance of Race: Blacks and Changing American Institutions*. Chicago: University of Chicago Press.

———. 1987. *The Truly Disadvantaged: The Inner City, the Underclass, and Public Policy*. Chicago: University of Chicago Press.

Wiltse, Jeff. 2007. *Contested Waters: A Social History of Swimming Pools in America*. Chapel Hill, NC: University of North Carolina Press.

Wise, Mike. 2005. "Opinions on the NBA's Dress Code are Far From Uniform," *Washington Post*. October 23. Available at http://www.washingtonpost.com/wp-dyn/content/article/2005/10/22/AR2005102201386.html. Last accessed May 7, 2017.

Woodbine, Onaje. 2016. *Black Gods of the Asphalt: Religion, Hip-Hop, and Street Basketball*. New York: Columbia University Press.

Zirin, Dave. 2005. *What's My Name, Fool? Sports and Resistance in the United States*. Chicago: Haymarket Books.

———. 2008. "The Explosive 1968 Olympics." *International Socialist Review*, 61, online edition (September-October). Available at http://www.isreview.org/issues/61/feat-zirin.shtml. Last accessed May 7, 2017.

Index

181

Onstott, Kyle, 123
OPHR. *See* Olympic Project for Human Rights
Oppression, 158, 159, 161
Orange County, 34–35

Parents, 28–30
Patronage, 89
Peaches, 28–31, 63
Peasant insolence, 16
Persona, on-court, 108–109, 161
Pickup basketball: assessment of, 105; crowd observing, 3; emotions released in, 71; as everyday resistance, 12, 41–42, 55, 74–75, 165, 166; evolution of, 7; formal basketball compared to, 12; freedom of, 161; rhythm of, 3–4; she-ballers in, 27–31, 59n4; size in, 106; sociological world of, 36; in suburbs, 32–33; symbolism of, 159, 166–167; white ballers uncomfortable with, 70–71. *See also* Black man's rules; Culture, pickup basketball
Pierce, Charles P., 6, 64–66
Play, 104; deep, 72–73; rule suspension during, 68, 74; styles of, 26, 99
Plessy v. Ferguson, 154, 168n8
Police, 14, 93; brutality, 44; racism influencing, 124–125; stop-and-frisk policies of, 147n8
Politics: of courts, 105; Culver City tension over, 88, 92–97; identity, 41; postracial, 166; race, 97–98, 136–137, 155–157; slavery institutions in, 166; sports intersection with, 53–58
Population: Clarkston social change of, 95–96; of Culver City and Los Angeles, 9; of Encino, 101
Post traumatic slave syndrome, 74–75
Posterization, 117n3
Postracial concept, 13, 115, 153, 166
Poverty: in America, 39; on East Coast, 7; in Washington D.C., 19n3
Power theater, 72
Prejudice, 64, 76n4; benign, 154; internalization of, 139–144; positive, 133; social processes underlying, 122, 124; subtlety of, 136
Pretextual stops, 147n7

"Prissy," 162
Privilege, white, 88, 95, 97, 156–158
Professional basketball, 16–17; ambition misdirected to, 47–48, 141, 144–145; loss of, 38–39; unlikelihood of, 37, 83
Projects, urban housing, 7, 28–31
Protocol, game, 2, 69–70, 101–102
"Pussy," 157

Race: baggage from, 106; black-white relations of, 66–67, 161; confrontations between, 87–91; consciousness of, 138; emotions displayed based on, 71; ethnoracial prison of, 71–73; gender intersection with, 17; interactions between, 115–116; language implying, 93, 136; legislation failing, 67; Los Angeles tensions over, 107; mind and body assumptions based on, 49–50; mixed, 33; narratives of, 13, 18, 167; perceptional disparities based on, 13–14, 138, 168n7; play distinction between, 26, 99, 104; politics, 97–98, 136–137, 155–158; postracial concept regarding, 13, 115, 153, 166; power dynamics of, 103; slavery ideologies regarding, 42–43; in Veterans Park, 92. *See also* Interactions, interracial; Narratives, race; Status quo, racial; White
Racial Healing (Dalton), 77n8
Racism: America imbued with, 43, 153–154; ideologies of, 140; of Key, 60n13; law enforcement practices influenced by, 124–125; Native American resistance to, 66; overt and subtle, 52; by race groups, 155; stealth, 75, 124–125; Supreme Court upholding, 150, 168n8
Rap, message, 112
Reagan administration, 111–112
Recognition, 57–58, 84; intersubjective, 87–88, 89, 117n4
The Redneck Store, 153
Refugee resettlement, 95–96
Reggae music, 112
Religion, 47
Representation, African American: of America, 6; in professional sports,

About the Book

What is it about basketball that makes it "the black man's game"? And what about pickup basketball in particular: can it tell us something about the state of blackness in the United States?

Reflecting on these questions, Rafik Mohamed presents pickup games as a text of the political, social, and economic struggles of African American men. In the process, he tells a story about race in its peculiarly American context, and about how the politics of race—and resistance—are mediated through sports.

A. Rafik Mohamed is professor of sociology and dean of the College of Social and Behavioral Sciences at California State University San Bernardino. He is coauthor of *Dorm Room Dealers: Drugs and the Privileges of Race and Class.*